FAVORITE BRAND NAME

P · I · E

COLLECTION

PUBLICATIONS INTERNATIONAL, LTD.

ISBN 1-56173-671-6

Library of Congress Catalog Card Number: 93-084428

Pictured on front cover: *Top row, left:* German Sweet Chocolate Pie *(page 170); Center:* Ice Cream Shop Pies — Rocky Road Pie, Toffee Bar Crunch Pie and Strawberry Banana Split Pie *(page 152); Right:* Jubilee Pie *(page 146). Bottom row, left:* Peach Delight Pie *(page 114); Center:* Nestlé® Candy Shop Pizza *(page 130); Right:* Pineapple Macadamia Cheese Pie *(page 85).*

Pictured on back cover: *Top row, left:* Apple Cinnamon Tart *(page 50); Center:* Chocolate-Filled Cream Puffs *(page 206),* Chocolate-Almond Tarts *(page 206)* and Napoleons *(page 207); Right:* Mushroom Quiche with Brown Rice Crust *(page 32). Bottom row, left:* Patriotic Pie *(page 159); Center:* Vegetable & Cheese Pot Pie *(page 31); Right:* Apple Almond Mince Pie *(page 189)* and Mince Cheesecake Pie *(page 188).*

8 7 6 5 4 3 2 1

Manufactured in U.S.A.

Microwave ovens vary in wattage and power output; cooking times given with microwave directions in this book may need to be adjusted. Consult manufacturer's instructions for suitable microwave-safe cooking dishes.

Contents

TIPS AND TECHNIQUES

Home-baked pie is one of America's all-time favorite desserts. Whether it has one crust or two, a crumb crust or a pastry crust, a custard filling or a fruit filling, there are pies to suit every craving. While apple pie remains America's darling, consider the popularity of savory main-dish pot pies and pizzas. And who hasn't spied a luscious lemon meringue, chocolate cream or pumpkin pie in a local diner and decided to have dessert after all?

There are as many types of pies as there are fillings. This book offers a broad sampling of recipes, some familiar and some not so familiar, including a chapter devoted to specialty pastries for those looking for a delicious change of pace. Following are some basic techniques to follow for surefire results.

BEFORE YOU BEGIN

Some tips that lay the foundation for successful pie baking:

• Before beginning, read the entire recipe to make sure you have all the necessary ingredients and utensils.

• Use the ingredients called for in the recipe. Do not assume that butter, shortening and margarine are interchangeable. Unless specified in a recipe, whipped, low-calorie, "light" or diet margarine products are not suitable for baking because of varying degrees of moisture content.

• Adjust oven racks and preheat the oven. Check oven temperature for accuracy with an oven thermometer.

• Do any necessary food preparation before assembling pies (i.e. separating eggs, slicing fruit, toasting nuts, melting chocolate).

• Follow recipe directions and baking times exactly. Check for doneness using the test given in the recipe.

GLOSSARY OF PIE TECHNIQUES

The following glossary of terms will help take the mystery out of pie baking:

Cutting in: Incorporating solid fat ingredients like shortening, butter or margarine, with dry ingredients like flour, using a pastry blender, fork or two knives. To cut in, use an up-and-down cutting motion to form crumbs of desired consistency.

Blind baking: Baking a pie crust without its filling to prevent it from becoming soggy when it is filled. To blind bake, line the pastry with foil, waxed paper or parchment paper. Spread dried beans, dried peas or pie weights over the bottom to prevent crust from puffing or losing its shape during baking. Cool blind-baked pie shells completely before filling. (You may reuse the beans or peas later for blind baking, but do not prepare them for eating; they are inedible after baking.)

Dotting: Adding additional butter or margarine to pie surface to achieve the desired flavor. To dot, cut butter or margarine into small pieces, or "dots," and distribute evenly over surface before baking.

Fluting: Shaping pie shell edges for decorative purposes. To flute, create desired design by using fingers or utensils to crimp or decorate pastry edge.

SUCCESSFUL CRUSTS

The secret behind a good pie is the success of its crust. Ensure no-fail crusts every time with these easy basics:

• For tender, flaky pie crusts, always keep solid and liquid ingredients *chilled*. If using butter in a pastry recipe, keep it *well chilled*. (However, vegetable shortening and lard do not need to be chilled.) Handle the dough as little as possible.

• Cut cold solid ingredients into dry ingredients for best results. Add *cold* water to dough, 1 tablespoon at a time, just until mixture holds together with slight pressure and can be formed into a ball. *Do not overwork the dough.* Wrap ball of dough in plastic wrap and refrigerate at least 1 hour before shaping into pie shells or using for specialty pastry recipes.

• To prevent soggy crust, place pie in lower third of oven.

• If using a commercially prepared frozen deep-dish crust, *do not thaw*. Instead, preheat oven and cookie sheet. Pour pie filling into frozen crust, place on preheated cookie sheet and bake.

• Kitchen shears are useful for trimming bottom crusts once they are pressed into pie plates. Trim dough about ½ inch beyond the edge of the pie plate. For single crust pies, fold the extra dough under to form a rim.

• If using a top crust, moisten edges of both top and bottom crusts lightly with water, then join and seal. Fold the extra dough from both crusts under to form a rim. *Always* cut slits or small decorative shapes into top crust before baking in order to allow steam to escape.

• To prevent a crust from overbrowning, cover the pie loosely with foil and continue baking.

• To speed up preparation, process dough ingredients in a food processor until ingredients form a ball. For flakiest crusts, freeze butter, margarine or shortening before processing.

• Thawed frozen puff pastry sheets and phyllo dough also make great specialty pastries and pie crusts; refer to specific recipes and package directions for more information.

FOOLPROOF MERINGUES

Knowing these simple tips can make meringue-baking a cinch:

• Weather can affect the success of meringues. The sugar in the mixture absorbs moisture in the air; high humidity can result in a gooey meringue. For best results, make meringues on sunny, low-humidity days.

• Make sure mixing bowls and beaters are *completely* clean and dry; any remaining food or moisture can affect the outcome.

• When separating eggs for meringue, make sure they are *cold*; they will separate more easily. However, let egg whites come to room temperature before beating; this produces a higher volume.

• Before adding sugar to a meringue mixture, beat egg whites and cream of tartar (if using) to soft peak stage. Always add sugar *gradually* to egg whites and continue beating until sugar is *completely dissolved*. Egg whites should be glossy and stiff, but *not* dry.

• When spreading meringues onto pies before baking, spread completely to edge to "seal" pie like a crust. Most meringue-topped pies are placed briefly under the broiler to brown the meringue.

• For best results, cool fully baked meringues slowly, away from drafts. They hold their shape and volume better.

CLASSIC CRISCO® CRUSTS

Ingredients for 9- or 10-inch Classic Crisco®
Single Crust
1⅓ cups all-purpose flour
½ teaspoon salt
½ cup CRISCO® Shortening
3 tablespoons cold water

Ingredients for 9-inch Classic Crisco®
Double Crust
2 cups all-purpose flour
1 teaspoon salt
¾ cup CRISCO® Shortening
5 tablespoons cold water

Ingredients for 10-inch Classic Crisco®
Double Crust
2⅔ cups all-purpose flour
1 teaspoon salt
1 cup CRISCO® Shortening
7 to 8 tablespoons cold water

2. Cut in Crisco® using pastry blender or 2 knives until flour is blended to form pea-size chunks.

1. Spoon flour into measuring cup and level. Combine flour and salt in medium bowl.

3. Sprinkle with water, 1 tablespoon at a time. Toss lightly with fork until dough forms a ball.

For Single Crust Pies

4. Press dough between hands to form a 5- to 6-inch "pancake." Flour rolling surface and rolling pin lightly. Roll dough into circle. Trim circle 1 inch larger than upside-down pie plate. Carefully remove trimmed dough. Set aside to reroll and use for pastry cutout garnish, if desired.

5. Fold dough into quarters. Unfold and press into pie plate. Fold edge under. Flute.

6. **For recipes using a baked pie crust,** heat oven to 425°F. Prick bottom and side thoroughly with fork (50 times) to prevent shrinkage. Bake at 425°F for 10 to 15 minutes or until lightly browned.

7. **For recipes using an unbaked pie crust,** follow baking directions given for that recipe.

For Double Crust Pies

Follow steps 1 to 3 for Classic Crisco® Crusts on page 6.

4. Divide dough in half. Roll out each half separately. Transfer bottom crust to pie plate. Trim edge even with plate.

5. Add desired filling to unbaked pie crust. Moisten pastry edge with water. Lift top crust onto filled pie. Trim ½ inch beyond edge of pie plate. Fold top edge under bottom crust. Flute. Cut slits in top crust to allow steam to escape. Bake according to specific recipe directions.

CONTEMPORARY TECHNIQUES
Waxed Paper Method

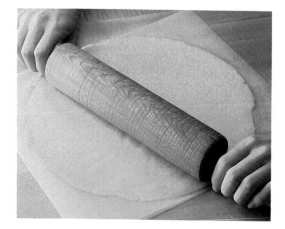

1. Flour "pancake" lightly on both sides. Roll between sheets of waxed paper (or plastic wrap) on dampened countertop. Peel off top sheet.

2. Flip dough into pie plate. Remove other sheet.

Plastic Food Storage Bag Method

1. Flour "pancake" lightly on both sides or lightly flour inside of 2-gallon (13×15-inch) food storage bag. Slide "pancake" into center of bag. Do not close open end.

Place on dampened countertop. Roll dough into circle almost touching side edges. Sprinkle a little more flour over dough if it sticks to bag. Turn bag for even rolling.

2. Slit bag with scissors or sharp knife on all 3 sides. Remove top sheet and discard.

3. Place pie plate over dough. Turn over to flip dough into pie plate. Peel off plastic.

HOW TO MAKE A LATTICE TOP CRUST

1. Leave overhang on bottom crust. Cut top crust into 10 (½-inch) strips. (Use a pastry wheel to cut lattice strips with scalloped edges.) Place 5 strips evenly across filling. Fold every other strip back. Lay first strip across in opposite direction.

2. Continue in this pattern, folding back every other strip each time you add a cross strip. Trim ends of lattice strips even with crust overhang. Press together to seal; fold edges under and flute.

GARNISH IDEAS

Garnishing a pie gives it that special touch. Try these decorative suggestions for dressing up your favorite pies:

• For decorative crust edges, use tiny cookie cutters, bottle caps or thimbles to cut out desired shapes from leftover pie dough. Place shapes on pastry edge, overlapping slightly, and press gently into place. Or, pastry cutouts can be arranged on top of single-crust pies before baking. Flowers, leaves, stars and other simple shapes make the best decorations.

• To use up leftover pastry for no-bake single crust pies, cut pastry into desired shapes and place on baking sheet. Bake cut-outs with the pastry shell; decorate pie with the pre-baked cut-out shapes once the pie has been filled and is ready to serve.

• For a golden crust, beat 1 egg yolk with 2 tablespoons water; brush mixture over crust with pastry brush before baking.

• For a browner crust, glaze crust with milk or cream before baking.

• For a sparkling crust, glaze crust with milk or cream and sprinkle with granulated sugar before baking.

• For a colorful crust, tint 1 beaten egg white with a few drops of desired food coloring. Brush onto crust with pastry brush before baking.

SIMPLY SAVORY

Sunflower Wheat Beef Pot Pie

Crust
1¾ cups all-purpose flour
¼ cup whole-wheat flour
1 teaspoon salt
⅛ teaspoon baking powder
⅔ cup CRISCO® Shortening
5 to 6 tablespoons cold water

Filling
¼ cup chopped celery
¼ cup chopped potatoes
¼ cup chopped carrots
¼ cup frozen corn
¼ cup frozen peas
3 tablespoons minced onion
3 tablespoons salted sunflower kernels
1 teaspoon minced fresh parsley
1½ cups water, divided
¾ cup beef broth
1½ tablespoons cornstarch
½ teaspoon instant beef flavor bouillon granules
½ teaspoon instant chicken flavor bouillon granules
¼ teaspoon pepper
⅛ teaspoon salt
1½ tablespoons ketchup
1 cup cubed cooked roast beef (about ⅓ pound)
¾ cup condensed Cheddar cheese soup
1 tablespoon butter or margarine
¼ cup (1 ounce) finely shredded American cheese

1. Heat oven to 400°F.

2. For Crust, combine dry ingredients in large bowl. See page 6, steps 2 and 3, for remaining dough preparation. Roll and press bottom crust into 9-inch pie plate. (See page 7, step 4, for Double Crust Pies.) *Do not bake.*

3. For Filling, combine vegetables, sunflower kernels, parsley and 1¼ cups water in medium saucepan. Bring to a boil. Reduce heat; simmer 10 minutes.

4. Heat beef broth in large saucepan. Combine cornstarch, bouillon granules, pepper, salt, ketchup and remaining ¼ cup water in small bowl. Add to beef broth. Cook and stir until thickened. Add beef, cooked vegetables with liquid and cheese soup. Stir well to combine. Spoon into unbaked pie crust. Dot with butter; sprinkle with American cheese. Moisten pastry edge with water.

5. Roll out top crust. Lift onto filled pie. Trim ½ inch beyond edge of pie plate. Fold top edge under bottom crust; flute. Cut slits or shapes into top crust to vent.

6. Bake at 400°F for 15 minutes. *Reduce oven temperature to 350°F.* Bake 20 to 25 minutes. Let stand 10 minutes before cutting and serving. Serve hot. Refrigerate leftover pie.   *Makes 1 (9-inch) pie*

Sunflower Wheat Beef Pot Pie

Reuben Pie

Caraway Crust (recipe follows)
4 eggs
12 ounces thinly sliced corned beef, chopped
1½ cups *well-drained* sauerkraut
½ cup prepared Thousand Island salad dressing
2 tablespoons flour
1 teaspoon WYLER'S® or STEERO® Beef-Flavor Instant Bouillon
¾ cup (3 ounces) shredded Swiss cheese

Prepare Caraway Crust. Meanwhile, in large bowl, beat eggs; stir in remaining ingredients except cheese. Mix well. Pour into prepared crust; bake at 350°F for 35 to 40 minutes or until set. Top with cheese; bake 5 minutes longer. Let stand 5 minutes. Garnish as desired. Refrigerate leftovers.   *Makes 1 (9-inch) pie*

Caraway Crust: Preheat oven to 400°F. In medium bowl, combine 1¼ cups unsifted flour, 2 teaspoons caraway seed and 1½ teaspoons Wyler's® or Steero® Beef-Flavor Instant Bouillon; cut in ⅓ cup shortening until crumbly. Adding 1 tablespoon at a time, sprinkle with ¼ cup cold water, stirring to form ball. On floured surface, roll dough into 10-inch circle. Turn into 9-inch pie plate; trim and flute edge. Prick with fork; bake 10 to 12 minutes. *Reduce oven temperature to 350°F.*

Reuben Pie

Louisiana Seafood Pie

Filling
½ cup butter or margarine
¼ cup all-purpose flour
1 cup chopped onion
½ cup thinly sliced green onion tops
⅓ cup chopped green bell pepper
3 tablespoons chopped celery
3 tablespoons chopped fresh parsley
2 teaspoons finely chopped garlic
¼ cup whipping cream
3 tablespoons brandy
1 teaspoon salt
¾ teaspoon black pepper
2 pounds shelled, cleaned crawfish tail meat *or* shelled, deveined raw shrimp
Crust
9-inch Classic Crisco® Double Crust (pages 6 and 7)

1. For Filling, melt butter in large skillet on low heat. Gradually add flour. Cook slowly, stirring constantly, until smooth, slightly thickened and light golden brown. Add chopped onion, green onion, green pepper, celery, parsley and garlic. Cook, stirring, until vegetables are very soft. Add cream, brandy, salt and black pepper. Mix gently, but thoroughly. Cook 3 minutes longer on low heat. Add crawfish. Cook until tender. Remove from heat; cool slightly. Heat oven to 350°F.

2. For Crust, prepare 9-inch Classic Crisco® Double Crust. Press bottom crust into 9-inch pie plate. Spoon in filling. Moisten pastry edge with water.

3. Cover pie with top crust. Cut slits or designs into top crust to allow steam to escape. Bake at 350°F for 25 to 30 minutes or until filling in center is bubbly and crust is golden brown. Serve warm.
Makes 1 (9-inch) pie

Crustless Carrot Quiche

Nonstick cooking spray
2 cups finely shredded carrots
3 eggs *plus* 6 egg whites, beaten
   together
1¼ cups skim milk
1 tablespoon minced dried onion
½ teaspoon garlic powder
¼ teaspoon salt
⅛ teaspoon ground ginger
⅛ teaspoon pepper
½ cup (2 ounces) shredded Cheddar
   cheese*

Preheat oven to 350°F. Spray 9-inch pie plate with cooking spray. Cook carrots in lightly salted boiling water about 5 minutes; drain well. Combine eggs, milk, onion, garlic powder, salt, ginger and pepper; stir in well-drained cooked carrots and cheese. Pour into prepared pie plate. Bake 30 to 50 minutes or until knife inserted near center comes out clean.

Makes 1 (9-inch) crustless quiche

*Use low-fat cheese, if available.

Favorite recipe from Sauder's Penn Dutch Eggs

Thirty Little Filled Pies

3¼ to 3¾ cups all-purpose flour, divided
1 package RED STAR® QUICK-RISE™
   Yeast or Active Dry Yeast
2 tablespoons sugar
1 teaspoon salt
1 cup water
½ cup butter or margarine
   Cheese Filling *or* Sausage Cheese
   Filling (recipes follow)
1 egg, beaten

In large mixer bowl, combine 2 cups flour, yeast, sugar and salt. Heat water and butter to 120° to 130°F (butter does not need to melt). Add liquid to flour mixture

Thirty Little Filled Pies

and blend at low speed until moistened; beat 3 minutes at medium speed. By hand, gradually stir in enough remaining flour to make soft dough. Knead on floured surface until smooth and elastic, 3 to 5 minutes. Divide dough into 6 portions and place each in small plastic sandwich bag. Flatten to disk shape and let rest 5 minutes. (Disk-shaped dough may be refrigerated or frozen. When ready to use, bring to room temperature.) Let dough rise 15 minutes before dividing and shaping.

Preheat oven to 400°F. Divide each portion into 5 pieces. Pat each piece into 4-inch circle and place on greased cookie sheet. Spoon about 1 tablespoon Cheese or Sausage Cheese Filling on each circle. Fold half of circle over filling. Seal edge with fingers, then fork. Brush tops with beaten egg. Bake 12 to 15 minutes or until golden brown. Remove from cookie sheet. Serve warm.

Makes 30 (4-inch) individual pies.

Cheese Filling: Combine 1 egg, ½ cup Ricotta cheese, 2 tablespoons Parmesan cheese, 2 teaspoons chopped fresh parsley and 1 cup (4 ounces) shredded mozzarella cheese. Makes enough filling for 15 pies.

Sausage Cheese Filling: Combine ½ pound pork sausage (browned and drained), ¾ cup (3 ounces) shredded Swiss cheese, 2 teaspoons prepared mustard and 1 tablespoon horseradish. Makes enough filling for 15 pies.

Note: Filling recipes can be doubled.

Mediterranean Phyllo Pie

1 cup sliced fresh mushrooms
¾ cup olive oil *or* melted butter
1 (26-ounce) jar CLASSICO® Di Napoli
    (Tomato & Basil) Pasta Sauce
2 cups chopped cooked chicken
1 (14-ounce) can artichoke hearts,
    drained and chopped *or* 1 (9-ounce)
    package frozen artichoke hearts,
    thawed, drained and chopped
½ cup sliced pitted ripe olives
1 teaspoon WYLER'S® or STEERO®
    Chicken-Flavor Instant Bouillon
1 (16-ounce) package frozen phyllo
    pastry dough, thawed
¾ cup grated Parmesan or Romano
    cheese

In large skillet, cook mushrooms in
2 tablespoons oil until tender. Add pasta
sauce, chicken, artichokes, olives and
bouillon. Bring to a boil; reduce heat and
simmer, uncovered, 20 minutes, stirring
occasionally. Preheat oven to 400°F.
Meanwhile, place 2 pastry sheets in
bottom of greased 15×10-inch baking
pan, pressing into corners. Brush with oil.
Working quickly, repeat with pastry and
oil, using 2 sheets pastry at a time until 14
sheets have been used. Sprinkle with ¼
cup cheese. Spread chicken mixture over
pastry; top with ¼ *cup* cheese. Repeat
layering with remaining pastry sheets and
oil until all pastry has been used. Trim
edges of pastry even with edges of pan.
Top with remaining ¼ *cup* cheese. Bake 25
to 30 minutes or until golden. Refrigerate
leftovers.   *Makes 8 to 10 servings*

Kentucky Burgoo Pie

Burgoo Filling
1½ pounds chicken, skinned
½ pound beef stew meat
½ pound pork shoulder roast
½ pound veal shoulder roast
1½ cups water
2 carrots, peeled and sliced
2 potatoes, peeled and cubed
2 tomatoes, peeled and chopped
1 rib celery, chopped
1 medium onion, chopped
1 small green pepper, chopped
1 cup fresh or drained, canned butter
    beans or lima beans
1 cup fresh or frozen whole kernel
    corn
½ cup tomato juice
1 can (10.5 ounces) tomato puree
1 tablespoon salt
1½ teaspoons hot pepper sauce
1½ teaspoons Worcestershire sauce
1 teaspoon black pepper
½ teaspoon ground red pepper

Crust
10-inch Classic Crisco® Double Crust
    (pages 6 and 7)

Sauce
⅓ cup butter or margarine
⅓ cup all-purpose flour
½ teaspoon salt
¼ teaspoon black pepper
⅔ cup milk

Decorations
9-inch Classic Crisco® Single Crust
    (pages 6 and 7)

1. For Burgoo Filling, combine chicken,
beef, pork, veal and water in 5-quart
Dutch oven. Cover and simmer, turning
chicken and meat frequently, until tender,
about 1½ to 2 hours. Add additional
water, if necessary. Drain, reserving liquid;

cool. Debone meat; cut into ¼-inch cubes. Place meat and reserved liquid in large container. Refrigerate several hours or overnight. Skim off and discard fat from surface.

2. Place meat and liquid in Dutch oven. Add carrots, potatoes, tomatoes, celery, onion, green pepper, butter beans, corn, tomato juice, tomato puree, 1 tablespoon salt, pepper sauce, Worcestershire sauce, 1 teaspoon black pepper and red pepper to Dutch oven. Simmer, covered, 1 hour. Uncover; simmer 2 hours. Remove from heat.

3. Prepare 10-inch Classic Crisco® Double Crust. Roll and press bottom crust into 10-inch pie plate or 1½-quart casserole. *Do not bake.* Heat oven to 425°F.

4. For Sauce, melt butter in medium saucepan. Stir in flour, ½ teaspoon salt and ¼ teaspoon black pepper. Cook and stir until bubbly. Remove from heat. Stir in milk. Return to heat; cook and stir 1

minute. Remove from heat. Stir in small amount of Burgoo Filling. Continue adding small amounts of Burgoo Filling until mixture in saucepan measures about 2 cups. Return to Dutch oven. Stir to blend. Spoon 3½ cups into unbaked pie crust. (Refrigerate or freeze remaining thickened burgoo for additional pie.) Moisten pastry edge with water.

5. Roll out top crust. Lift onto filled pie. Trim ½ inch beyond edge of pie plate. Fold top edge under bottom crust. *Do not flute.*

6. For Decorations, prepare 9-inch Classic Crisco® Single Crust. Roll dough into 10×8-inch rectangle. Cut 12 (⅜-inch) strips and 4 leaf shapes from crust. Braid strips. Moisten edge of top crust with water. Place braids on edge of pie. Moisten underside of leaves. Arrange on top of crust. Cut slits or shapes into top to allow steam to escape.

7. Bake at 425°F for 30 to 35 minutes. Serve warm. Refrigerate leftover pie.
Makes 1 (10-inch) pie

Kentucky Burgoo Pie

Chicken Hash Pie

4 large potatoes, peeled and diced
1 cup (½ pint) heavy cream, divided
6 tablespoons butter or margarine,
    divided
¼ teaspoon *plus* ⅛ teaspoon freshly
    ground pepper
    Pinch ground nutmeg
    Salt to taste
1 cup chopped green onions with tops
½ cup chopped celery
2 tablespoons all-purpose flour
1 cup chicken stock or broth
3 cups chopped cooked PERDUE®
    Chicken or Turkey
¼ teaspoon dried thyme leaves,
    crumbled
4 eggs

Preheat oven to 350°F. Grease 9-inch pie plate. In large saucepan over medium-high heat, bring potatoes to a boil in enough salted water to cover. Reduce heat to low; cook until tender, about 15 minutes. Drain and mash, adding ¼ cup cream, 2 tablespoons butter, ¼ teaspoon pepper, nutmeg and salt. Cover; set aside.

In large skillet over medium-high heat, melt remaining 4 tablespoons butter. Cook and stir green onions and celery in butter 3 minutes. Whisk in flour; cook 3 minutes. Add stock and remaining ¾ cup cream; bring to a boil, whisking constantly. Stir in chicken, thyme, salt and ⅛ teaspoon pepper. Spread chicken mixture into prepared pie plate; top with potatoes. Make four depressions in potatoes with back of spoon. Bake 15 minutes. Remove from oven; carefully break eggs into depressions. Season with salt and pepper; bake 15 minutes or until eggs are set to desired doneness.

Makes 1 (9-inch) deep-dish pie

Top to bottom: Fancy Chicken Puff Pie, Cajun Pie (page 18), Empanada Pie (page 18), Chicken Hash Pie

Fancy Chicken Puff Pie

¼ cup butter or margarine
¼ cup chopped shallots
¼ cup all-purpose flour
1 cup chicken stock or broth
¼ cup sherry
    Salt to taste
⅛ teaspoon white pepper
    Pinch ground nutmeg
¼ pound ham, cut into 2×¼-inch strips
3 cups cooked PERDUE® Chicken or
    Turkey, cut into 2×¼-inch strips
1½ cups fresh asparagus *or* 1 package
    (10 ounces) frozen asparagus, cut
    into 2-inch pieces
1 cup (½ pint) heavy cream
    Pastry for 1-crust 9-inch pie *or* 1 sheet
    frozen puff pastry, thawed
1 egg, beaten

Preheat oven to 425°F. In medium saucepan over medium-high heat, melt butter; lightly cook and stir shallots. Whisk in flour; cook 3 minutes. Add stock and sherry. Bring to a boil, whisking constantly; season with salt, pepper and nutmeg. Reduce heat to low; simmer 5 minutes. Stir in ham, chicken, asparagus and cream. Pour chicken mixture into 9-inch pie plate.

Cut 1 (8-inch) crust from pastry, using plate to trace pattern. Cut pastry shapes from extra pastry with cookie cutter, if desired. Place crust on cookie sheet moistened with cold water; prick with fork. Brush crust with egg. Decorate with shapes and brush shapes with egg.

Place crust and decorative shapes with filled pie plate in oven. Bake 10 minutes. *Reduce oven temperature to 350°F;* bake 10 to 15 minutes or until crust is golden brown and filling is hot and set. Remove crust, decorative shapes and filled pie plate from oven. With spatula, place crust over hot filling; arrange decorative shapes on top. Serve immediately. *Makes 4 servings*

Cajun Pie

Buttermilk Biscuits (recipe follows)
¼ pound lean bacon
   Vegetable oil
 3 tablespoons all-purpose flour
½ cup chopped onion
½ cup chopped green pepper
½ cup fresh ripe or canned chopped
      tomatoes
 2 tablespoons Worcestershire sauce
   Hot pepper sauce to taste
1¼ cups water
   Salt to taste
½ cup frozen corn
½ cup frozen lima beans
 2 cups chopped cooked PERDUE®
      Chicken or Turkey

Preheat oven to 425°F. Prepare Buttermilk Biscuits; set aside. Grease 1 deep-dish 9-inch pie plate or ovenproof dish. In large heavy skillet over medium-high heat, cook bacon until crisp. Remove bacon with slotted spoon; crumble. Pour drippings into measuring cup; add enough oil to measure ½ cup. Return to skillet; stir in flour. Cook over medium heat, stirring constantly, 5 to 10 minutes or until well browned. Add onions; cook 1 minute. Stir in green peppers, tomatoes, Worcestershire sauce, pepper sauce and water; season with salt. Simmer 1 to 3 minutes or until slightly thickened; stir in corn, lima beans, bacon and chicken. Pour into prepared dish. Cover chicken mixture with biscuits so edges touch. Bake 15 to 20 minutes or until golden.

Makes 1 (9-inch) deep-dish pie

Buttermilk Biscuits

2 cups all-purpose flour
1 teaspoon salt
1 teaspoon baking powder
1 teaspoon baking soda
¼ cup shortening *or* butter
   About ¾ cup buttermilk

Preheat oven to 425°F. In large bowl, sift together flour, salt, baking powder and baking soda. Cut in shortening until mixture resembles coarse crumbs. Stir in just enough buttermilk so dough holds together; turn out onto floured surface. Pat to ½-inch thickness; cut into 2-inch rounds.

Empañada Pie

Short Pastry
 2 cups all-purpose flour
¾ teaspoon salt
 6 tablespoons butter or margarine
 2 tablespoons lard or shortening
   About ⅓ cup ice-cold water

Filling
 2 tablespoons butter or margarine
½ cup thinly sliced onion
 1 cup thinly sliced green pepper
 1 hot green chili pepper, chopped
 1 cup chopped fresh or stewed
      tomatoes
 1 cup raisins
½ cup pitted green olives sliced into
      rounds
¼ cup cider vinegar
 1 tablespoon tomato paste
⅛ teaspoon ground cinnamon
   Salt to taste
 3 cups chopped cooked PERDUE®
      Chicken or Turkey
 1 egg, beaten

Preheat oven to 425°F. In small bowl, combine flour and ¾ teaspoon salt. With pastry blender, fork or two knives, cut in butter and lard until mixture resembles coarse crumbs. Gradually stir in water until dough forms ball; *do not overmix.*

Grease 1 deep-dish 9-inch pie plate or ovenproof dish. Roll out two thirds of the pastry; line bottom of pie plate. Pierce well with fork. Roll remaining pastry to ⅛-inch thickness. (Pastry can be prepared ahead and refrigerated until filling is ready.)

In medium saucepan over medium-high heat, melt butter. Add onion, green pepper and chili pepper; cook and stir 3 minutes or until softened. Add tomatoes, raisins, olives, vinegar and tomato paste; cook 5 minutes. Season with cinnamon and salt; stir in chicken. Spread chicken mixture in prepared pie plate; top with pastry. Flute edges. Cut decorative slits in top; brush with beaten egg. Bake on bottom shelf of oven 30 minutes or until browned.

Makes 1 (9-inch) deep-dish pie

Turkey-Olive Ragoût en Crust

½ **pound Boneless White or Dark Turkey Meat, cut into 1-inch cubes**
1 **clove garlic, minced**
1 **teaspoon vegetable oil**
¼ **cup (about 10) small whole frozen onions**
½ **cup reduced-sodium chicken bouillon *or* turkey broth**
½ **teaspoon dried parsley flakes**
⅛ **teaspoon dried thyme leaves, crumbled**
1 **small bay leaf**
1 **medium red potato, skin on, cut into ½-inch cubes**
10 **frozen snow peas**
8 **whole small pitted ripe olives**
1 **can (4 ounces) refrigerated crescent rolls**
½ **teaspoon dried dill weed, crumbled**

1. Preheat oven to 375°F.

2. In medium skillet over medium heat, cook and stir turkey in garlic and oil 3 to 4 minutes or until no longer pink; remove and set aside. Add onions to skillet; cook and stir until lightly browned. Add bouillon, parsley, thyme, bay leaf and potatoes. Bring mixture to a boil. Reduce heat; cover and simmer 10 minutes or until potatoes are tender. Remove and discard bay leaf.

3. Combine turkey mixture with potato mixture. Stir in snow peas and olives. Divide mixture between 2 (1¾-cup) individual ovenproof casseroles.

4. Divide crescent rolls into 2 rectangles; press perforations together to seal. If necessary, roll out each rectangle to make dough large enough to cover top of each casserole. Sprinkle dough with dill weed, pressing lightly into dough. Cut small decorative shape from each dough piece; discard cutouts or place on baking sheet and bake in oven with casseroles. Place dough over turkey-vegetable mixture in casseroles. Trim dough to fit; press dough to edge of each casserole to seal. Bake 7 to 8 minutes or until pastry is golden brown.

Makes 2 individual deep-dish pies

Lattice Crust Variation: With pastry wheel or knife, cut each rectangle lengthwise into 6 strips. Arrange strips, lattice-fashion, over turkey-vegetable mixture; trim dough to fit. Press ends of dough to edge of each casserole to seal.

Note: For more golden crust, brush top of dough with beaten egg yolk before baking.

*Favorite recipe from **National Turkey Federation***

Turkey-Olive Ragoût en Crust

Gratin of Apples, Onion and Gruyère

Tart Shells
¾ cup flour
½ teaspoon sugar
   Pinch salt
5 tablespoons butter
1 tablespoon cold water
1 egg yolk

Filling
2 tablespoons butter, divided
1 medium yellow onion, thinly sliced
1 WASHINGTON Granny Smith apple, cored and thinly sliced
8 thin slices WASHINGTON Winesap apple
4 thin slices Gruyère cheese
2 tablespoons finely chopped fresh chives (optional)

Preheat oven to 400°F. For Tart Shells, combine flour, sugar and salt in food processor or blender. Add butter; process until mixture resembles coarse crumbs. Add water and egg yolk; process until dough forms a ball (add additional water, if necessary).

Gratin of Apples, Onion and Gruyère

Divide dough into 4 pieces. On lightly floured surface, roll out each piece to 5-inch round. Fit each round into 4-inch tart pan. Bake 12 to 15 minutes or until golden. *Reduce oven temperature to 350°F.*

For Filling, melt 1 tablespoon butter in skillet. Add onions; cook, covered, 10 minutes, stirring occasionally. Set aside. Melt remaining butter in separate skillet. Add apple slices; cook and stir until tender and golden. Fill each shell with cooked onions; top with apple slices arranged in fan pattern, alternating Winesap slices with Granny Smith slices for each tart. Cover apple fans with cheese; bake 5 minutes. If desired, garnish tarts with chopped chives.   *Makes 4 (4-inch) tarts*

Favorite recipe from Washington Apple Commission

Turkey Cottage Pie

¼ cup butter or margarine
¼ cup all-purpose flour
1 envelope LIPTON® Recipe Secrets Golden Onion Recipe Soup Mix
2 cups water
2 cups cut-up cooked turkey *or* chicken
1 package (10 ounces) frozen mixed vegetables, thawed
1¼ cups (about 5 ounces) shredded Swiss cheese
⅛ teaspoon pepper
5 cups hot mashed potatoes

Preheat oven to 375°F. In large saucepan, melt butter and cook flour over medium-low heat, stirring constantly, 5 minutes or until golden. Stir in golden onion recipe soup mix thoroughly blended with water. Bring to a boil, then simmer 15 minutes or until thickened. Stir in turkey, vegetables, 1 cup cheese and pepper. Turn into lightly greased 2-quart casserole; top with hot potatoes, then remaining cheese. Bake 30 minutes or until bubbling.

Makes about 8 servings

Potato la Creme Pie

Crust
   9-inch Classic Crisco® Double Crust
      (pages 6 and 7)
   ⅛ teaspoon garlic salt
   ⅛ teaspoon onion salt

Filling
   3 tablespoons butter or margarine
   1 small onion, diced
   1 or 2 small carrots, cooked and diced
   2 or 3 medium Idaho (russet) potatoes,
      cooked and shredded
   2 green onion tops, chopped
   1½ cups dairy sour cream
   1 can (10¾ ounces) condensed cream of
      chicken soup
   1 cup (4 ounces) shredded sharp
      Cheddar cheese
   ½ teaspoon salt
   ⅛ teaspoon white pepper
   ¾ cup chopped cooked chicken *or*
      turkey breast (optional)

1. Prepare 9-inch Classic Crisco® Double Crust, adding garlic salt and onion salt to flour mixture. Press bottom crust into 9-inch pie plate. *Do not bake.* Heat oven to 425°F.

2. For Filling, melt butter in small saucepan. Add onion; cook until tender. Add carrots; cook and stir 1 or 2 minutes. Place potatoes in large bowl. Add vegetable mixture and green onion tops.

3. Combine sour cream and soup in small bowl. Add to potato mixture along with cheese, salt, white pepper and chicken. Spoon filling into unbaked pie crust. Moisten pastry edge with water.

4. Cover pie with top crust. Cut slits into top crust to allow steam to escape. Bake at 425°F for 20 to 25 minutes or until crust is golden brown. Serve warm.

Makes 1 (9-inch) pie

Rosemary Chicken Sauté Pizza

Rosemary Chicken Sauté Pizza

   2 boneless skinless chicken breast
      halves, cut into strips
   1 medium onion, sliced
   ½ teaspoon dried rosemary leaves,
      crushed
   1 tablespoon vegetable oil
   1 (12-inch) prepared, pre-baked pizza
      crust*
   1 can (14½ ounces) DEL MONTE®
      Pizza Style Chunky Tomatoes
   2 cups (8 ounces) shredded mozzarella
      cheese
   1 green, yellow or red pepper, sliced

Preheat oven to 450°F. In large skillet, cook chicken, onion and rosemary in oil over medium-high heat; drain. Place crust on baking sheet. Spread tomatoes evenly over crust. Layer with half of the cheese. Top with chicken mixture, pepper slices and remaining 1 cup cheese. Bake 10 minutes or until hot and bubbly.

Makes 1 (12-inch) pizza

*Substitute 4 (6-inch) prepared, pre-baked pizza crusts, if desired. Refrigerated or frozen pizza dough may also be used; prepare and bake as package directs.

Clam Bake Pie

3 slices bacon
¼ cup chopped onion
¼ cup unsifted flour
1 (15-ounce) can SNOW'S® or
    DOXSEE® Condensed New
    England Clam Chowder
1 (6½-ounce) can SNOW'S® or
    DOXSEE® Chopped or Minced
    Clams, drained, reserving
    ¼ cup liquid
1 cup whole kernel corn
½ cup BORDEN® or MEADOW
    GOLD® Half-and-Half
2 tablespoons chopped fresh parsley *or*
    1 tablespoon dried parsley flakes
Pastry for 2-crust 9-inch pie

Place rack in lowest position in oven; preheat oven to 425°F. In medium skillet, cook bacon until crisp; remove and crumble. In 2 tablespoons drippings, cook onion until tender; stir in flour until smooth. Add chowder, reserved clam liquid, corn and half-and-half; cook and stir until thickened. Stir in clams, bacon and parsley. Turn into pastry-lined 9-inch pie plate. Cover with top crust; cut slits near center. Seal and flute. Bake 30 minutes or until golden. Let stand 20 minutes before serving. Garnish as desired. Refrigerate leftovers.

Makes 1 (9-inch) pie

Quiche Lorraine
Grey Poupon® Style

1 cup (4 ounces) shredded Swiss cheese
4 slices bacon, cooked and crumbled
2 tablespoons chopped green onions
8 unbaked (3-inch) tart shells *or*
    1 unbaked (9-inch) pie shell
3 eggs, slightly beaten
1 cup light cream or half-and-half
¼ cup GREY POUPON® Dijon Mustard
    or Country Dijon Mustard

Preheat oven to 375°F. Place cheese, bacon and green onions evenly into tart shells. In small bowl, combine eggs, cream and mustard. Pour evenly over cheese mixture. Bake 25 to 30 minutes for tarts (35 to 40 minutes for pie) or until knife inserted in filling comes out clean.

Makes 8 servings

Note: If prepared pie crust in foil pie plate is used, reduce baking time by 5 to 10 minutes.

Fish & Chowder Pie

½ pound white fish fillets, fresh or
    frozen, thawed, cut into small
    pieces
1 (15-ounce) can SNOW'S® or
    DOXSEE® Condensed New
    England Clam Chowder
2 (6½-ounce) cans SNOW'S® or
    DOXSEE® Chopped or Minced
    Clams, drained, reserving ¼ cup
    liquid
⅓ cup BORDEN® or MEADOW
    GOLD® Half-and-Half or Milk
1 (10-ounce) package frozen peas and
    carrots, thawed
¼ cup unsifted flour
½ teaspoon dried thyme leaves,
    crumbled
⅛ to ¼ teaspoon pepper
Pastry for 1-crust 10-inch pie

Preheat oven to 400°F. In 1½-quart baking dish, combine all ingredients except pastry. Top with pastry; cut slits near center. Seal and flute. Bake 1 hour or until golden brown. Let stand 10 minutes before serving. Refrigerate leftovers.

Makes 6 to 8 servings

Top to bottom: Fish & Chowder Pie,
Clam Bake Pie

String Pie

String Pie

1 pound ground beef
½ cup chopped onion
¼ cup chopped green pepper
1 jar (15½ ounces) spaghetti sauce
8 ounces spaghetti, cooked and drained
⅓ cup grated Parmesan cheese
2 eggs, beaten
2 teaspoons butter
1 cup cottage cheese
½ cup (2 ounces) shredded mozzarella
 cheese

Preheat oven to 350°F. Cook beef, onion
and green pepper in large skillet over
medium-high heat until meat is browned,
stirring to separate meat. Drain fat. Stir in
spaghetti sauce; mix well. Combine hot
spaghetti, Parmesan cheese, eggs and
butter in large bowl; mix well. Place in
bottom of 13×9-inch pan. Spread cottage
cheese over top. Pour sauce mixture over
cottage cheese. Sprinkle mozzarella
cheese over top. Bake about 20 minutes or
until cheese melts. *Makes 6 to 8 servings*

Favorite recipe from **North Dakota Beef Commission**

Leek Mushroom Pie

Crust
 9-inch Classic Crisco® Double Crust
  (pages 6 and 7)
Filling
 8 leeks (about 3 pounds), halved
  lengthwise, washed, patted dry
 ¼ cup CRISCO® Shortening
 8 ounces fresh mushrooms, coarsely
  chopped
 5 tablespoons whipping cream, divided
 ½ teaspoon salt
  Dash white pepper

1. Prepare 9-inch Classic Crisco® Double
Crust. Roll and press bottom crust into
9-inch pie plate. *Do not bake.* Heat oven to
425°F.

2. For Filling, remove green part of leeks.
Chop white part coarsely.

3. Melt Crisco® in large skillet. Add
chopped leeks. Cook and stir 5 minutes.
Add mushrooms. Cook and stir 5 minutes.
Add 4 tablespoons cream, 1 tablespoon at
a time. Cook and stir 2 minutes after each
addition. Add salt, white pepper and
remaining 1 tablespoon cream. Cool
mixture 10 minutes. Spoon into unbaked
pie crust. Moisten pastry edge with water.

4. Roll out top crust. Lift onto filled pie.
Trim ½ inch beyond edge of pie plate. Fold
top edge under bottom crust; flute. Cut
slits into top crust to allow steam to
escape.

5. Bake at 425°F for 30 minutes or until
lightly browned. Let stand 10 minutes
before cutting and serving. Refrigerate
leftover pie. *Makes 1 (9-inch) pie*

Santa Fe Corn Pie

1 pound ground beef
⅓ cup chopped onion
1 clove garlic, minced
¼ cup DEL MONTE® Tomato Ketchup
2 teaspoons chili powder
¼ teaspoon salt
¾ teaspoon dried oregano leaves, crumbled, divided
1 can (12 ounces) DEL MONTE® Vacuum Packed Whole Kernel Golden Sweet Corn
1 package (8 ounces) corn muffin mix
1 tablespoon melted butter or margarine
1 can (14½ ounces) DEL MONTE® Original Recipe Stewed Tomatoes
2 teaspoons cornstarch
½ teaspoon sugar
   Parsley

Preheat oven to 400°F. Brown meat with onion and garlic; drain. Add ketchup, chili powder, salt and ½ teaspoon oregano. Line 9-inch pie plate with meat mixture. Pour corn into center of meat shell. Prepare muffin mix as package directs, stirring in melted butter. Spread evenly over meat and corn. Bake 30 minutes. Loosen edge with knife. Invert pie onto serving dish. Drain tomatoes, reserving juice in saucepan. Add cornstarch, sugar and ¼ teaspoon oregano to juice in saucepan. Cook, stirring constantly, until thickened. Add tomatoes. Heat through and serve over pie. Garnish with parsley.

Makes 1 (9-inch) pie

No-Crust Holiday Quiche

   Nonstick cooking spray
1 package (10 ounces) frozen chopped spinach, thawed and drained well
¼ pound smoked turkey breast, diced
½ cup sliced green onions
2 tablespoons diced pimiento
1 cup (4 ounces) shredded Swiss cheese
4 eggs
1 can (5 ounces) evaporated skim milk (about ⅔ cup)
2 tablespoons flour
1 teaspoon Worcestershire sauce
¼ teaspoon dried rosemary leaves, crumbled
   Whole almonds (optional)
   Additional pimiento and fresh rosemary sprigs for garnish

Preheat oven to 375°F. Generously coat 9-inch pie plate with cooking spray. Layer spinach, turkey, green onions and 2 tablespoons pimiento in prepared pie plate. Sprinkle with cheese. Whisk together eggs, milk, flour, Worcestershire sauce and dried rosemary; pour over layered ingredients. Arrange almonds over top to make pine-cone shape, if desired. Bake 25 to 30 minutes or until knife inserted near center comes out clean. Garnish with additional pimiento and fresh rosemary.

Makes 1 (9-inch) crustless quiche

*Favorite recipe from **Sauder's Penn Dutch Eggs***

No-Crust Holiday Quiche

Simply Special Vegetable Pie

1 package (10 ounces) frozen chopped
    spinach, thawed and well drained
1 can (2.8 ounces) DURKEE® French
    Fried Onions
1 egg
½ teaspoon garlic salt
1 package (1⅛ ounces) cheese sauce mix
1 cup milk
1 bag (16 ounces) frozen vegetable
    combination (broccoli, carrots, red
    pepper, water chestnuts), thawed
    and drained

Preheat oven to 350°F. In small bowl,
combine spinach, ½ *can* French Fried
Onions, egg and garlic salt; stir until well
mixed. Using back of spoon, spread
spinach mixture onto bottom and up side
of greased 9-inch pie plate to form shell.
In medium saucepan, prepare cheese
sauce mix as package directs using milk;
stir in vegetables. Pour vegetable mixture
into spinach shell. Bake, covered, 30
minutes or until heated through. Top with
remaining onions; bake, uncovered, 5
minutes or until onions are golden brown.
Makes 1 (9-inch) pie

Heartland Shepherd's Pie

¾ pound ground beef
1 onion, chopped
1 can (14½ ounces) DEL MONTE®
    Original Recipe Stewed Tomatoes
1 can (8 ounces) DEL MONTE® Tomato
    Sauce
1 can (17 ounces) DEL MONTE® Mixed
    Vegetables, drained
    Salt and pepper to taste
    Instant mashed potato flakes
3 cloves garlic, minced
    Milk
    Butter

Preheat oven to 375°F. In skillet, brown
meat with onions; drain. Drain tomatoes,
reserving liquid. Add liquid and tomato
sauce to skillet; cook over high heat until
reduced and thickened. Chop tomatoes;
stir into meat mixture with vegetables.
Season with salt and pepper. In saucepan,
prepare potatoes, using garlic, milk and
butter as specified on package to make 6
servings. Cook as package directs. Salt
and pepper to taste. In 2-quart casserole
dish, layer meat mixture and potatoes.
Bake 20 minutes or until heated through.
Makes 4 to 6 servings

Hearty Sausage & Hash Browns Pie

1 (24-ounce) package frozen *shredded*
    hash browns potatoes, thawed
    (about 4½ cups)
⅓ cup margarine or butter, melted
1½ teaspoons WYLER'S® or STEERO®
    Beef-Flavor Instant Bouillon
1 pound bulk country sausage
⅓ cup chopped onion
3 eggs, beaten
1 cup BORDEN® or MEADOW
    GOLD® Cottage Cheese
4 slices BORDEN® Process American
    Cheese Food, cut into pieces

Preheat oven to 400°F. In medium bowl,
combine potatoes, margarine and
bouillon. Spoon into lightly greased 10-
inch pie plate; press onto bottom and up
side to rim to form crust. Bake 25 minutes.
Reduce oven temperature to 350°F. In large
skillet, cook sausage and onion; pour off
fat. Stir in eggs, cottage cheese and cheese
food pieces. Pour into prepared crust. Bake
30 to 35 minutes or until set. Let stand 5
minutes. Garnish as desired. Refrigerate
leftovers.   *Makes 1 (10-inch) pie*

Top to bottom: Dilly Meat Pies, Hearty Sausage & Hash Browns Pie

Dilly Meat Pies

1 (15-ounce) package refrigerated pie shells
½ pound lean ground beef
½ cup chopped onion
1½ cups diced cooked potatoes
6 slices BORDEN® Process American Cheese Food, cut into pieces
1 (8-ounce) container BORDEN® or MEADOW GOLD® Sour Cream, at room temperature
½ cup shredded carrot
3 tablespoons finely chopped dill pickle
1 teaspoon WYLER'S® or STEERO® Beef-Flavor Instant Bouillon

Preheat oven to 400°F. On large baking sheet, unfold pie crusts; press out fold lines. In medium skillet, brown meat with onion; pour off fat. Add remaining ingredients; mix well. On half of each crust, spread half of the meat mixture to within 1 inch of outside edge. Brush crust edge with water. Fold over and seal edges. Bake 20 to 25 minutes or until golden brown. Cut into wedges to serve. Refrigerate leftovers.

Makes 4 to 6 servings

China Choy Quiche

1 unbaked (9-inch) pie shell
3 eggs
2/3 cup milk
1 (8-ounce) can LA CHOY® Sliced
   Water Chestnuts, drained and
   coarsely chopped
1 cup (4 ounces) shredded Monterey
   Jack cheese
3/4 cup *each*: finely chopped red bell
   peppers and sliced fresh
   mushrooms
1/3 cup sliced green onions
1 tablespoon LA CHOY® Soy Sauce
1/2 teaspoon *each*: garlic powder and dry
   mustard
1/4 teaspoon *each*: black pepper and
   Oriental sesame oil

Preheat oven to 425°F. Bake pie shell 5
minutes; set aside. *Reduce oven temperature
to 350°F.* In large bowl, beat together eggs
and milk; stir in *remaining* ingredients.
Pour into partially baked shell. Bake 50 to
55 minutes or until knife inserted 1 inch
from edge comes out clean. Let stand 10
minutes before serving. Garnish, if
desired. *Makes 1 (9-inch) quiche*

Turkey 'n Stuffing Pie

1 1/4 cups water*
1/4 cup butter or margarine*
3 1/2 cups seasoned stuffing crumbs*
1 can (2.8 ounces) DURKEE® French
   Fried Onions
1 can (10 3/4 ounces) condensed cream of
   celery soup
3/4 cup milk
1 1/2 cups (7 ounces) cubed cooked turkey
1 package (10 ounces) frozen peas,
   thawed and drained

Preheat oven to 350°F. In medium
saucepan, heat water and butter; stir until
butter melts. Remove from heat. Stir in
seasoned stuffing crumbs and *1/2 can*
French Fried Onions. Spoon stuffing
mixture into 9-inch round or fluted baking
dish. Press stuffing evenly onto bottom
and up side of dish to form shell. In
medium bowl, combine soup, milk, turkey
and peas; pour into stuffing shell. Bake,
covered, 30 minutes or until heated
through. Top with remaining onions;
bake, uncovered, 5 minutes or until onions
are golden brown. *Makes 1 (9-inch) pie*

*Substitute 3 cups leftover stuffing for
butter, water and stuffing crumbs, if
desired. If stuffing is dry, stir in water,
1 tablespoon at a time, until moist but
not wet.

Coney Dog Pie

1 (6- or 8 1/2-ounce) package corn muffin
   mix
1 pound lean ground beef
1 (12-ounce) jar BENNETT'S® Chili
   Sauce
1 teaspoon WYLER'S® or STEERO®
   Beef-Flavor Instant Bouillon
1 teaspoon prepared mustard
1 pound frankfurters, cut into quarters

Preheat oven to 350°F. Prepare muffin mix
as package directs. In 12-inch ovenproof
skillet, brown beef; pour off fat. Add chili
sauce, bouillon, mustard and frankfurters;
bring to a boil. Top with prepared corn
muffin batter. Bake 20 minutes or until
golden brown. Refrigerate leftovers.
Makes 6 to 8 servings

China Choy Quiche

All-American Apple-Pork Pie

1 pound lean pork, cut into thin,
  narrow strips
2 tablespoons vegetable oil
1 small onion, thinly sliced and
  separated into rings
½ cup shredded peeled potato
1 teaspoon salt
¼ to ½ teaspoon caraway seed
¼ to ½ teaspoon pepper
2 WASHINGTON Golden Delicious
  apples, sliced
¼ cup apple juice
1 tablespoon butter or margarine
  Pastry for 1 crust 9-inch pie

Preheat oven to 425°F. Cook pork in hot
oil in large skillet until browned; add
onion and cook until tender. Stir in potato.
Place half of mixture in 9-inch deep-dish
pie plate. Combine seasonings; sprinkle
half over pork mixture. Layer half of the
apples over pork. Repeat layers. Pour juice
over top; dot with butter. Roll pastry to fit
pie plate. Place over filling and flute
edges; cut vents into crust. Bake 15
minutes. *Reduce oven temperature to 350°F.*
Bake 30 to 35 minutes longer or until
apples are tender. Serve hot.
Makes 1 (9-inch) deep-dish pie

Tip: Keep shredded peeled potato in
cold water until ready to use to avoid
discoloration; drain potato well just before
using.

Favorite recipe from **Washington Apple Commission**

All-American Apple-Pork Pie

Tuna Melt Turnovers

1 (15-ounce) package refrigerated pie
  shells
1 (12½-ounce) can tuna, drained
2 hard-cooked eggs, chopped
⅓ cup BENNETT'S® Tartar Sauce
3 cups chopped celery
¼ cup finely chopped carrot
¼ cup chopped onion
2 tablespoons REALEMON® Lemon
  Juice from Concentrate
6 slices BORDEN® Process American
  Cheese Food, quartered
  Additional REALEMON® Lemon
  Juice from Concentrate
Sesame seed

Preheat oven to 425°F. On large baking
sheet, unfold pie shells; press out fold
lines. In medium bowl, combine tuna,
eggs, tartar sauce, celery, carrot, onion and
2 tablespoons ReaLemon® brand. On half
of each crust, place half of cheese food;
top with half of the tuna mixture to within
1 inch of outside edge. Fold over and seal
edges. Brush with additional ReaLemon®
brand; sprinkle with sesame seed. Bake 15
to 18 minutes or until golden brown. Cut
into wedges to serve. Refrigerate leftovers.
Makes 4 to 6 servings

Pizza Style Quiche

1 unbaked (9-inch) pie or tart shell
⅓ cup chopped pepperoni
½ cup chopped onion
⅓ cup chopped green pepper
¾ cup (3 ounces) shredded mozzarella
  cheese
¾ cup (3 ounces) shredded Cheddar
  cheese
1⅓ cups milk
3 eggs
3 tablespoons flour
½ teaspoon garlic salt
⅛ teaspoon black pepper
1 tablespoon grated Parmesan cheese
1 cup CONTADINA® Pizza Sauce

Preheat oven to 425°F. Bake pie shell 6 minutes; remove from oven. *Reduce oven temperature to 350°F.* Cook and stir pepperoni, onion, and green pepper in medium saucepan over medium heat; pour into pie shell. Add mozzarella and Cheddar cheeses. Process milk, eggs, flour, garlic salt, and black pepper in food processor or blender until blended. Pour over ingredients in pie shell. Sprinkle with Parmesan cheese. Bake 25 to 35 minutes or until knife inserted halfway between center and edge comes out clean. Let stand 10 minutes. Serve with warmed pizza sauce. Garnish as desired.

Makes 1 (9-inch) quiche

Vegetable & Cheese Pot Pie

Vegetable & Cheese Pot Pie

2 tablespoons butter or margarine
½ cup sliced green onions
1¾ cups water
1 package LIPTON® Noodles & Sauce–Chicken Flavor
1 package (16 ounces) frozen mixed vegetables, partially thawed
1 cup (4 ounces) shredded mozzarella cheese
1 teaspoon prepared mustard
½ cup milk
1 tablespoon all-purpose flour
Salt and pepper
Pastry for 1-crust 9-inch pie
1 egg yolk
1 tablespoon water

Preheat oven to 425°F. In large saucepan, melt butter and cook green onions over medium heat 3 minutes or until tender. Add 1¾ cups water and bring to a boil. Stir in noodles & chicken flavor sauce and vegetables; continue boiling over medium heat, stirring occasionally, 7 minutes or until noodles are almost tender. Stir in cheese, mustard and milk blended with flour. Cook over medium heat, stirring frequently, 2 minutes or until thickened. Season to taste with salt and pepper.

Turn into greased 1-quart round casserole or soufflé dish, then top with pastry. Press pastry around edge of casserole to seal; trim excess pastry, then flute edges. (Use extra pastry to make decorative shapes.) Brush pastry with egg yolk beaten with 1 tablespoon water. With tip of knife, make small slits in pastry. Bake 12 minutes or until crust is golden brown.

Makes about 4 servings

Meat Variation: Stir in 1 cup cut-up cooked turkey, chicken or ham with salt and pepper. Use greased 1½-quart casserole or soufflé dish and bake 20 minutes.

Mushroom Quiche with Brown Rice Crust

2½ cups cooked brown rice
3 eggs, divided
1 teaspoon chopped fresh rosemary, divided
2 cups (8 ounces) VELVEETA® Shredded Pasteurized Process Cheese Food
1 cup chopped cooked chicken
1 cup mushroom slices
¾ cup milk
⅛ teaspoon pepper

- Heat oven to 350°F.

- Mix rice, 1 of the eggs, beaten, and ½ teaspoon of the rosemary. Press onto bottom and up sides of lightly greased 9-inch quiche dish or pie plate to form crust.

- Bake 10 minutes.

- Mix remaining 2 eggs, beaten, remaining ½ teaspoon rosemary and all other remaining ingredients. Pour into crust.

- Bake 50 to 55 minutes or until filling is set.   *Makes 1 (9-inch) quiche*

Prep time: 20 minutes
Cooking time: 1 hour and 55 minutes

Mushroom Quiche with Brown Rice Crust

Spinach Pizza

3/4 cup chopped onion
2 cloves garlic, crushed
3 tablespoons olive oil
1 cup (10-ounce package) thawed
    frozen chopped spinach, well
    drained
2 tablespoons capers, rinsed
1/2 teaspoon salt
1/4 teaspoon pepper
1 (1-pound) loaf frozen bread dough,
    thawed
1 cup CONTADINA® Pizza Sauce
3/4 cup (3 ounces) shredded mozzarella
    cheese
1/4 cup grated Romano cheese
2 tablespoons toasted pine nuts

Place rack in lowest position in oven.
Preheat oven to 400°F. Cook and stir
onion and garlic in oil in medium
saucepan over medium heat until tender
but not browned. Add spinach, capers,
salt, and pepper. Cook 5 to 10 minutes,
stirring occasionally, until mixture is dry
and crumbly. Roll or stretch bread dough
to fit 12-inch dark metal pizza pan.
Spread pizza sauce over bread dough to
within 1/2 inch of edge. Spread spinach
mixture evenly over sauce. Sprinkle with
cheeses and pine nuts. Bake 15 to 20
minutes or until cheese and crust are
browned. *Makes 1 (12-inch) pizza*

Steak Pot Pie

1 cup chopped onion
2 tablespoons margarine
2 tablespoons all-purpose flour
1 1/2 cups beef broth
1/2 cup A.1.® Steak Sauce
3 cups diced cooked steak
    (about 1 1/2 pounds)
2 cups frozen peas and carrots, thawed
    Pastry for 2-crust 9-inch pie

Preheat oven to 400°F. In 2-quart
saucepan over medium-high heat, cook
onion in margarine until tender. Blend in
flour; cook 1 minute. Add beef broth and
steak sauce; cook and stir until mixture
thickens and begins to boil. Stir in steak
and vegetables. Spoon mixture evenly into
4 (16-ounce) individual ovenproof
casseroles. Roll out and cut pastry crust to
fit over casseroles. Seal crusts to edges of
casseroles. Slit tops of crusts to vent. Bake
at 400°F, 25 minutes or until golden
brown. Serve warm. *Makes 4 servings*

Little Chicken Pies

1/2 cup chopped onion
1/3 cup BLUE BONNET® Margarine
1/3 cup all-purpose flour
1/2 teaspoon dried thyme leaves,
    crumbled
1/4 teaspoon ground black pepper
1 (13 3/4-ounce) can COLLEGE INN®
    Chicken Broth
1 cup half-and-half or light cream
3 cups cubed cooked chicken
1 (10-ounce) package frozen peas and
    carrots, thawed
    Pastry crust for 1-crust 9-inch pie
1 egg yolk, beaten with 1 tablespoon
    water

Preheat oven to 400°F. In large saucepan
over medium-high heat, cook and stir
onion in margarine until tender. Stir in
flour, thyme and pepper; cook and stir
over low heat until smooth. Stir in broth
and half-and-half; heat, stirring often,
until thickened. Add chicken and
vegetables. Divide mixture among 5
(1 1/2-cup) greased casseroles.

Cut pastry to fit top of each casserole; cut
1/2-inch hole into center of each. Place over
chicken mixture; seal edge of pastry and
brush with egg mixture. Bake at 400°F for
20 to 25 minutes or until browned and
bubbly. *Makes 5 servings*

Quick Classic Pizza

1 (12-inch) Italian bread shell *or* prepared pizza crust
1 cup (4 ounces) shredded mozzarella cheese
1 (14-ounce) jar CLASSICO® Pasta Sauce, any flavor
  Pizza toppings: chopped onion, peppers, sliced mushrooms, pepperoni, sliced pitted ripe olives, cooked sausage, cooked ground beef, cooked bacon

Preheat oven to 450°F. Top bread shell with half of the cheese, pasta sauce, desired toppings and remaining cheese. Bake 10 to 12 minutes or until hot and bubbly. Let stand 5 minutes. Serve warm. Refrigerate leftovers.

Makes 1 (12-inch) pizza

Pizza Calzones

½ pound Italian sausage
1 (26-ounce) jar CLASSICO® D'Abruzzi (Beef & Pork) Pasta Sauce
1 cup sliced fresh mushrooms
½ cup chopped green bell pepper
½ cup chopped onion
2 (8-ounce) packages refrigerated crescent rolls
1 egg, beaten
1 tablespoon water
1 cup (4 ounces) shredded mozzarella cheese

Preheat oven to 350°F. In large skillet, brown sausage; pour off fat. Add ¾ *cup* pasta sauce, mushrooms, green pepper and onion; simmer, uncovered, 10 minutes. Meanwhile, unroll crescent roll dough; separate into 8 rectangles. Firmly press perforations together and flatten slightly. In small bowl, mix egg and water; brush on dough edges. Stir cheese into meat mixture. Spoon equal amounts of meat mixture on half of each rectangle to within ½ inch of edges. Fold dough over filling; press to seal edges. Arrange on baking sheet; brush with egg mixture. Bake 15 minutes or until golden brown. Heat remaining pasta sauce; serve sauce with calzones. Refrigerate leftovers.

Makes 8 calzones

Meatza Pizza Pie

1 pound ground round
½ cup fresh bread crumbs (1 slice)
1 egg
2 teaspoons WYLER'S® or STEERO® Beef-Flavor Instant Bouillon
½ teaspoon Italian seasoning
½ cup CLASSICO® Di Napoli (Tomato & Basil) Pasta Sauce
1 (2½-ounce) jar sliced mushrooms, drained
2 tablespoons chopped green bell pepper
2 tablespoons chopped onion
1 cup (4 ounces) shredded mozzarella cheese

Preheat oven to 350°F. In medium bowl, combine meat, crumbs, egg, bouillon and seasoning; mix well. Press evenly onto bottom and up side to rim of 9-inch pie plate to form crust. Bake 15 minutes; pour off fat. Spoon pasta sauce over crust. Top with mushrooms, green pepper, onion and cheese. Bake 10 minutes longer or until cheese melts. Garnish as desired. Refrigerate leftovers.

Makes 1 (9-inch) pie

Top to bottom: Quick Classic Pizza, Pizza Calzone, Meatza Pizza Pie

Old-Fashioned Beef Pot Pie

1 pound ground beef
1 can (11 ounces) condensed beef with
   vegetables and barley soup
½ cup water
1 package (10 ounces) frozen peas and
   carrots, thawed and drained
½ teaspoon seasoned salt
⅛ teaspoon garlic powder
⅛ teaspoon ground black pepper
1 cup (4 ounces) shredded Cheddar
   cheese
1 can (2.8 ounces) DURKEE® French
   Fried Onions
1 package (7.5 ounces) refrigerated
   biscuits

Preheat oven to 350°F. In large skillet,
brown ground beef in large chunks; drain.
Stir in soup, water, vegetables and
seasonings; bring to a boil. Reduce heat
and simmer, uncovered, 5 minutes.
Remove from heat; stir in ½ *cup* cheese and
½ *can* French Fried Onions. Pour into
12×8-inch baking dish. Cut each biscuit in
half; place, cut side down, around edge of
casserole. Bake, uncovered, 15 to 20
minutes or until biscuits are done. Top
with remaining cheese and onions; bake,
uncovered, 5 minutes or until onions are
golden brown.   *Makes 4 to 6 servings*

Old-Fashioned Beef Pot Pie

Sour Cream Chicken Quiche

Crust
   9-inch Classic Crisco® Single Crust
      (pages 6 and 7)
Filling
   2 tablespoons CRISCO® Shortening
   2 tablespoons chopped green bell
      pepper
   2 tablespoons chopped onion
   1 cup cubed cooked chicken
   1 tablespoon all-purpose flour
   ¼ teaspoon salt
      Dash ground nutmeg
      Dash black pepper
   ½ cup (2 ounces) shredded sharp
      Cheddar cheese
   ¼ cup (1 ounce) shredded Swiss cheese
   2 eggs, slightly beaten
   ¾ cup milk
   ¾ cup dairy sour cream

1. Prepare 9-inch Classic Crisco® Single
Crust. *Do not bake.* Heat oven to 400°F.

2. For Filling, melt Crisco® in small skillet.
Add green pepper and onion. Cook on
medium-high heat 3 minutes, stirring
frequently. Add chicken and flour. Cook
and stir 2 minutes. Spread in bottom of
unbaked pie crust. Sprinkle with salt,
nutmeg and black pepper. Top with
Cheddar and Swiss cheeses.

3. Combine eggs, milk and sour cream in
medium bowl. Stir until smooth. Pour
carefully over cheeses.

4. Bake at 400°F for 20 minutes. *Reduce
oven temperature to 350°F.* Bake 30 to 35
minutes or until knife inserted near center
comes out clean. Cool 10 minutes before
cutting and serving. Refrigerate leftovers.
                    Makes 1 (9-inch) pie

Tuna-Swiss Pie

2 cups cooked unsalted long-grain rice
    (⅔ cup uncooked)
1 tablespoon butter or margarine
¼ teaspoon garlic powder
3 eggs
1 can (2.8 ounces) DURKEE® French
    Fried Onions
1 cup (4 ounces) shredded Swiss cheese
1 can (9¼ ounces) water-packed tuna,
    drained and flaked
1 cup milk
¼ teaspoon salt
¼ teaspoon ground black pepper

Preheat oven to 400°F. To hot rice in
saucepan, add butter, garlic powder and
1 slightly beaten egg; mix thoroughly. Spoon
rice mixture into *ungreased* 9-inch pie plate.
Press rice mixture firmly onto bottom and
up side of pie plate to form crust. Layer
½ can French Fried Onions, *½ cup* cheese
and the tuna evenly over rice crust. In
small bowl, combine milk, remaining eggs
and the seasonings; pour over tuna filling.
Bake, uncovered, 30 to 35 minutes or until
center is set. Top with remaining cheese
and onions; bake, uncovered, 1 to
3 minutes or until onions are golden
brown.   *Makes 1 (9-inch) pie*

Apple and Cheese Appetizer Tart

¾ cup fresh parsley sprigs
½ cup walnut pieces
3 tablespoons olive oil
2 tablespoons lemon juice, divided
2 teaspoons dried basil leaves
2 medium apples, cored, thinly sliced
½ package (15 ounces) refrigerated pie
    crust (1 crust)
¾ pound VELVEETA® Pasteurized
    Process Cheese Spread, sliced

Apple and Cheese Appetizer Tart

- Heat oven to 450°F.

- Place parsley, walnuts, oil, 1 tablespoon
  of the juice and basil in food processor or
  blender; cover. Process until walnuts are
  finely chopped.

- Toss apples with remaining 1 tablespoon
  juice.

- Unfold pie crust. Place in 10-inch tart
  pan; trim excess. Prick bottom and sides
  with fork.

- Bake 10 minutes; remove from oven.
  Reduce oven temperature to 400°F.

- Spread parsley mixture over crust.
  Arrange apples and Velveeta®
  Pasteurized Process Cheese Spread
  over parsley mixture.

- Bake 10 minutes or until crust is lightly
  browned. Sprinkle with additional
  chopped parsley and fresh basil leaves, if
  desired. Serve immediately.
                    Makes 1 (10-inch) tart

Prep time: 10 minutes
Cooking time: 20 minutes

Tuna Pot Pies

Filling
2 tablespoons CRISCO® Oil
3 medium carrots, thinly sliced
1 small onion, diced
2 tablespoons all-purpose flour
1 can (12 ounces) evaporated skim milk
1 cup water
1 package (9 ounces) frozen cut green beans *or* peas
1 can (16 ounces) whole potatoes, drained and diced
1 can (12½ to 13 ounces) solid white tuna in water, drained and broken up
1 tablespoon minced fresh dill *or* ¼ teaspoon dried dill weed
¼ teaspoon salt

Crust
1¼ cups all-purpose flour
1 teaspoon baking powder
3 tablespoons CRISCO® Oil
¼ cup cold water

1. For Filling, heat Crisco® Oil in large saucepan on medium heat. Add carrots and onion. Cook until tender. Stir in flour. Cook 1 minute. Gradually stir in milk and water. Cook and stir until mixture thickens slightly.

2. Add green beans, stirring to separate. Remove saucepan from heat. Stir in potatoes, tuna, dill and salt. Spoon into four 14-ounce ramekins.*

3. Heat oven to 400°F.

4. For Crust, combine flour and baking powder in medium bowl.

5. Combine Crisco® Oil and water. Add to flour mixture. Stir with fork until mixture forms large clumps. Press with fingers to form ball. Divide into 4 sections. Flatten between hands to form four crusts.

6. Roll each crust between unfloured sheets of waxed paper or plastic wrap on dampened countertop. Peel off top sheet.

7. Trim each crust to 1 inch larger than top of ramekin. Moisten outside edge of each ramekin with water. Flip crust over onto each ramekin. Remove remaining waxed paper; fold crust edges under and flute. Cut slits into crust to allow steam to escape. Place ramekins on baking sheet.

8. Bake at 400°F for 25 to 30 minutes or until filling is bubbly and crust is golden brown. *Makes 4 servings*

*Use 2-quart casserole if ramekins are unavailable. Roll pastry to fit top of casserole. Bake at 400°F for 30 to 35 minutes.

Chile Quiche Olé

½ cup chopped onion
2 tablespoons BLUE BONNET® Margarine
4 eggs, slightly beaten
1⅓ cups milk
1 tablespoon all-purpose flour
1 (4-ounce) can ORTEGA® Diced Green Chiles
⅛ teaspoon liquid hot pepper seasoning
1 partially baked (9-inch) pie shell
1 (12-ounce) jar ORTEGA® Mild, Medium or Hot Thick and Chunky Salsa

Preheat oven to 350°F. In small skillet over medium-high heat, cook onion in margarine until tender; set aside.

In medium bowl, beat together eggs, milk and flour; stir in onion mixture, chiles and hot pepper seasoning. Pour mixture into pie shell.

Bake 30 to 35 minutes or until knife inserted in center comes out clean. Let stand 10 minutes. To serve, cut into wedges; top with salsa.

Makes 1 (9-inch) quiche

Easy Spinach-Zucchini Pie

1 to 2 medium zucchini (*each* about
    8 inches long)
Hot water
2 packages (10 ounces *each*) frozen
    chopped spinach, thawed and well
    drained
½ cup sour cream
1 package (3 ounces) cream cheese,
    softened
¼ cup (1 ounce) grated Parmesan cheese
3 tablespoons dry bread crumbs
1 egg, slightly beaten
½ teaspoon garlic salt
½ teaspoon sweet basil
1 can (2.8 ounces) DURKEE® French
    Fried Onions
½ cup (2 ounces) shredded Cheddar
    cheese

Preheat oven to 375°F. Using sharp knife,
trim off one long side of zucchini to form
straight edge. Starting at straight edge, cut
zucchini lengthwise into eight thin strips
(about ⅛ inch thick). Place zucchini strips
in shallow dish filled with hot water about
3 minutes to soften; drain.

In large bowl, using fork, thoroughly
combine spinach, sour cream, cream
cheese, Parmesan cheese, bread crumbs,
egg, seasonings and ⅔ can French Fried
Onions. Line bottom and side of 9-inch
pie plate or quiche dish with zucchini
strips, allowing 3 inches of one end of
each strip to hang over edge. Spoon
spinach mixture evenly into pie plate. Fold
zucchini strips over spinach mixture,
tucking ends into center of mixture. Cover
pie plate with foil. Bake, covered, 40
minutes or until zucchini is tender. Top
center of pie with cheese and remaining
onions; bake, uncovered, 3 minutes or
until onions are golden brown.

Makes 1 (9-inch) pie

Beef Tamale Pie

2½ cups (12 ounces) cooked beef, cut into
    ½-inch pieces
1 can (15¾ ounces) mild chili beans in
    chili sauce
1 can (4 ounces) chopped green chilies
¼ cup sliced green onion
¼ teaspoon *each*: ground cumin and
    pepper
1 package (8½ ounces) corn muffin mix
1 cup cold water
½ cup (2 ounces) shredded sharp
    Cheddar cheese

Preheat oven to 425°F. Combine beef, chili
beans, chilies, green onion, cumin and
pepper; mix well. Set aside. Combine corn
muffin mix and water (mixture will be
very thin). Grease sides and bottom of
9-inch square baking pan or 10-inch metal
skillet. Pour corn muffin batter into pan.
Spoon beef mixture into center of corn
muffin mixture, leaving 1-inch border.
Bake 30 minutes or until corn muffin
mixture is slightly browned and begins to
pull away from edge of pan. Sprinkle with
cheese; let stand 5 minutes before serving.

Makes 4 servings

Favorite recipe from **National Live Stock and Meat Board**

Beef Tamale Pie

Spaghetti Pie

Spaghetti Pie

8 ounces dry spaghetti, cooked and drained
1 tablespoon vegetable oil
⅓ cup grated Parmesan cheese
2 eggs, beaten
1 cup (8 ounces) cottage cheese
8 ounces ground beef *or* pork sausage
½ cup chopped onion
¼ cup chopped green pepper
1¾ cups (14½-ounce can) CONTADINA® Stewed Tomatoes, cut up and drained
⅔ cup (6-ounce can) CONTADINA® Tomato Paste
1 teaspoon dried oregano leaves, crushed
½ teaspoon garlic powder
½ teaspoon ground black pepper
¼ teaspoon salt (optional)
½ cup (2 ounces) shredded mozzarella cheese

In large bowl, toss hot spaghetti with oil; reserve *1 cup* spaghetti for filling. Toss *remaining* spaghetti with Parmesan cheese and eggs. Press spaghetti mixture into bottom and up side of 10-inch skillet. Spread cottage cheese over spaghetti mixture. Cook and stir ground beef, onion, and green pepper until meat is browned; drain. Stir in tomatoes, tomato paste, oregano, garlic powder, black pepper, salt, and *reserved* 1 cup spaghetti. Heat thoroughly; spoon over cottage cheese. Cover loosely with greased foil. Bake 20 minutes. Sprinkle with mozzarella cheese; continue baking, covered, 8 to 10 minutes or until cheese is melted. *Makes 6 servings*

"Sprouting Out" Custard Pie

1 cup KELLOGG'S® ALL-BRAN®
   Cereal
½ cup whole-wheat flour
¼ cup *plus* 1 tablespoon all-purpose
   flour
1 tablespoon sugar
¼ cup margarine
3 tablespoons water
   Nonstick cooking spray
1 egg white, slightly beaten
2 tablespoons chopped onion
1 small clove garlic, finely chopped
1 cup sliced mushrooms
½ cup chopped green pepper
1 cup low-fat cottage cheese
1½ cups (12-ounce can) evaporated skim
   milk
½ teaspoon dry mustard
¼ teaspoon salt
¼ teaspoon black pepper
4 egg whites
¾ cup (3 ounces) shredded mozzarella
   cheese
1½ cups alfalfa sprouts
1 medium tomato, sliced

1. Preheat oven to 350°F. Combine
Kellogg's® All-Bran® cereal, whole-wheat
flour, ¼ cup all-purpose flour and sugar;
cut in margarine until mixture resembles
coarse crumbs. Stir in 2 tablespoons water
until stiff dough forms. Press evenly and
firmly into bottom and up side of 9-inch
pie plate coated with cooking spray. Brush
crust with 1 slightly beaten egg white,
coating completely.

2. Bake crust about 6 minutes or until
lightly browned. Remove from oven; set
aside. *Reduce oven temperature to 325°F.*

3. In medium skillet, cook onion, garlic,
mushrooms and green pepper in
remaining 1 tablespoon water until
tender; drain. Set aside.

4. Place cottage cheese, ½ cup milk,
remaining 1 tablespoon all-purpose flour,
mustard, salt, black pepper and 4 egg
whites in food processor or blender.
Process on medium speed until smooth.
Add remaining milk, processing until
combined. Spread vegetable mixture
evenly in crust; sprinkle with mozzarella
cheese. Pour milk mixture over all.

5. Bake about 45 minutes or until center is
set. Let stand 10 minutes before slicing.
Garnish pie with alfalfa sprouts and
tomato slices before serving.
                    Makes 1 (9-inch) pie

Traditional Quiche

1 unbaked (9-inch) pie shell, pricked
12 slices bacon, cooked and crumbled
1½ cups (6 ounces) shredded Swiss
   cheese
4 eggs
2 cups (1 pint) BORDEN® or
   MEADOW GOLD® Half-and-Half
¼ teaspoon salt
⅛ teaspoon ground nutmeg
   Dash ground red pepper

Preheat oven to 425°F. Bake pie shell
8 minutes; remove from oven. Sprinkle
bacon and cheese on bottom of pie shell.
In medium bowl, beat eggs; add
remaining ingredients. Pour into prepared
pie shell. Bake 15 minutes. *Reduce oven
temperature to 350°F;* bake 25 minutes or
until center is set. Cool slightly. Serve
warm or chilled. Refrigerate leftovers.
                    Makes 1 (9-inch) quiche

Turkey Cranberry Loaf Wedges

1 (12-ounce) container cranberry-
    orange sauce
1½ pounds ground fresh turkey
1½ cups fresh bread crumbs (3 slices)
¼ cup REALEMON® Lemon Juice from
    Concentrate
1 egg
1 tablespoon WYLER'S® or STEERO®
    Chicken-Flavor Instant Bouillon *or*
    3 Chicken-Flavor Bouillon Cubes
1 to 2 teaspoons poultry seasoning

Preheat oven to 350°F. Reserve ½ cup
cranberry-orange sauce. In large bowl,
combine remaining ingredients; mix well.
Turn into 9-inch pie plate. Bake 50
minutes or until set. Top with reserved
sauce. Let stand 5 minutes before serving.
Cut into wedges; garnish as desired.
Refrigerate leftovers.

Makes 1 (9-inch) pie

Hot Chicken Salad in Stuffing Crust

4 cups herb-seasoned stuffing mix
½ cup margarine or butter, melted
3 eggs, beaten
2 cups diced cooked chicken
1 cup chopped celery
1 (8-ounce) can water chestnuts,
    drained and chopped
½ cup mayonnaise or salad dressing
1 (2-ounce) jar sliced pimiento, drained
    (optional)
3 tablespoons REALEMON® Lemon
    Juice from Concentrate
1½ teaspoons WYLER'S® or STEERO®
    Chicken-Flavor Instant Bouillon

*Top to bottom: Hot Chicken Salad in Stuffing
Crust, Turkey Cranberry Loaf Wedge, Fruited
Chicken Salad Tarts*

Preheat oven to 350°F. In medium bowl,
combine stuffing mix and margarine;
reserve ½ cup. To remaining stuffing, add
eggs; mix well. Spoon into greased 9-inch
pie plate; press onto bottom and up side to
rim to form crust. In large bowl, combine
remaining ingredients except reserved
stuffing; spoon into prepared crust. Top
with reserved stuffing. Bake 40 to 45
minutes or until hot. Let stand 10 minutes.
Garnish as desired. Refrigerate leftovers.

Makes 1 (9-inch) pie

Fruited Chicken Salad Tarts

1 cup mayonnaise or salad dressing
¼ cup REALIME® Lime Juice from
    Concentrate
2 teaspoons WYLER'S® or STEERO®
    Chicken-Flavor Instant Bouillon
4 cups cubed cooked chicken
1 (11-ounce) can mandarin orange
    segments, drained
1 cup seedless grape halves
1 (8-ounce) can crushed pineapple,
    drained
½ cup slivered almonds, toasted
12 baked (3-inch) tart crusts

In large bowl, combine mayonnaise,
ReaLime® brand and bouillon; stir in
remaining ingredients except tart crusts.
Chill thoroughly. Serve in tart crusts.
Refrigerate leftovers.

Makes 12 (3-inch) tarts

Smoked Chicken Pizza

3 tablespoons yellow cornmeal, divided
1 (1-pound) loaf frozen bread dough, thawed
1 tablespoon olive or vegetable oil
1½ cups (6 ounces) shredded Monterey Jack cheese, divided
4 plums *or* 2 fresh California nectarines, sliced
6 ounces shredded smoked or roasted chicken
2 serrano or jalapeño peppers, seeds removed, thinly sliced
2 teaspoons chopped fresh cilantro

Preheat oven to 425°F. In 10-inch oiled cast-iron skillet, sprinkle 2 tablespoons cornmeal. Stretch dough to fit bottom of skillet. Sprinkle with oil. Sprinkle with remaining 1 tablespoon cornmeal. Cover with half of the cheese. Top with fruit, chicken, peppers, cilantro and remaining cheese. Bake 15 to 20 minutes or until cheese is melted. *Makes 6 servings*

Favorite recipe from **California Tree Fruit Agreement**

Smoked Chicken Pizza

Monk's Pie

1 (11-ounce) package pie crust mix, prepared as package directs
4 eggs
2 (15-ounce) containers ricotta cheese
¾ cup grated Parmesan cheese
¼ cup GREY POUPON® Dijon Mustard
1 (10-ounce) package frozen chopped spinach, thawed and well drained
¼ cup chopped onion
¼ teaspoon pepper
2 cups diced cooked ham

Preheat oven to 375°F. Shape two thirds of the prepared pastry into large ball; shape remaining pastry into small ball, pinching off small piece to use for decoration. On floured surface, roll larger ball into 15-inch circle. Transfer to 9-inch springform pan; lightly press pastry onto bottom and up side of pan. Set aside.

Separate one egg; set aside egg white. In large bowl, with electric mixer at medium speed, blend egg yolk, remaining eggs, ricotta cheese, Parmesan cheese, mustard, spinach, onion and pepper; stir in ham. Spoon mixture into pastry-lined pan.

Roll smaller ball of pastry into 9-inch circle; place over filling, pressing lightly around edge to seal. Roll out remaining piece of dough; cut out leaves and use to decorate pastry top. Slit top of pie to allow steam to escape. Beat reserved egg white; brush over pastry top. Bake 1 hour. Serve warm or cold.

Makes 1 (9-inch) deep-dish pie

Reduced Cholesterol Spinach Quiche

Corn Oil Pie Crust (recipe follows)
1 tablespoon MAZOLA® Corn Oil
2 cups sliced mushrooms
½ cup finely chopped onion
1 clove garlic, minced
3 egg whites
2 teaspoons Dijon-style mustard
¼ teaspoon salt
¼ teaspoon pepper
1 container (8 ounces) lowfat cottage cheese
1 package (10 ounces) frozen chopped spinach, thawed and squeezed dry

Prepare Corn Oil Pie Crust. *Reduce oven temperature to 350°F.* In medium skillet, heat corn oil over medium heat. Add mushrooms, onion and garlic; cook and stir 5 minutes or until tender. In medium bowl, slightly beat egg whites, mustard, salt and pepper until blended. Stir in cottage cheese, onion mixture and spinach. Spoon into baked pie crust. Bake 45 minutes or until knife inserted in center comes out clean.   *Makes 1 (9-inch) quiche*

Corn Oil Pie Crust

1⅓ cups flour
½ teaspoon salt
⅓ cup MAZOLA® Corn Oil
1 egg white, slightly beaten
1 tablespoon cold water

Preheat oven to 450°F. In medium bowl, combine flour and salt. Add corn oil, egg white and water. Mix with fork until mixture holds together; press firmly into ball. Flatten pastry slightly between 2 pieces of waxed paper; immediately roll to 12-inch circle. Peel off top paper. Place pastry in 9-inch pie plate, paper side up. Peel off paper; fit pastry loosely into pie plate. Pierce with fork before baking. Bake 10 to 12 minutes or until golden brown, piercing once with fork during baking.

Cheeseburger Pie

Cheeseburger Pie

1 unbaked (9-inch) pie shell, pricked
8 slices BORDEN® Process American Cheese Food
1 pound lean ground beef
1 (8-ounce) can tomato sauce
⅓ cup chopped green bell pepper
⅓ cup chopped onion
2 cloves garlic, finely chopped
1 teaspoon WYLER'S® or STEERO® Beef-Flavor Instant Bouillon *or* 1 Beef-Flavor Bouillon Cube
2 eggs, well beaten

Preheat oven to 425°F. Bake pie shell 8 minutes; remove from oven. *Reduce oven temperature to 350°F.* Cut 6 *slices* cheese food into pieces. In large skillet, brown meat; pour off fat. Add tomato sauce, green pepper, onion, garlic and bouillon; cook and stir until bouillon dissolves. Remove from heat; stir in eggs and cheese pieces. Turn into prepared shell. Bake 20 to 25 minutes or until hot. Cut each of the remaining 2 *slices* cheese food into 4 triangles. Arrange on top of pie. Bake 3 to 5 minutes longer or until cheese food begins to melt. Garnish as desired. Refrigerate leftovers.

Makes 1 (9-inch) pie

Barbecue Rancheros Pie

1 pound lean ground beef
¾ cup BENNETT'S® Chili Sauce
½ cup chopped onion
½ cup chopped green bell pepper
⅓ cup BAMA® Grape Jelly
1 teaspoon chili powder
1 teaspoon WYLER'S® or STEERO®
   Beef-Flavor Instant Bouillon
⅛ teaspoon black pepper
   BORDEN® Country Store® Instant
   Mashed Potato Flakes, prepared as
   package directs for 4 servings
   (about 2 cups)
   Yellow corn meal
   Paprika

Preheat oven to 400°F. In large skillet,
brown meat; pour off fat. Add remaining
ingredients except potatoes, corn meal and
paprika. Over medium heat, cook and stir
until bubbly. Pour into lightly greased
1½-quart baking dish; top with potatoes.
Sprinkle lightly with corn meal and
paprika; bake 20 minutes or until bubbly
and top is lightly browned. Refrigerate
leftovers.   *Makes 4 to 6 servings*

Tiropitas

1 envelope LIPTON® Recipe Secrets
   Golden Onion Recipe Soup Mix
1 container (15 ounces) ricotta or
   creamed cottage cheese
3 eggs, beaten
8 ounces feta cheese, crumbled
½ cup plain dry bread crumbs
1 tablespoon snipped fresh dill
28 phyllo strudel sheets*
¾ cup butter or margarine, melted

Preheat oven to 425°F. In medium bowl,
combine golden onion recipe soup mix,
ricotta, eggs, feta cheese, bread crumbs
and dill; set aside.

Unfold phyllo strudel sheets; cover with
waxed paper, then damp cloth. Using two
sheets at a time, brush lightly with melted
butter; cut sheets lengthwise into four
equal strips. Place 1 tablespoon cheese
mixture on top corner of each strip; fold
corner over to opposite edge, forming
triangle. Continue folding, keeping
triangular shape with each fold, until
rolled completely to end. Arrange on
ungreased baking sheets; repeat with
remaining phyllo. Bake 20 minutes or
until golden.

Makes about 4½ dozen tiropitas

*Substitute 3 packages (8 ounces *each*)
refrigerated crescent rolls, if desired.
Separate dough as package directs. Cut
each triangle in half and flatten slightly.
Place 1 tablespoon mixture in center of
dough and fold over sides to form triangle.
Bake as package directs.

Cottage Spinach Un-Quiche

4 eggs
1 (16-ounce) container BORDEN®
   Lite-line® or Viva® Lowfat Cottage
   Cheese
1 (10-ounce) package frozen chopped
   spinach, thawed and *well drained*
2 tablespoons flour
1 teaspoon WYLER'S® or STEERO®
   Chicken-Flavor Instant Bouillon
2 teaspoons Dijon-style mustard

Preheat oven to 350°F. In large bowl, beat
eggs; add remaining ingredients. Pour into
lightly oiled 9-inch pie plate. Bake 35 to
40 minutes or until set. Let stand 10
minutes before serving. Refrigerate
leftovers.   *Makes 1 (9-inch) quiche*

Fiesta Beef Pot Pie

Crust
1²/₃ cups all-purpose flour
⅓ cup yellow cornmeal
2 tablespoons toasted wheat germ
1 teaspoon salt
⅓ cup (about 1⅓ ounces) shredded
    Cheddar cheese
¾ cup CRISCO® Shortening
5 to 7 tablespoons cold water

Filling
1 pound lean boneless beef chuck, cut
    into ¼- to ½-inch chunks
1 tablespoon CRISCO® Shortening
½ cup chopped green pepper
½ cup chopped onion
1 can (14½ ounces) Mexican-style
    stewed tomatoes,* undrained
1 can (8½ ounces) whole kernel corn,
    drained
1 can (4 ounces) sliced mushrooms,
    drained
½ cup water
⅓ cup tomato paste
2 teaspoons sugar
1 teaspoon chili powder
½ teaspoon ground cumin
¼ teaspoon salt
⅛ teaspoon crushed red pepper
    (optional)
⅓ cup sliced pitted ripe olives

Glaze and Topping
1 egg, beaten
¼ teaspoon salt
⅓ cup (about 1⅓ ounces) shredded
    Cheddar cheese

1. For Crust, combine flour, cornmeal, wheat germ and 1 teaspoon salt in large bowl. Cut in ⅓ cup cheese and ¾ cup Crisco®. See pages 6 and 7, steps 3 and 4, for remaining double-crust preparation. Roll and press bottom crust into 9-inch pie plate. *Do not bake.*

Fiesta Beef Pot Pie

2. For Filling, brown beef in 1 tablespoon Crisco® in large skillet and cook until tender. Add green pepper, onion, tomatoes with liquid, corn, mushrooms, water, tomato paste, sugar, chili powder, cumin, ¼ teaspoon salt and red pepper; cover. Bring to a boil. Reduce heat; simmer 30 minutes, stirring occasionally. Remove from heat. Stir in olives. Spoon hot filling into unbaked pie crust. Moisten pastry with water.

3. Heat oven to 425°F. Roll out top crust; lift onto filled pie. Trim ½ inch beyond edge of pie plate. Fold top edge under bottom crust; flute. Cut slits or design into top crust to allow steam to escape.

4. For Glaze and Topping, combine egg and ¼ teaspoon salt. Brush lightly over top crust. Bake at 425°F for 30 to 40 minutes or until crust is golden brown. Sprinkle with ⅓ cup cheese. Let stand 10 minutes before cutting and serving. Serve hot or warm. Refrigerate leftover pie.
Makes 1 (9-inch) pie

*If Mexican-style tomatoes are unavailable, use plain stewed tomatoes. Increase green pepper and onion to ⅔ cup *each*. Add 1 tablespoon minced jalapeño pepper and ¼ teaspoon garlic powder.

Top to bottom: Chicken Primavera Pasta Pie, California Salmon Pie

Chicken Primavera Pasta Pie

Pasta Crust (recipe follows)
2 cups frozen broccoli, carrot and
    cauliflower combination, thawed
    and drained
1½ cups diced cooked chicken
  ¼ cup unsifted flour
  2 eggs, beaten
  1 cup BORDEN® or MEADOW
    GOLD® Half-and-Half
  ⅓ cup grated Parmesan cheese
  2 teaspoons WYLER'S® or STEERO®
    Chicken-Flavor Instant Bouillon
  1 clove garlic, finely chopped
  ½ teaspoon dried basil leaves, crumbled
  ½ teaspoon dried oregano leaves,
    crumbled

Preheat oven to 350°F. Prepare Pasta
Crust; set aside. In large bowl, toss
vegetables and chicken with flour to coat;
add remaining ingredients. Mix well.
Spoon into prepared crust. Cover tightly
with foil; bake 25 to 30 minutes or until
set. Uncover; let stand 5 minutes. Garnish
as desired. Refrigerate leftovers.

Makes 1 (10-inch) pie

Pasta Crust: Cook ½ (1-pound) package
CREAMETTE® Spaghetti as package
directs; drain. In large bowl, combine hot
spaghetti, 2 beaten eggs, ⅓ cup grated
Parmesan cheese and 2 tablespoons
melted margarine or butter. Spoon into
well-greased 10-inch pie plate; press onto
bottom and up side to rim to form crust.

California Salmon Pie

4 eggs
1 (15½-ounce) can salmon, drained and
    flaked
1 (9-ounce) package frozen artichoke
    hearts, cooked, drained and
    chopped, *or* 1 (14-ounce) can
    artichoke hearts, drained and
    chopped
¼ cup chopped green onions
¼ cup grated Parmesan cheese
2 tablespoons margarine or butter,
    melted
3 tablespoons REALEMON® Lemon
    Juice from Concentrate
1½ teaspoons WYLER'S® or STEERO®
    Chicken-Flavor Instant Bouillon
1 unbaked (9-inch) pie shell
1 (8-ounce) container BORDEN® or
    MEADOW GOLD® Sour Cream, at
    room temperature
1½ teaspoons dried dill weed, crumbled

Preheat oven to 425°F. In large bowl, beat
eggs; add salmon, artichokes, green
onions, cheese, margarine, *1 tablespoon*
ReaLemon® brand and *1 teaspoon* bouillon.
Pour into pie shell. Bake 25 minutes. In
small bowl, combine sour cream,
remaining *2 tablespoons* ReaLemon® brand,
remaining *½ teaspoon* bouillon and dill
weed. Spread over salmon filling; bake 5
minutes longer or until set. Serve warm or
chilled. Garnish as desired. Refrigerate
leftovers.   *Makes 1 (9-inch) pie*

Vegetable Cheese Tart

3 eggs, beaten
1½ cups half-and-half
2 cups (8 ounces) shredded Swiss
    cheese
1 package (1.4 ounces) KNORR®
    Vegetable Soup and Recipe Mix
1 package (10 ounces) frozen chopped
    spinach, thawed and squeezed dry
1 pre-baked (11-inch) tart crust*

Preheat oven to 375°F. In large bowl, stir
together eggs, half-and-half, Swiss
cheese, soup mix and spinach until
blended. Spoon into tart crust. Bake 45
minutes or until knife inserted between
center and edge comes out clean.
          Makes 1 (11-inch) tart

*Substitute 1 *unbaked* (9-inch) pie shell for
pre-baked tart crust, if desired.

Pan-Fried Noodle Pie

1 package LIPTON® Noodles &
    Sauce–Butter
2 eggs, beaten
¼ cup *plus* 1 tablespoon grated
    Parmesan cheese
1 cup (4 ounces) shredded mozzarella
    cheese
⅛ teaspoon pepper
1 tablespoon butter or margarine
2 teaspoons finely chopped garlic
1 tablespoon finely chopped parsley
¼ teaspoon paprika

Prepare noodles & butter sauce as package
directs, omitting butter; let cool slightly.

In medium bowl, thoroughly combine
eggs, ¼ cup Parmesan cheese, mozzarella
cheese, pepper and noodles & butter
sauce.

In large skillet, melt butter and cook garlic
over medium heat 30 seconds. Add noodle
mixture; spread evenly. Simmer, covered,
15 minutes or until set. Sprinkle with
remaining 1 tablespoon Parmesan cheese,
parsley and paprika. To serve, cut into
wedges.   *Makes about 6 servings*

CREAMY CREATIONS

Apple Cinnamon Tart

1½ cups quick-cooking oats
1 tablespoon *plus* ½ teaspoon ground
    cinnamon, divided
¾ cup frozen apple juice concentrate,
    thawed and divided
2 large apples, peeled (if desired) and
    thinly sliced
1 teaspoon lemon juice
⅓ cup cold water
1 envelope unflavored gelatin
2 cups DANNON® Plain Nonfat or
    Lowfat Yogurt
½ cup honey
½ teaspoon almond extract
    Fresh mint leaves (optional)

Preheat oven to 350°F. In small bowl, combine oats and 1 tablespoon cinnamon. Toss with ¼ cup apple juice concentrate. Press onto bottom and up side of 9-inch pie plate. Bake 5 minutes or until set. Cool on wire rack.

In medium bowl, toss apple slices with lemon juice; arrange on cooled crust in pan and set aside. In small saucepan, combine cold water and remaining ½ cup apple juice concentrate. Sprinkle gelatin over water mixture; let stand 3 minutes to soften. Cook and stir over medium heat until gelatin is completely dissolved;

remove from heat. Add yogurt, honey, remaining ½ teaspoon cinnamon and almond extract; blend well. Pour over apples in crust. Chill several hours or overnight. Garnish with mint leaves.

Makes 1 (9-inch) tart

Coconut Cream Pie

1⅓ cups BAKER'S® ANGEL FLAKE®
    Coconut, divided
1 baked (9-inch) pie crust, cooled
2⅔ cups cold milk
1 package (6-serving size) JELL-O®
    Vanilla Flavor Instant Pudding or
    Pie Filling
1¾ cups (4 ounces) thawed COOL
    WHIP® Non-Dairy Whipped
    Topping

• Sprinkle ⅔ cup coconut in bottom of pie shell; set aside.

• Pour milk into small mixing bowl. Add pie filling mix. Beat with wire whisk about 1 minute or until well blended. (Mixture will be thin.) Pour at once into pie crust. Chill at least 1 hour.

• Spread whipped topping over pie and top with remaining ⅔ cup coconut.

Makes 1 (9-inch) pie

Apple Cinnamon Tart

Café Cream Pie

Café Cream Pie

Choco-Nut Crust
  1 cup (6-ounce package) NESTLÉ® Toll
    House® Semi-Sweet Chocolate
    Morsels
  1 tablespoon shortening
1½ cups finely chopped nuts

Filling
  ½ pound marshmallows (about 40 large)
  ⅓ cup milk
  ¼ teaspoon salt
  3 tablespoons coffee-flavored liqueur
  3 tablespoons vodka
1½ cups heavy cream, whipped

Choco-Nut Crust: Combine Nestlé® Toll
House® Semi-Sweet Chocolate Morsels
and shortening over hot, not boiling,
water; stir until morsels are melted and
mixture is smooth. Stir in nuts. Spread
evenly onto bottom and up sides (not over
rim) of foil-lined 9-inch pie plate. Chill
until firm (about 1 hour). Lift chocolate
crust out of pan; peel off foil and place
crust back into pie plate or onto serving
plate. Chill until ready to use.

Filling: Combine marshmallows, milk,
and salt over hot, not boiling, water; stir
until marshmallows are melted. Remove
from heat. Add liqueur and vodka; stir
until well blended. Transfer to medium
bowl. Chill until slightly thickened (45 to
60 minutes), stirring occasionally. Gently
fold in whipped cream. Pour into Choco-
Nut Crust; chill until firm (about 1 hour).
Garnish as desired.   *Makes 1 (9-inch) pie*

Cherry Cream Pie

Crust
1⅓ cups all-purpose flour
  ½ teaspoon salt
  ⅓ cup CRISCO® Oil
  3 tablespoons skim milk

Filling
  ¾ cup skim milk
  1 envelope (about 1 tablespoon)
    unflavored gelatin
  ⅓ cup sugar
  1 container (16 ounces) 2% lowfat
    cottage cheese
  1 teaspoon vanilla extract

Topping
  1 can (21 ounces) light cherry pie
    filling
  ½ teaspoon almond extract

1. Heat oven to 375°F.

2. For Crust, combine flour and salt in
medium bowl. Blend Crisco® Oil and milk
in small bowl. Add to flour mixture. Stir
with fork until mixture forms large
clumps. Press with fingers to form ball.
Flatten between hands to form 5- to 6-
inch crust. Roll crust circle between
unfloured sheets of waxed paper (or
plastic wrap) on dampened countertop.
Peel off top sheet of waxed paper. Trim
crust to 1 inch larger than upside-down
9-inch pie plate. Flip crust into pie plate.
Remove remaining waxed paper. Press
crust into place. Fold edge under; flute.
Prick bottom and side thoroughly with
fork 50 times to prevent shrinkage.

3. Bake at 375°F for 12 to 15 minutes or
until lightly browned. Cool completely.

4. For Filling, pour milk into small saucepan. Sprinkle with gelatin. Let stand 5 minutes to soften. Heat until almost boiling. Stir to dissolve gelatin. Pour into food processor or blender. Add sugar. Process at high speed 30 seconds.

5. Add cottage cheese and vanilla. Blend 1½ minutes or until smooth. Pour into cooled baked crust. Refrigerate 1½ hours or until firm.

6. For Topping, combine pie filling and almond extract. Spoon over cream layer. Refrigerate at least 1 hour.

7. Cut into wedges to serve. Refrigerate leftovers.   *Makes 1 (9-inch) pie*

Peanut Butter Cream Pie

1 package (3½ ounces) instant vanilla
    pudding and pie filling
1 cup dairy sour cream
1 cup milk
1½ cups REESE'S® Peanut Butter Chips
2 tablespoons vegetable oil
1 (8-inch) prepared graham cracker or
    other flavor crumb crust
    Thawed frozen non-dairy whipped
    topping

Microwave Directions: In small mixer bowl, blend pudding mix, sour cream and milk; set aside. In top of double boiler over hot (*not boiling*) water, melt peanut butter chips with oil, stirring constantly to blend. (Or, place chips and oil in small microwave-safe bowl. Microwave at HIGH [100%] 45 seconds; stir. If necessary, microwave at HIGH additional 15 seconds or until melted and smooth when stirred.) Gradually add melted chips to pudding; blend well. Pour into crust. Cover; chill several hours or overnight. Garnish with whipped topping.   *Makes 1 (8-inch) pie*

Lemon Cloud Pie

1 (14-ounce) can EAGLE® Brand
    Sweetened Condensed Milk
    (NOT evaporated milk)
½ cup REALEMON® Lemon Juice from
    Concentrate
    Yellow food coloring (optional)
1 cup (½ pint) BORDEN® or
    MEADOW GOLD® Whipping
    Cream, whipped
1 baked (9-inch) pie crust *or* 1 (9-inch)
    prepared graham cracker crumb
    crust

In medium bowl, stir together sweetened condensed milk, ReaLemon® brand and food coloring. Fold in whipped cream. Pour into prepared pie crust. Chill 3 hours or until set. Garnish as desired. Refrigerate leftovers.   *Makes 1 (9-inch) pie*

Top to bottom: Black Forest Pie (page 136), Lemon Cloud Pie

Microwave Butterscotch Praline Pie

Praline (recipe follows)
1 baked (9-inch) pie crust
⅔ cup packed brown sugar
3 tablespoons ARGO® or
   KINGSFORD'S® Corn Starch
¼ teaspoon salt
1½ cups water
3 egg yolks
¼ cup MAZOLA® Margarine, melted
1 teaspoon vanilla extract
   Whipped cream for garnish

Prepare Praline. Reserve ¼ cup chopped Praline for garnish; sprinkle remaining Praline on bottom of baked pie crust. In large microwavable bowl with fork or wire whisk, combine sugar, corn starch and salt. Beat in water, egg yolks and margarine until smooth. Microwave on High (100%), stirring twice, 6 to 7 minutes or until mixture boils and thickens. Beat vigorously until smooth. Stir in vanilla. Pour into prepared crust. Cover surface with plastic wrap. Chill 1½ to 2 hours or until set. Garnish with whipped cream and reserved Praline.

Makes 1 (9-inch) pie

Praline

MAZOLA® No-Stick™ Corn Oil
   Cooking Spray
½ cup granulated sugar
¼ cup KARO® Light Corn Syrup
   Pinch salt
½ cup chopped pecans

Spray cookie sheet and metal spatula with cooking spray. In 2-cup microwavable glass measuring cup or bowl, stir sugar, corn syrup and salt with wooden spoon until well mixed. Microwave on High (100%) 4½ to 5 minutes or until syrup is pale yellow. *Candy syrup is very hot; handle carefully. Do not touch hot mixture.* Stir in nuts. Microwave 30 seconds to 1 minute or until nuts are lightly browned. Immediately pour onto cookie sheet; spread evenly with spatula. Cool. Chop finely.

Egg Custard Pie

Crust
   9-inch Classic Crisco® Single Crust
      (pages 6 and 7)

Filling
   4 eggs
   ½ cup sugar
   1 teaspoon vanilla extract
   ¼ teaspoon salt
2½ cups milk
   Ground nutmeg (optional)

1. Heat oven to 425°F. Prepare 9-inch Classic Crisco® Single Crust. *Do not bake.*

2. Bake at 425°F for 5 minutes.

3. For Filling, beat eggs with fork or at low speed of electric mixer until lemon colored. Stir in sugar, vanilla and salt. Gradually stir in milk. Mix well. Pour into partially baked pie crust. Sprinkle with nutmeg.

4. Bake at 425°F for 15 minutes. *Reduce oven temperature to 350°F.* Bake 20 to 25 minutes or until knife inserted in center comes out clean. Cool to room temperature before serving. Refrigerate leftovers.   *Makes 1 (9-inch) pie*

Coconut Custard Pie: Stir ½ cup flake coconut into egg mixture before pouring into crust and baking.

Left to right: Rocky Road Pie (page 123), Classic Peanut Butter Pie

Classic Peanut Butter Pie

½ cup peanut butter
¾ cup confectioners' sugar
¼ cup chopped peanuts
1 (14-ounce) can EAGLE® Brand
    Sweetened Condensed Milk
    (NOT evaporated milk)
4 egg *yolks*
½ cup water
1 (4-serving size) package vanilla flavor
    pudding mix *(not instant)*
1 (8-ounce) container BORDEN® or
    MEADOW GOLD® Sour Cream, at
    room temperature
1 baked (9-inch) pie crust
    BORDEN® or MEADOW GOLD®
    Whipping Cream, whipped, *or*
    thawed frozen non-dairy whipped
    topping

In small bowl, cut peanut butter into sugar until crumbly; stir in peanuts. Sprinkle into prepared pie crust. In medium saucepan, combine sweetened condensed milk, egg *yolks*, water and pudding mix. Over medium heat, cook and stir until thickened. Cool 15 minutes; beat in sour cream. Spoon into prepared pie crust. Chill thoroughly. Spread top with whipped cream. Garnish as desired. Refrigerate leftovers.

Makes 1 (9-inch) pie

Microwave: Prepare peanut butter mixture as directed. In 2-quart glass measure with handle, combine sweetened condensed milk, egg *yolks*, water and pudding mix; mix well. Cook on 100% power (high) 5 to 8 minutes, stirring after 2 minutes, then every minute until thickened and smooth. Proceed as directed.

CREAMY CREATIONS   55

Bananas Foster Chiffon Pie

1¼ cups graham cracker crumbs
5 tablespoons melted margarine
1¼ cups sugar, divided
4 eggs, separated
1 cup milk
¼ teaspoon salt
1 envelope unflavored gelatin
¼ cup dark rum
1 (9-inch) prepared graham cracker
  crumb crust
2 firm, medium DOLE® Bananas,
  peeled, sliced
  Whipping cream, additional banana
  slices and additional graham
  cracker crumbs for garnish

- Preheat oven to 350°F. Combine crumbs, margarine and ¼ cup sugar. Press into 9-inch pie plate. Bake 10 minutes. Cool.

- In saucepan, combine egg yolks with milk, ½ cup sugar and salt. Cook over medium heat, stirring, until slightly thickened and mixture coats back of spoon. Remove from heat. Stir gelatin into rum to dissolve, then into hot mixture. Cool.

- Beat egg whites until foamy. Gradually beat in remaining ½ cup sugar until stiff peaks form. Fold egg white mixture into yolk mixture.

- Line pie crust with sliced bananas. Pour filling over bananas. Refrigerate 1 hour or until firm. Garnish with whipped cream, banana slices and crumbs just before serving.   *Makes 1 (9-inch) pie*

Prep time: 20 minutes
Cook time: 10 minutes
Chill time: 1 hour

Toffee-Topped Peach Pie

Almond Crunch Topping
½ cup granulated sugar
2 tablespoons water
½ cup slivered almonds, toasted*

Pie
1 package (8 ounces) Neufchâtel cheese
  or light cream cheese, softened
⅓ cup powdered sugar
⅓ cup light sour cream
½ teaspoon vanilla extract
3 fresh California peaches, very thinly
  sliced, divided
1 (8-inch) prepared graham cracker
  crust

For Almond Crunch Topping, in small saucepan combine granulated sugar and water. Cook 4 minutes or until syrup turns light golden brown. Add almonds; pour at once onto buttered baking sheet. Cool. When cooled, break up and coarsely crush in food processor or blender.**

For Pie, in large bowl, beat cheese, powdered sugar and sour cream until smooth. Stir in vanilla and ¼ cup Almond Crunch Topping. Place two thirds of the peach slices in pie crust. Spread cheese mixture over fruit. Sprinkle with remaining topping. Arrange remaining peaches on top.   *Makes 1 (8-inch) pie*

*To toast almonds, spread on baking sheet and toast in preheated 350°F oven 7 to 10 minutes or until golden brown.

**Substitute an equal amount of crushed English toffee candies for Almond Crunch Topping, if desired.

Tip: After cooking syrup, immediately rinse pan with hot water to dissolve sugar syrup easily.

Serving Suggestion: Almond Crunch Topping is also delicious served over sliced peaches, ice cream or pudding.

*Favorite recipe from **California Tree Fruit Agreement***

Toffee-Topped Peach Pie

Easy Piña Colada Pie

Easy Piña Colada Pie

2 cups crisp macaroon cookie crumbs
   (about 12 cookies)
3 tablespoons margarine, melted
1 can (8¼ ounces) DOLE® Crushed
   Pineapple in Syrup or Juice
1 package (8 ounces) light cream
   cheese, softened
¼ cup sugar
½ cup milk
2 tablespoons dark rum
¼ teaspoon coconut extract
1 package (3½ ounces) instant vanilla
   pudding and pie filling mix

- Preheat oven to 350°F. In bowl, combine
  cookie crumbs and margarine; mix well.
  Press into 9-inch pie plate. Bake 10
  minutes. Cool.

- Drain pineapple; reserve syrup.

- In bowl, beat cream cheese with sugar
  until smooth. Add milk, reserved
  pineapple syrup, rum and coconut
  extract; blend well. Add pudding mix,
  beating 1 to 2 minutes longer. Stir in
  pineapple.

- Pour filling into crust. Chill at least
  4 hours.   *Makes 1 (9-inch) pie*

Prep time: 15 minutes
Cook time: 10 minutes
Chill time: 4 hours

Microwave Vanilla Cream Pie

1 (14-ounce) can EAGLE® Brand
   Sweetened Condensed Milk
   (NOT evaporated milk)
4 egg *yolks*
½ cup water
1 (4-serving size) package vanilla flavor
   pudding mix (*not instant*)
1 (8-ounce) container BORDEN® or
   MEADOW GOLD® Sour Cream
1 baked (9-inch) pie crust *or* 1 (9-inch)
   prepared graham cracker crumb
   crust
   Whipped cream *or* thawed frozen
   non-dairy whipped topping

In 2-quart glass measure, beat sweetened
condensed milk, egg *yolks,* water and
pudding; mix well. Cook on 100% power
(high) 5 to 8 minutes, stirring every minute
until thickened and *smooth.* Cool 15
minutes, stirring occasionally. Beat in sour
cream. Pour into pie crust. Chill. Top with
whipped cream. Garnish as desired.
Refrigerate leftovers.

Makes 1 (9-inch) pie

Banana Cream Pie: Prepare filling as
directed. Slice 2 bananas; dip in
ReaLemon® Lemon Juice from
Concentrate and drain. Arrange in crust.
Top with filling. Chill. Top with whipped
cream and banana slices.

Butterscotch Cream Pie: Substitute
butterscotch flavor pudding mix for
vanilla.

Bread Crumb Dessert Crust

**1 cup PROGRESSO® Plain Bread
    Crumbs**
¼ cup packed brown sugar
⅓ cup butter or margarine, melted

For unfilled baked crust:
1. Preheat oven to 350°F.

2. In medium bowl, combine bread
crumbs and brown sugar. Add butter; mix
well with fork. Press crumb mixture into
9-inch pie plate.

3. Bake 8 to 9 minutes or until lightly
browned; cool on wire rack. Fill as desired.

For filled crust:
1. Preheat oven and prepare filling as
recipe directs.

2. Combine crust ingredients; press into
9-inch pie plate.

3. Pour filling into crust. Bake as recipe
directs.   *Makes 1 (9-inch) pie crust*

Preparation time: 5 minutes
Baking time for empty crust: 8 minutes

Peanut Pie

Crust
  **9-inch Classic Crisco® Single Crust
    (pages 6 and 7)**

Filling
  ½ cup granulated sugar
  ¼ cup packed brown sugar
  ¼ cup all-purpose flour
  2 tablespoons cornstarch
  ¼ teaspoon salt
  3 cups milk
  ½ cup peanut butter chips
  4 egg yolks
  3 tablespoons butter or margarine
1½ teaspoons vanilla extract
  **1 bag (7 ounces) chocolate-covered
    peanuts, chopped**

1. Prepare and bake 9-inch Classic
Crisco® Single Crust. Cool completely.
Heat oven to 350°F.

2. For Filling, combine granulated sugar,
brown sugar, flour, cornstarch and salt in
saucepan. Gradually add milk and peanut
butter chips. Cook and stir on medium
heat until mixture comes to a boil and
thickens; reduce heat. Cook and stir 2
minutes; remove from heat.

3. Beat egg yolks lightly in small bowl. Stir
1 cup hot mixture slowly into yolks,
mixing thoroughly. Return mixture to
saucepan. Bring to a boil. Cook and stir on
low heat 2 minutes; remove from heat. Stir
in butter and vanilla. Pour mixture into
baked pie crust.

4. Bake at 350°F for 12 minutes.
Immediately sprinkle with chocolate-
covered peanuts. Cool to room
temperature before serving. Refrigerate
leftover pie.   *Makes 1 (9-inch) pie*

Peanut Pie

Lemon Meringue Pie

Lemon Meringue Pie

1⅓ cups sugar, divided
¼ cup ARGO® or KINGSFORD'S®
    Corn Starch
1½ cups cold water
  3 egg yolks, slightly beaten (reserve
      egg whites)
    Grated peel of 1 lemon
¼ cup lemon juice
  1 tablespoon MAZOLA® Margarine
  1 baked (9-inch) pie crust

Preheat oven to 350°F. In medium saucepan, combine 1 cup sugar and corn starch. Gradually stir in water until smooth. Stir in egg yolks. Stirring constantly, bring to a boil over medium heat; boil 1 minute. Remove from heat.

Stir in lemon peel, lemon juice and margarine. Spoon hot filling into pie crust. In small bowl with mixer at high speed, beat reserved egg whites until foamy. Gradually beat in remaining ⅓ cup sugar; continue beating until stiff peaks form. Spread meringue evenly over hot filling, sealing to edge of crust. Bake 15 to 20 minutes or until golden. Cool on wire rack; refrigerate.   *Makes 1 (9-inch) pie*

Microwave: In large microwavable bowl, combine 1 cup sugar and corn starch. Gradually stir in water until smooth. Stir in egg yolks. Microwave on High (100%), stirring twice with fork or wire whisk, 6 to 8 minutes or until mixture boils; boil 1 minute. Stir in lemon peel, lemon juice and margarine. Spoon hot filling into pie crust. Continue as directed.

Blueberry Bavarian Sweet Dough Pie

Crust
10-inch Classic Crisco® Single Crust
   (pages 6 and 7)
1 teaspoon vanilla extract

White Confectioners Coating
1½ to 2 ounces white baking bar

Filling
5 cups fresh blueberries, divided
1¼ cups sugar
¼ cup cornstarch
2 teaspoons lemon juice

Bavarian Layer
1 envelope (about 1 tablespoon)
   unflavored gelatin
¼ cup cold water
1 cup fresh blueberries
¼ cup *plus* 1½ teaspoons sugar
1½ cups whipping cream

Topping
   Sweetened whipped cream
   Fresh blueberries

1. Prepare 10-inch Classic Crisco® Single Crust, substituting 1 teaspoon vanilla for 1 teaspoon water. Bake and cool completely.

2. For White Confectioners Coating, melt baking bar in top of double boiler over hot water. Brush on inside of baked pie crust.

3. For Filling, place 2½ cups blueberries in large saucepan. Crush berries. Stir in 1¼ cups sugar and cornstarch. Cook and stir on medium heat until mixture comes to a boil and thickens. Cool. Stir in remaining 2½ cups blueberries and lemon juice. Refrigerate.

4. For Bavarian Layer, place gelatin in cold water to soften. Process 1 cup blueberries in food processor or blender container. Heat processed blueberries in small saucepan on low heat. Add gelatin; stir

until dissolved. Stir in ¼ cup *plus* 1½ teaspoons sugar. Remove from heat. Cool until almost set. Beat whipping cream in small bowl at high speed of electric mixer until stiff peaks form. Fold one third of the whipped cream into blueberry mixture. Fold blueberry mixture into remaining whipped cream. Refrigerate.

5. To assemble pie, spoon two thirds of the Filling into coated pie crust. Cover with Bavarian layer. Spoon remaining one third of the Filling in center of Bavarian.

6. For Topping, top with whipped cream. Garnish with blueberries. Refrigerate until firm.   *Makes 1 (10-inch) pie*

Peach Almond Cream Tart

1 unbaked (9- or 10-inch) pie shell,
   pricked
1 (14-ounce) can EAGLE® Brand
   Sweetened Condensed Milk
   (NOT evaporated milk)
1 (8-ounce) container BORDEN® or
   MEADOW GOLD® Sour Cream, at
   room temperature
2 tablespoons REALEMON® Lemon
   Juice from Concentrate
1 teaspoon almond extract
1 (21-ounce) can peach pie filling
   Sliced almonds, lightly toasted

Preheat oven to 375°F. Bake pie shell 15 minutes. Meanwhile, in medium bowl, combine sweetened condensed milk, sour cream, ReaLemon® brand and extract; mix well. Reserving 6 peach slices, spread remaining pie filling on bottom of prepared pie shell. Top with sour cream mixture. Top with reserved peach slices and almonds. Bake 30 minutes or until set; cool. Chill. Refrigerate leftovers.
   Makes 1 (9- or 10-inch) pie

Raspberry Chiffon Pie

Crust
  2 cups graham cracker crumbs
  ¼ cup sugar
  ½ cup margarine or butter, melted

Filling
  ¼ cup raspberry juice *or* water
  1 envelope *plus* 1 teaspoon unflavored gelatin
  ⅔ cup sugar, divided
  8 plums *or* 4 fresh California peaches, divided
  1 cup fresh raspberries, crushed
  1 cup plain low-fat yogurt
  3 egg whites
  ¼ teaspoon cream of tartar

For Crust, preheat oven to 375°F. In lightly greased 10-inch pie plate, combine crumbs, ¼ cup sugar and margarine. Press evenly onto bottom and up side of pie plate. Bake 5 minutes; cool.

For Filling, in medium saucepan combine juice and gelatin; let stand 5 minutes. Add ⅓ cup sugar; stir over medium heat to dissolve gelatin. In food processor or blender, process 6 plums (*or* 3 peaches) until blended. Add processed fruit and raspberries to gelatin mixture. Refrigerate until mixture begins to set, about 1 hour. Stir yogurt into fruit mixture. In large bowl, beat egg whites until frothy.

Raspberry Chiffon Pie

Gradually add cream of tartar and remaining ⅓ cup sugar; beat until stiff peaks form. Gently fold egg whites into fruit mixture. Spoon into crust. Refrigerate 4 hours or overnight. Thinly slice remaining 2 plums (*or* 1 peach); garnish pie. *Makes 1 (10-inch) pie*

Favorite recipe from California Tree Fruit Agreement

Boston Cream Pastry Pie

  1 (15-ounce) package refrigerated pie shells
  1 (14-ounce) can EAGLE® Brand Sweetened Condensed Milk (NOT evaporated milk)
  ⅓ cup cold water
  1 (4-serving size) package *instant* vanilla flavor pudding mix
  1 cup (½ pint) BORDEN® or MEADOW GOLD® Whipping Cream, whipped
  Confectioners' sugar
  ¼ cup semisweet chocolate chips *or* 1 (1-ounce) square semisweet chocolate
  1 teaspoon shortening

Preheat oven to 425°F. Line 9-inch pie plate with 1 crust; turn under edge and flute. Cut second crust into 8-inch circle, then into 8 wedges; place on ungreased baking sheet. Bake crust and wedges 8 to 10 minutes or until golden brown; cool. Meanwhile, in large bowl, combine sweetened condensed milk and water. Add pudding mix; beat well. Chill 5 minutes. Fold in whipped cream. Spoon into prepared crust. Top with crust wedges. Sprinkle with sugar. Melt chocolate chips with shortening; drizzle over crust wedges. Chill. Refrigerate leftovers. *Makes 1 (9-inch) pie*

Creamy Cheese Pie

Crust
  4 cups Rice CHEX® Brand Cereal,
    crushed to 1 cup
  ¼ cup packed brown sugar
  ¼ teaspoon ground cinnamon
  5 tablespoons butter or margarine,
    melted

Filling
  ½ cup *plus* 3 tablespoons granulated
    sugar
2½ tablespoons cornstarch
  ¼ teaspoon salt
  1 cup milk
  2 eggs, separated
  1 teaspoon vanilla extract
  8 ounces cream cheese, softened, cut
    into cubes
    Fresh fruit (optional)

To prepare Crust, preheat oven to 300°F.
Butter 9-inch pie plate. In medium bowl,
combine cereal, brown sugar and
cinnamon. Gradually add butter, stirring
until cereal pieces are evenly coated. Press
evenly onto bottom and up side of pie
plate. Bake 10 minutes; cool completely.

To prepare Filling, in medium saucepan
combine ½ cup granulated sugar,
cornstarch and salt. Stir in milk and egg
yolks. Cook over medium heat just until
mixture comes to a boil, stirring
constantly. (Mixture will be very thick and
lemon colored. If lumps form, beat
vigorously until smooth.) Remove from
heat. Stir in vanilla. Stir cheese into
mixture until smooth; set aside. In
medium bowl, beat egg whites until
foamy. Gradually add remaining 3
tablespoons granulated sugar, beating
until stiff. Fold into cheese mixture. Pour
into crust. Chill 4 hours or until firm.
Serve with fresh fruit.

Makes 1 (9-inch) pie

Almond Pie

Almond Pie

  1 (5-ounce) can LA CHOY® Chow Mein
    Noodles
  1 (2½-ounce) package sliced almonds,
    divided
  5 tablespoons butter or margarine,
    melted
  ¼ cup sugar
  1 (3.5-ounce) package vanilla instant
    pudding and pie filling mix
2½ cups milk
  ½ cup sour cream
  ½ teaspoon almond extract

Preheat oven to 375°F. In food processor
or blender, process noodles and ½ *cup*
almonds until finely ground. In medium
bowl, combine noodle mixture, butter and
sugar; mix well. Place in 9-inch pie plate;
press mixture onto bottom and up side of
pie plate to form crust. Bake 10 to 15
minutes or until lightly browned.

Meanwhile, place *remaining* almonds on
baking sheet. Place in oven with pie
crust. Bake until lightly toasted, stirring
occasionally. Cool pie crust and almonds.
In separate medium bowl, combine
pudding mix, milk, sour cream and
almond extract; beat 1 to 2 minutes or
until well blended. Pour into *cooled* pie
crust. Refrigerate at least 1 hour. Top with
toasted almonds just before serving.
Garnish, if desired.   *Makes 1 (9-inch) pie*

Vanilla Chip Fruit Tart

¾ cup (1½ sticks) butter or margarine,
  softened
½ cup confectioners' sugar
1½ cups all-purpose flour
  Vanilla Filling (recipe follows)
  Fruit Topping (recipe follows)

Heat oven to 300°F. In small mixer bowl,
beat butter and confectioners' sugar until
smooth; blend in flour. Press mixture onto
bottom and up side of 12-inch round
pizza pan. Flute edge, if necessary. Bake
20 to 25 minutes or until lightly browned;
cool completely. Prepare Vanilla Filling;
spread over cooled crust. Cover; refrigerate. Prepare Fruit Topping. Cover;
refrigerate. Assemble tart just before
serving.   *Makes 1 (12-inch) tart*

Vanilla Filling: In microwave-safe bowl,
place 1⅔ cups (10-ounce package)
HERSHEY₅S Vanilla Milk Chips and
¼ cup whipping cream. Microwave at
HIGH (100%) 1 to 1½ minutes or until
chips are melted and mixture is smooth
when stirred vigorously. Beat in 1 package
(8 ounces) softened cream cheese.

Fruit Topping: In small saucepan, stir
together ¼ cup granulated sugar and
1 tablespoon cornstarch; stir in ½ cup
pineapple juice and ½ teaspoon lemon
juice. Cook over medium heat, stirring
constantly, until thickened; cool.
Meanwhile, slice and arrange assorted
fresh fruit on top of filling; carefully pour
or brush juice mixture over fruit.

Orange Dessert Pie

  Tart Shell (recipe follows)
⅓ cup all-purpose flour
⅓ cup sugar
1½ cups milk
  2 large eggs
½ teaspoon almond extract
  8 Florida oranges, peeled and sectioned

Prepare Tart Shell. In medium saucepan,
mix flour and sugar. Beat together milk
and eggs in small mixing bowl. Gradually
stir milk mixture into flour mixture. Cook
over low heat, stirring constantly, until
custard thickens. Remove from heat; stir in
almond extract. Place piece of plastic wrap
directly on surface of filling. Cool custard.
Spoon custard into prepared tart shell;
chill. Before serving, arrange orange
sections over custard.
               Makes 1 (9-inch) pie

Tart Shell

1⅓ cups unsifted all-purpose flour
¼ cup sugar
½ cup butter or margarine, at room
    temperature
  2 egg yolks

Preheat oven to 400°F. In medium bowl,
mix flour and sugar. Stir in butter and egg
yolks with fork until mixture forms a ball.
Press dough into 9-inch tart pan with
removable bottom. Chill 15 minutes. *Do
not prick bottom.* Bake 10 minutes; *reduce
oven temperature to 350°F.* Bake 10 to 15
minutes longer or until shell is lightly
browned. Transfer to wire rack; cool
completely.

*Favorite recipe from **Florida Department of Citrus***

Vanilla Chip Fruit Tart

Southern Nights Ambrosia Cream Pie

Crust
  9-inch Classic Crisco® Single Crust
    (pages 6 and 7)
  1 teaspoon grated orange peel

Filling
  ½ cup *plus* 2 tablespoons granulated
    sugar
  ¼ cup cornstarch
  ½ teaspoon salt
  2½ cups milk
  4 egg yolks, slightly beaten
  2 tablespoons butter or margarine
  2 teaspoons vanilla extract
  3½ cups flake coconut, finely chopped
    and divided
  2 teaspoons grated orange peel, divided

Topping
  1 can (8 ounces) crushed pineapple,
    drained
  2 large navel oranges, peeled,
    sectioned, chopped and drained
  1 cup whipping cream
  2 tablespoons confectioners sugar
  ½ teaspoon vanilla extract
  1 tablespoon finely chopped pecans

1. Prepare 9-inch Classic Crisco® Single Crust, adding 1 teaspoon orange peel to flour mixture. Bake and cool.

2. For Filling, combine granulated sugar, cornstarch and salt in medium saucepan. Beat milk and egg yolks in separate bowl. Stir gradually into sugar mixture. Cook and stir on medium heat until mixture comes to a boil. Boil 1 minute; remove from heat. Stir in butter and 2 teaspoons vanilla. Reserve 1 teaspoon coconut and 1 teaspoon grated orange peel for Topping. Stir remaining coconut and 1 teaspoon grated orange peel into egg mixture. Pour into cooled baked pie crust. Place plastic wrap on surface of Filling. Refrigerate 2 to 3 hours. Remove plastic wrap.

3. For Topping, arrange pineapple on top of Filling to form ring 1 inch from pastry edge. Arrange chopped orange in a ring inside ring of pineapple. Beat whipping cream until stiff. Beat in confectioners sugar and ½ teaspoon vanilla. Garnish outer edge and center of pie with whipped cream. Sprinkle top with reserved 1 teaspoon coconut, reserved 1 teaspoon grated orange peel and nuts. Refrigerate until ready to serve.

Makes 1 (9-inch) pie

Southern Nights Ambrosia Cream Pie

Cool 'n Easy Pie

  1 package (4 to 6 serving size) JELL-O®
    Brand Gelatin, any flavor
  ⅔ cup boiling water
  ½ cup cold water
    Ice cubes
  3½ cups (8 ounces) thawed COOL
    WHIP® Non-Dairy Whipped
    Topping *or* COOL WHIP® Extra
    Creamy Dairy Recipe Whipped
    Topping*
  1 baked (9-inch) prepared graham
    cracker crumb crust, cooled

- Completely dissolve gelatin in boiling water. Combine cold water and enough ice cubes to measure 1¼ cups. Add to gelatin, stirring until slightly thickened. Remove any unmelted ice.

- Using wire whisk, blend in whipped topping; beat until smooth. Chill about 15 minutes or until mixture mounds. Spoon into pie crust. Chill 2 hours or freeze until firm.   *Makes 1 (9-inch) pie*

*Or, use 2 envelopes DREAM WHIP® Whipped Topping Mix, prepared as package directs.

Lemon Blueberry Pie

3 egg *yolks*
1 (14-ounce) can EAGLE® Brand Sweetened Condensed Milk (NOT evaporated milk)
½ cup REALEMON® Lemon Juice from Concentrate
1½ teaspoons grated lemon peel (optional)
   Yellow food coloring (optional)
1 (9-inch) prepared graham cracker crumb crust *or* 1 baked (9-inch) pie crust
1 (21-ounce) can blueberry pie filling, chilled
   BORDEN® or MEADOW GOLD® Whipping Cream, whipped *or* non-dairy whipped topping

Preheat oven to 325°F. In medium bowl, beat egg *yolks*; stir in sweetened condensed milk, ReaLemon® brand, peel and food coloring. Pour into prepared crust; bake 30 minutes. Cool. Chill. Top with blueberry pie filling. Garnish with whipped cream. Refrigerate leftovers.

Makes 1 (9-inch) pie

Banana Strawberry Yogurt Cream Pie

Banana Strawberry Yogurt Cream Pie

3 extra-ripe, medium DOLE® Bananas
1 large package (6 ounces) strawberry-banana gelatin
¾ cup boiling water
1 carton (16 ounces) vanilla lowfat yogurt
1 baked (9-inch) deep-dish pie crust
   Banana and strawberry slices for garnish

- Process peeled bananas in food processor or blender; measure 1½ cups and discard remainder.

- Dissolve gelatin in boiling water, stirring until completely dissolved.

- Stir processed bananas and yogurt into gelatin mixture. Chill 30 minutes until mixture mounds. Pour into baked pie crust. Chill until firm, about 3 hours. Garnish with banana and strawberry slices.   *Makes 1 (9-inch) pie*

Prep time: 15 minutes
Chill time: 3 hours

Ambrosial Cheeseless Cheese Pie

1 can (20 ounces) DOLE® Pineapple
   Chunks in Syrup or Juice
1 package (3¾ ounces) instant French
   vanilla pudding mix
1 cup dairy sour cream
1 (8-inch) prepared graham cracker
   crumb crust
¼ cup orange marmalade, heated
¼ cup flaked coconut

• Drain pineapple well; reserve ½ cup
  syrup.

• Combine pudding mix and sour cream
  until blended. Stir in reserved pineapple
  syrup. Pour into graham cracker crust.
  Chill 15 minutes.

• Top pie with pineapple. Spoon
  marmalade over pineapple to glaze.
  Sprinkle with coconut. Chill 1 hour
  before serving.   *Makes 1 (8-inch) pie*

Prep time: 20 minutes
Chill time: 1¼ hours

Creamy Blackberry Swirl Pie

Crust
   9-inch Classic Crisco® Single Crust
      (pages 6 and 7)

Filling
3½ cups fresh blackberries *or* 1 package
      (16 ounces) thawed frozen dry pack
      blackberries, divided
   1 cup sugar
   3 tablespoons cornstarch
   ⅛ teaspoon salt

Custard
   2 eggs, beaten
   ½ cup dairy sour cream
   ¼ cup orange-flavored liqueur*

1. Prepare 9-inch Classic Crisco® Single
Crust. *Do not bake.* Heat oven to 375°F.

2. For Filling, pat blackberries dry between
paper towels. Combine sugar, cornstarch
and salt in large bowl. Add blackberries.
Toss well to mix. Spoon 1 cup filling into
unbaked pie crust.

3. For Custard, combine eggs, sour cream
and liqueur. Beat at low speed of electric
mixer until blended. Spoon over filling in
pie crust. Spoon remaining filling over
custard.

4. Bake at 375°F for 45 to 55 minutes or
until center is set and crust is golden
brown. Cool.
                              Makes 1 (9-inch) pie

*Substitute ¼ cup orange juice *plus* ½
teaspoon grated orange peel for orange-
flavored liqueur, if desired.

Almond Velvet Custard Pie

1 unbaked (9-inch) pie shell, pricked
1 (14-ounce) can EAGLE® Brand
   Sweetened Condensed Milk
   (NOT evaporated milk)
1 cup (½ pint) BORDEN® or
   MEADOW GOLD® Whipping
   Cream, *unwhipped*
2 eggs
1 teaspoon almond extract
½ cup sliced almonds, lightly toasted

Preheat oven to 375°F. Bake pie shell 15
minutes; remove from oven. *Reduce oven
temperature to 300°F.* Meanwhile, in large
mixer bowl, beat sweetened condensed
milk, unwhipped cream, eggs and extract
until well blended. Stir in almonds. Pour
into prepared pie shell. Bake 50 minutes or
until set. Serve warm or chilled. Garnish
as desired. Refrigerate leftovers.
                              Makes 1 (9-inch) pie

Left to right: Old-Fashioned Buttermilk Pie, Almond Velvet Custard Pie

Old-Fashioned Buttermilk Pie

3 eggs
1¼ cups sugar
3 tablespoons flour
¼ teaspoon ground nutmeg
1 cup BORDEN® or MEADOW
   GOLD® Buttermilk
⅓ cup butter or margarine, melted
1 teaspoon vanilla extract
1 unbaked (9-inch) pie shell

Preheat oven to 400°F. In large mixer bowl, beat eggs. Add sugar, flour and nutmeg; mix well. Beat in buttermilk, butter and vanilla. Pour into pie shell. Bake 10 minutes. *Reduce oven temperature to 325°F;* bake 35 to 40 minutes longer or until knife inserted near edge comes out clean. Cool. Serve with fresh fruit, if desired. Refrigerate leftovers.

Makes 1 (9-inch) pie

Buttermilk Coconut Pie: Add ½ cup flaked coconut to filling. Bake as directed.

Buttermilk Lemon Pie: Add 2 tablespoons ReaLemon® Lemon Juice from Concentrate to filling. Bake as directed.

Buttermilk Pecan Pie: Add 1 cup chopped pecans to filling. Bake as directed.

Lemon Sponge Pie

1 unbaked (9-inch) pie shell, pricked
3 eggs, separated
1¼ cups granulated sugar
¼ cup unsifted flour
¼ cup margarine or butter, melted
⅓ cup REALEMON® Lemon Juice from Concentrate
1 cup BORDEN® or MEADOW GOLD® Milk
Confectioners' sugar

Preheat oven to 350°F. Bake pie shell 8 minutes; remove from oven. Meanwhile, in small mixer bowl, beat egg *whites* until foamy; gradually add *¼ cup* granulated sugar, beating until soft peaks form. In large mixer bowl, combine remaining *1 cup* granulated sugar, flour, margarine and egg *yolks*; beat well. Stir in ReaLemon® brand. Gradually add milk; mix well. Fold egg white mixture into lemon mixture. Pour into prepared pastry shell; bake 40 minutes or until knife inserted near center comes out clean. Cool. Sprinkle with confectioners' sugar. Garnish as desired. Refrigerate leftovers.

Makes 1 (9-inch) pie

Lemon Sponge Pie

Microwave Sunny Citrus Pie

⅔ cup sugar
3 tablespoons ARGO® or KINGSFORD'S® Corn Starch
⅔ cup low-fat milk
¾ cup orange juice
2 egg yolks, slightly beaten
2 tablespoons lemon juice
1 cup light sour cream
1 (8-inch) prepared graham cracker crumb crust

In large microwavable bowl, combine sugar and corn starch. Gradually stir in milk until smooth. Stir in orange juice, egg yolks and lemon juice until blended. Microwave on High (100%) 5 to 7 minutes or until mixture boils, stirring twice with fork or wire whisk; boil 1 minute. Stir until smooth. Cover; chill 1 hour. Stir mixture until smooth; fold in sour cream. Pour into crust. Refrigerate several hours or overnight. Garnish as desired.

Makes 1 (8-inch) pie

Butterscotch Rum Chiffon Pie

1 envelope unflavored gelatin
¼ cup cold water
4 eggs, separated
½ cup milk
½ teaspoon salt
½ (12-ounce) package (1 cup) NESTLÉ® Toll House® Butterscotch Flavored Morsels
1 tablespoon rum
¼ cup sugar
½ cup heavy cream, whipped
1 *baked* (9-inch) pie crust

In cup, combine gelatin and cold water; set aside. Combine egg yolks, milk, and salt over hot, not boiling, water. Cook, stirring constantly with wire whisk, until slightly thickened. Remove from heat. Stir in gelatin. Add Nestlé® Toll House® Butterscotch Flavored Morsels and rum; stir until morsels are melted and mixture is smooth. Transfer to large bowl. Chill 20 to 30 minutes, stirring occasionally, until mixture mounds slightly when dropped from spoon.

In 1½-quart bowl, beat egg whites until foamy. Gradually add sugar; beat until stiff peaks form. Fold egg whites and whipped cream into butterscotch mixture. Pour into prepared pie crust.* Chill about 4 hours or until firm.

Makes 1 (9-inch) pie

*If using frozen pie crust, use deep-dish style.

Coconut Chiffon Pumpkin Pie

1¾ cups (16-ounce can) LIBBY'S® Solid
    Pack Pumpkin
 1 cup whipping cream, unwhipped
 ¾ cup packed brown sugar, divided
 2 eggs, separated
 ½ teaspoon salt
1½ teaspoons ground cinnamon
 ½ teaspoon ground nutmeg
 ¼ teaspoon ground ginger
 1 envelope (1 ounce) unflavored gelatin
 1 teaspoon vanilla extract
 ¾ cup flaked coconut, toasted
 1 *baked* (9-inch) pie crust, cooled
    Whipped cream (optional)
    Additional toasted coconut (optional)

Coconut Chiffon Pumpkin Pie

In medium saucepan, combine pumpkin, cream, ½ *cup* brown sugar, egg yolks, salt, cinnamon, nutmeg, and ginger. Cook over medium heat, stirring constantly, about 8 to 10 minutes or until mixture thickens slightly. Remove from heat. Sprinkle gelatin over top; stir until completely dissolved. Stir in vanilla. Pour into large bowl; chill until mixture just begins to set. In small mixer bowl, beat egg whites until soft peaks form. Gradually add *remaining* ¼ cup brown sugar; beat until stiff and shiny. Fold into pumpkin mixture. Gently fold in coconut. Spoon into pie crust; chill about 2 hours or until set. Garnish with whipped cream and toasted coconut, if desired.

Makes 1 (9-inch) pie

Cookie Crust Lemon Pie

1 (20-ounce) package refrigerated sugar
    cookie dough
1⅓ cups sugar
⅓ cup cornstarch
2 eggs
½ cup REALEMON® Lemon Juice from
    Concentrate
1½ cups boiling water
2 tablespoons margarine or butter
    Yellow food coloring (optional)
    Additional sugar

Preheat oven to 350°F. On floured surface, press *half* of the cookie dough into 6-inch circle. With floured side down, press firmly onto bottom and up side to rim of 9-inch pie plate to form crust. In heavy saucepan, combine sugar, cornstarch and eggs; mix well. Over medium heat, gradually stir in ReaLemon® brand, then water, stirring constantly. Cook and stir until thickened. Cook 1 minute longer. Remove from heat. Add margarine; stir until melted. Add food coloring. Pour into prepared crust. Slice remaining dough into 16 (¼-inch) rounds; arrange on top of filling. Bake 15 minutes or until golden. Sprinkle with additional sugar. Cool. Chill. Refrigerate leftovers.

Makes 1 (9-inch) pie

Cookie Crust Lime Pie: Substitute REALIME® Lime Juice from Concentrate for ReaLemon® brand and green food coloring for yellow.

French Apple Cream Tart

    Golden Nut Crust (recipe follows)
1 (14-ounce) can EAGLE® Brand
    Sweetened Condensed Milk
    (NOT evaporated milk)
1 (16-ounce) container BORDEN® or
    MEADOW GOLD® Sour Cream
½ cup frozen apple juice concentrate,
    thawed
2 eggs, beaten
1 teaspoon vanilla extract
2 medium all-purpose apples, cored,
    peeled and thinly sliced
2 tablespoons margarine or butter
½ cup BAMA® Apricot Preserves
5 teaspoons water
1 teaspoon cornstarch

Preheat oven to 350°F. Prepare Golden Nut Crust. Meanwhile, in medium bowl, combine sweetened condensed milk and sour cream; add juice concentrate, eggs and vanilla. Mix well. Pour into prepared crust. Bake 30 to 35 minutes or until center is set. Cool. In skillet, cook apples in margarine until tender-crisp. Arrange on top of tart. In small saucepan, combine preserves, water and cornstarch; cook and stir until slightly thickened. Spoon over apples. Chill thoroughly. Refrigerate leftovers.

Makes 1 (9-inch) tart

Golden Nut Crust: In small mixer bowl, beat ½ cup softened margarine or butter and ¼ cup packed light brown sugar until fluffy. Stir in 1 cup unsifted flour, ¼ cup quick-cooking oats and ¼ cup finely chopped walnuts; press firmly onto bottom and halfway up side of lightly greased 9-inch springform pan. Bake 15 to 20 minutes or until golden.

*Top to bottom: Frozen Lemon Satin Pie
(page 161), Cookie Crust Lemon Pie*

Creamy Key Lime Tart

Creamy Key Lime Tart

Crust
   3 cups HONEY ALMOND DELIGHT®
      Brand Cereal, crushed to 1½ cups
   ¼ cup packed brown sugar
   ¼ cup (½ stick) margarine or butter,
      melted

Filling
   8 ounces cream cheese, softened
   1 can (14 ounces) sweetened condensed
      milk
   ⅓ cup lime juice
   1 teaspoon freshly grated lime peel
   2 drops green food coloring (optional)
   1 cup non-dairy whipped topping

To prepare Crust, preheat oven to 350°F.
In medium bowl, combine cereal, sugar
and margarine; mix well. Press firmly onto
bottom and up side of ungreased 9-inch
fluted tart pan or pie plate. Bake 8 to 9
minutes or until lightly browned. Cool
completely.

To prepare Filling, in large bowl beat
cream cheese and milk. Gradually add

juice, peel and food coloring, beating until
smooth. Fold in whipped topping. Pour
evenly into cooled crust. Chill 1 hour or
until set. Garnish with additional lime
peel and whipped topping, if desired.

Makes 1 (9-inch) tart

Pineapple-Coconut Chess Pie

Crust
   9-inch Classic Crisco® Single Crust
      (pages 6 and 7)

Filling
1⅔ cups sugar
   ½ cup BUTTER FLAVOR CRISCO®
   3 eggs
   1 teaspoon yellow cornmeal
   1 teaspoon all-purpose flour
   1 teaspoon vanilla extract
   1 can (8 ounces) crushed pineapple in
      unsweetened pineapple juice,
      undrained
   ½ cup flake coconut

1. Heat oven to 325°F. Prepare 9-inch
Classic Crisco® Single Crust. *Do not bake.*

2. For Filling, combine sugar and Butter
Flavor Crisco® in large bowl. Beat at
medium speed of electric mixer until light
and fluffy. Add eggs, one at a time,
beating well after each addition. Add
cornmeal, flour and vanilla. Mix well.

3. Combine undrained pineapple and
coconut in small bowl. Gently stir into
filling. Pour into unbaked pie crust.

4. Bake at 325°F for 45 to 50 minutes or
until knife inserted in center comes out
clean. Cool to room temperature before
serving. Refrigerate leftover pie.

Makes 1 (9-inch) pie

Lemon Blueberry Mousse Pie

Crust
9-inch Classic Crisco® Single Crust
   (pages 6 and 7)
2 teaspoons grated lemon peel

Filling
3 tablespoons sugar
2 tablespoons cornstarch
3 egg yolks, beaten
½ cup milk
⅓ cup thawed frozen lemonade
   concentrate
1¼ cups fresh or thawed frozen dry pack
   blueberries
1 cup whipping cream, whipped
   Grated lemon peel (optional)
   Blueberries (optional)

1. Prepare 9-inch Classic Crisco® Single Crust, adding lemon peel to flour mixture. Bake and cool.

2. For Filling, combine sugar and cornstarch in small saucepan. Add egg yolks and milk. Stir in lemonade concentrate. Cook and stir on low heat until thickened and translucent. Cool to room temperature. Spread ⅓ cup Filling into bottom of cooled baked pie crust.

3. Pat blueberries dry between paper towels; arrange in single layer over filling in pie crust. Stir small amount of whipped cream into remaining filling. Fold in remaining whipped cream. Spoon over blueberries in pie crust. Refrigerate 2 to 3 hours before serving. Garnish with grated lemon peel and blueberries.

Makes 1 (9-inch) pie

Banana Cream Pie

Vanilla wafers
Teddy bear cookies
1 large banana, sliced
2½ cups cold milk
1 package (6-serving size) JELL-O®
   Chocolate, Banana Cream *or*
   Vanilla Flavor Instant Pudding and
   Pie Filling
1 cup thawed COOL WHIP® Non-
   Dairy Whipped Topping (optional)
   Gumdrop slices (optional)

• Cover bottom of 9-inch pie plate with vanilla wafers. Arrange additional vanilla wafers and teddy bear cookies alternately around sides. Place banana slices over wafers on bottom of plate.

• Pour milk into small bowl. Add pie filling mix. Beat with wire whisk until well blended, 1 to 2 minutes. Pour over bananas in pie plate. Chill 2 hours. Garnish with whipped topping and additional banana slices, if desired.

Makes 1 (9-inch) pie

Banana Cream Pie

Peanut Cream Pie

Peanut Cream Pie

Crust
9-inch Classic Crisco® Single Crust
(pages 6 and 7)

Crumb Layer
⅓ cup JIF® Extra Crunchy Peanut
Butter
½ cup confectioners sugar

Fudge Sauce
1 square (1 ounce) unsweetened
chocolate
1½ teaspoons butter or margarine
⅓ cup *plus* ½ teaspoon boiling water
½ cup granulated sugar
1 tablespoon light corn syrup
½ teaspoon vanilla extract

Filling
½ cup granulated sugar
⅓ cup all-purpose flour
2 cups milk
3 egg yolks, slightly beaten
½ cup peanut butter chips
2 tablespoons butter or margarine
1 teaspoon vanilla extract

Topping
1½ cups whipping cream
1½ teaspoons granulated sugar
½ teaspoon vanilla extract

Drizzle
¼ cup peanut butter chips
½ teaspoon CRISCO® Shortening

1. Prepare and bake 9-inch Classic
Crisco® Single Crust; cool completely.

2. For Crumb Layer, combine peanut butter and confectioners sugar in small bowl. Stir with fork until crumbly.

3. For Fudge Sauce, combine chocolate and 1½ teaspoons butter in small saucepan. Cook on low heat until chocolate melts. Stir in water. Add ½ cup granulated sugar and corn syrup; stir well. Increase heat to medium. Cook until mixture simmers. Cover; simmer 3 minutes. *Do not stir.* Uncover; reduce heat to medium-low. Simmer 2 minutes without stirring. Stir in ½ teaspoon vanilla. Cool until slightly warm.

4. For Filling, combine ½ cup granulated sugar and flour in medium saucepan. Stir in milk. Cook and stir on medium-high heat until mixture comes to a boil; cook and stir 2 minutes. Remove from heat. Stir about one third of the hot mixture slowly into egg yolks. Mix well. Return mixture to saucepan. Cook and stir 2 minutes. Remove from heat. Add ½ cup peanut butter chips, 2 tablespoons butter and 1 teaspoon vanilla. Stir until chips are melted.

5. Sprinkle Crumb Layer into baked pie crust. Pour Fudge Sauce over crumbs. Spoon Filling over Fudge Sauce. Cover with plastic wrap. Refrigerate until set, about 2 to 3 hours.

6. For Topping, combine whipping cream, 1½ teaspoons granulated sugar and ½ teaspoon vanilla in medium bowl. Beat at high speed of electric mixer until stiff peaks form. Spread over Filling. Refrigerate.

7. For Drizzle, combine ½ cup peanut butter chips and Crisco® in small microwave-safe cup. Microwave at 50% (MEDIUM) 1 minute. Stir. Repeat until smooth (or melt on rangetop in small saucepan on very low heat). Drizzle over whipped cream. Cut into wedges immediately before drizzle hardens. Serve or store in refrigerator.

Makes 1 (9-inch) pie

Velvety Lemon Lime Pie

Almond Pastry Crust (recipe follows)
1 (8-ounce) package cream cheese, softened
1 (14-ounce) can EAGLE® Brand Sweetened Condensed Milk (NOT evaporated milk)
1 (8-ounce) container BORDEN® Lite-line® or Viva® Lemon Yogurt
⅓ cup REALIME® Lime Juice from Concentrate
1 teaspoon grated lime or lemon peel (optional)
Green or yellow food coloring (optional)
1 (4-ounce) container thawed frozen non-dairy whipped topping (1¾ cups)

Prepare Almond Pastry Crust. In large mixer bowl, beat cheese until fluffy. Gradually beat in sweetened condensed milk until smooth. Beat in yogurt and ReaLime® brand. Stir in peel and food coloring. Fold in whipped topping. Pour into prepared pastry crust. Chill 3 hours or until set. Garnish as desired. Refrigerate leftovers. *Makes 1 (9-inch) pie*

Almond Pastry Crust: Preheat oven to 425°F. In medium bowl, combine 1⅓ cups unsifted flour, 2 tablespoons ground almonds and ½ teaspoon salt; cut in ½ cup shortening until crumbly. Adding 1 tablespoon at a time, sprinkle with 3 tablespoons cold water, stirring to form a ball. On floured surface, roll dough into 10-inch circle. Turn dough into 9-inch pie plate; trim and flute edge. Prick bottom and side with fork. Bake 10 to 15 minutes or until lightly browned; cool.

Double Blueberry Cheese Pie

Crust
9-inch Classic Crisco® Single Crust
(pages 6 and 7)

Filling
2 packages (8 ounces *each*) cream
   cheese, softened
1 cup granulated sugar
2 tablespoons all-purpose flour
2 eggs
2 teaspoons vanilla extract
½ cup whipping cream
2 cups fresh blueberries

Topping
2 cups whipping cream
2 tablespoons confectioners sugar
1 teaspoon vanilla extract
1 cup fresh blueberries

1. Prepare 9-inch Classic Crisco® Single Crust in 9- or 9½-inch deep-dish pie plate. *Do not bake.* Heat oven to 350°F.

2. For Filling, place cream cheese and granulated sugar in food processor. Process until smooth. Add flour, eggs, 2 teaspoons vanilla and ½ cup whipping cream through feed tube while processor is running. Process until blended. Add 2 cups blueberries. Pulse (quick on and off) twice. Pour into unbaked pie crust.

3. Bake at 350°F for 45 minutes. Turn oven off. Allow pie to remain in oven with door ajar 1 hour. Cool to room temperature. Refrigerate 6 hours or overnight.

4. For Topping, beat 2 cups whipping cream in large bowl at high speed of electric mixer until stiff peaks form. Beat in confectioners sugar and 1 teaspoon vanilla. Spread over top of pie. Garnish with 1 cup blueberries. Serve immediately. Refrigerate leftover pie.

Makes 1 (9- or 9½-inch) deep-dish pie

Pineapple Citrus Pie

1 cup DOLE® Chopped Almonds
½ cup *plus* 2 tablespoons sugar, divided
1 tablespoon flour
3 tablespoons margarine, softened
¼ cup flaked coconut
1 envelope unflavored gelatin
1½ cups DOLE® Pineapple Juice
2 egg whites
1½ cups frozen whipped topping, thawed
   Grated peel from 1 *each:* DOLE®
   Orange, Lemon and Lime
1 DOLE® Fresh Pineapple

• Preheat oven to 350°F.

• Pulverize almonds in food processor or blender. Combine with 2 tablespoons sugar and flour. Cut in margarine. Stir in coconut. Press into 9-inch pie plate.

• Bake 15 minutes.

• Combine gelatin, ¼ cup sugar and pineapple juice in saucepan. Cook, stirring, to dissolve gelatin. Chill until slightly thickened.

• Beat egg whites until foamy. Gradually add remaining ¼ cup sugar, beating until stiff peaks form. Fold into chilled gelatin with ½ cup whipped topping and citrus peel. Pour into crust. Chill 3 hours.

• Spread top of pie with remaining 1 cup whipped topping.

• Twist crown from pineapple. Cut pineapple lengthwise in half. Refrigerate half for another use, such as for stir-fry. Cut fruit from shell. Cut fruit into thin wedges; arrange in petal fashion on top. Chill until firm.   *Makes 1 (9-inch) pie*

Prep Time: 30 minutes
Bake Time: 15 minutes
Chill Time: 4 hours

Double Blueberry Cheese Pie

Peaches and Cream Pie

Peaches and Cream Pie

Crust
　**9-inch Classic Crisco® Double Crust
　　(pages 6 and 7)**
　**1 egg white, slightly beaten
　　Granulated sugar**

Nut Layer
　½ cup sliced natural almonds
　2 teaspoons butter or margarine

Filling
　**1 package (8 ounces) cream cheese,
　　softened**
　1 cup confectioners sugar
　1 teaspoon vanilla extract
　1 cup whipping cream, whipped

Topping and Glaze
**3½ cups sliced, peeled peaches* (about
　　2 pounds *or* 5 to 6 medium),
　　divided**
　1 tablespoon lemon juice
　½ cup granulated sugar
　2 tablespoons cornstarch

1. Prepare 9-inch Classic Crisco® Double Crust; press bottom crust into 9-inch pie plate. Heat oven to 425°F. Roll out second half and cut out small leaf shapes using cookie cutter. Place around edge of pie crust. Brush with egg white; sprinkle with granulated sugar. Thoroughly prick bottom and sides with fork 50 times to prevent shrinkage. Cover with plastic wrap and freeze 10 minutes. Remove plastic wrap and bake pie crust 10 to 15 minutes or until lightly browned; cool. *Increase oven temperature to 450°F.*

2. For Nut Layer, place nuts and butter in baking pan. Bake 7 to 8 minutes or until golden brown, stirring often; cool. Sprinkle nuts over bottom of cooled baked pie crust.

3. For Filling, combine cream cheese, confectioners sugar and vanilla in medium bowl. Beat at medium speed of electric mixer until well blended. Fold in whipped cream. Spoon over nuts in pie crust. Refrigerate 1 hour.

4. For Topping and Glaze, combine 1¾ cups peaches and lemon juice in food processor or blender. Process until well mixed. Combine ½ cup granulated sugar and cornstarch. Add to food processor; process to mix. Pour mixture into small saucepan. Cook and stir on medium heat until mixture thickens and boils; boil 1 minute. Remove from heat; cool. Arrange remaining 1¾ cups peach slices on top of pie. Spoon glaze over peaches. Refrigerate until firm. 　　*Makes 1 (9-inch) pie*

*Use 1 bag (20 ounces) frozen unsweetened freestone peach slices if fresh peaches are not available. Use half of the package for glaze and half for topping.

Lime Mousse Pie

1 package (4-serving size) lime gelatin
1 cup boiling water
1 cup marshmallow creme
1 cup DANNON® Plain Nonfat or
    Lowfat Yogurt
1 (8-inch) prepared graham cracker
    crumb crust
    Sliced strawberries and kiwi fruit

Combine gelatin and boiling water in blender or with electric mixer. Blend on low speed 1 minute; blend on high speed 1 minute or until gelatin is completely dissolved. Add marshmallow creme; blend well on low speed. Add yogurt; blend on high speed. Pour into crust. Cover; chill several hours or overnight. Garnish with strawberries and kiwi fruit just before serving. *Makes 1 (8-inch) pie*

Any Season Light and Fruity Pie

1 package (4-serving size) JELL-O®
    Brand Gelatin, any flavor
⅔ cup boiling water
½ cup cold water
    Ice cubes
3½ cups (8 ounces) COOL WHIP®
    Whipped Topping, thawed
    Any Season Ingredients*
1 (8-inch) prepared graham cracker
    crumb crust

- Dissolve gelatin in boiling water. Combine cold water and enough ice cubes to measure 1¼ cups. Add to gelatin, stirring until slightly thickened. Remove any unmelted ice.

- Blend whipped topping into gelatin using wire whisk. Fold in Any Season Ingredients. Chill until mixture is very thick.

- Spoon gelatin mixture into crust. Chill 2 hours. Garnish with additional fruit and whipped topping, if desired.
Makes 1 (8-inch) pie

*Citrus Snowflake Pie (winter): Use orange flavor gelatin. Fold in 1 cup drained mandarin orange sections, 1 small banana, sliced, and 2 tablespoons orange liqueur (optional). Garnish with additional whipped topping, mandarin orange sections and toasted coconut (optional).

*Any Berry Pie (spring): Use raspberry *or* strawberry flavor gelatin. Fold in ½ cup *each*: blueberries, raspberries and sliced strawberries and 2 tablespoons raspberry liqueur (optional). Garnish with additional whipped topping and berries (optional).

*Creamy Daiquiri Pie (summer): Use lime flavor gelatin. Add ½ teaspoon grated lime peel, 2 tablespoons lime juice and 3 tablespoons rum (optional). Garnish with additional whipped topping and citrus curls (optional).

*Autumn Harvest Pie (fall): Use lemon flavor gelatin. Fold in 1 ripe pear, chopped, and 1 tablespoon lemon juice. Garnish with additional whipped topping and lemon slices (optional).

Prep time: 20 minutes
Chill time: 2 hours

Citrus Snowflake Pie

Easy Pineapple Pie

1 can (20 ounces) DOLE® Crushed
   Pineapple in Juice
1 package (3.5 ounces) instant lemon
   pudding and pie filling mix
1 cup milk
1 carton (4 ounces) frozen non-dairy
   whipped topping, thawed
   Grated peel and juice from
   1 DOLE® Lemon
1 (8- or 9-inch) prepared graham
   cracker crumb crust

- Drain pineapple well; reserve juice for
  another use.

- Combine pudding mix with milk. Beat
  2 to 3 minutes or until very thick.

- Fold in whipped topping, pineapple,
  1 teaspoon lemon peel and 2
  tablespoons lemon juice.

- Pour into pie crust. Chill overnight.

Makes 1 (8- or 9-inch) pie

Prep time: 5 minutes
Chill time: 8 hours or overnight

Pumpkin Custard Pie

⅓ cup FLEISCHMANN'S® Margarine
1¼ cups all-purpose flour
 4 to 5 tablespoons cold water
¾ cup EGG BEATERS® 99% Real Egg
   Product
1 (16-ounce) can solid-pack pumpkin
½ cup packed light brown sugar
1½ teaspoons pumpkin pie spice
1 (12-ounce) can evaporated skim milk

Preheat oven to 400°F. In medium bowl,
cut margarine into flour until mixture is
crumbly; stir in enough water until
mixture forms a ball. Set aside one fourth
of the dough; roll remaining dough into
11-inch circle. Place in 9-inch pie plate;
trim and smooth edges. Roll out reserved
dough and cut into 1-inch leaves; attach to
edge of pie using 1 tablespoon egg
product.

In large bowl with electric mixer at
medium speed, beat remaining egg
product, pumpkin, brown sugar and spice
until well blended. Gradually blend in
evaporated milk. Pour into prepared pie
shell. Bake 45 minutes or until knife
inserted in center comes out clean. Cool
on wire rack. Chill before serving.

Makes 1 (9-inch) pie

Lemon Cheesecake Pie

1 (8-ounce) package cream cheese,
   softened
1 (14-ounce) can EAGLE® Brand
   Sweetened Condensed Milk
   (NOT evaporated milk)
2 eggs
2 tablespoons REALEMON® Lemon
   Juice from Concentrate
1 teaspoon grated lemon peel (optional)
1 (9-inch) prepared graham cracker
   crumb crust
2 cups assorted cut-up fresh fruit,
   chilled
   Lemon Sauce (recipe follows)

Preheat oven to 350°F. In small mixer
bowl, beat cheese until fluffy; gradually
beat in sweetened condensed milk. Add
eggs and ReaLemon® brand; mix well. Stir
in peel. Pour into prepared crust. Bake 20
minutes or until set. Cool. Chill
thoroughly. Serve with fruit and Lemon
Sauce. Refrigerate leftovers.

Makes 1 (9-inch) pie

Lemon Sauce: In small saucepan, combine
⅓ cup sugar, 2 teaspoons cornstarch and
dash salt. Add ½ cup water, ¼ cup
ReaLemon® brand and 1 egg *yolk*; mix
well. Over medium heat, cook and stir
until thickened. Remove from heat; stir in
1 tablespoon margarine or butter and
yellow food coloring (optional). Cool.
Chill. Makes about 1 cup.

Banana Blueberry Pudding Pie

Vanilla wafers
2 medium bananas, sliced, dipped in REALEMON® Lemon Juice from Concentrate and well drained
1 cup fresh blueberries, rinsed and drained
2 (3-ounce) packages cream cheese, softened
1 (14-ounce) can EAGLE® Brand Sweetened Condensed Milk (NOT evaporated milk)
¾ cup cold water
1 (4-serving size) package *instant* vanilla *or* banana cream flavor pudding mix
1 cup (½ pint) BORDEN® or MEADOW GOLD® Whipping Cream, whipped

Line 9-inch pie plate with vanilla wafers; top with bananas and blueberries. In large mixer bowl, beat cheese until fluffy; gradually beat in sweetened condensed milk until smooth. On low speed, beat in water and pudding mix until smooth. Chill 10 minutes. Fold in whipped cream. Pour into prepared pie plate. Chill. Garnish as desired. Refrigerate leftovers.

Makes 1 (9-inch) pie

Banana Blueberry Pudding Pie

Pineapple Macadamia Cheesepie

1 cup chopped macadamia nuts
¾ cup graham cracker crumbs
6 tablespoons melted margarine, divided
½ cup *plus* 2 tablespoons sugar
1 can (8¼ ounces) DOLE® Crushed Pineapple in Syrup or Juice
12 ounces light cream cheese, softened
1 egg
¾ cup plain yogurt
1 teaspoon vanilla extract

- Preheat oven to 350°F. Combine nuts, crumbs, margarine and 2 tablespoons sugar. Press into bottom and up side of 8-inch pie plate. Refrigerate.

- Drain pineapple well; reserve syrup for another use. Reserve 2 tablespoons pineapple for garnish. Spread remaining pineapple over crust.

- Combine remaining ingredients. Pour filling over pineapple.

- Bake 20 minutes. Cool; refrigerate at least 2 hours. Garnish with reserved pineapple. *Makes 1 (8-inch) pie*

Prep time: 10 minutes
Cook time: 20 minutes
Chill time: 2 hours

Never Fail Meringue

1 tablespoon ARGO® or KINGSFORD'S® Corn Starch
⅔ cup water
3 egg whites, at room temperature
Dash salt
6 tablespoons sugar

Preheat oven to 350°F. In 1-quart saucepan, combine corn starch and water until smooth. Stirring constantly, bring to a boil over medium heat and boil 1 minute. Cover surface of corn starch mixture with waxed paper or plastic wrap; cool at room temperature.

In small bowl with mixer at high speed, beat egg whites and salt until foamy. Add sugar, 1 tablespoon at a time, beating well after each addition. Continue beating just until stiff peaks form. Beat in cooled corn starch mixture until well blended. Spread over desired pie filling, sealing to edge of desired crust. Bake 20 minutes or until meringue is lightly browned.
Makes enough meringue for 1 (9-inch) pie

Chess Pie

Crust
10-inch Classic Crisco® Single Crust (pages 6 and 7)

Filling
3 cups sugar
½ cup butter or margarine, softened
5 eggs, slightly beaten
3 tablespoons cornmeal
2 teaspoons vanilla extract
⅛ teaspoon salt
1 cup milk

1. Prepare 10-inch Classic Crisco® Single Crust. *Do not bake.* Heat oven to 325°F.

2. For Filling, combine sugar and butter in large bowl. Beat at low speed of electric mixer until blended. Beat in eggs, cornmeal, vanilla and salt. Add milk; beat at low speed until blended. Pour into unbaked pie crust.

3. Bake at 325°F for 60 to 80 minutes or until filling is set. Cover edge of pie with foil, if necessary, to prevent overbrowning. Cool to room temperature before serving. Refrigerate leftover pie.
Makes 1 (10-inch) pie

Pineapple Macadamia Cheesepie

Microwave Banana Caramel Pie

¼ cup margarine or butter
1 (14-ounce) can EAGLE® Brand Sweetened Condensed Milk (NOT evaporated milk)
1 teaspoon vanilla extract
1 cup (½ pint) BORDEN® or MEADOW GOLD® Whipping Cream, *unwhipped*
3 medium bananas
   REALEMON® Lemon Juice from Concentrate
1 (8-inch) prepared graham cracker crumb crust

In 2-quart glass measure with handle, melt margarine on 100% power (high) 1 minute. Stir in sweetened condensed milk and vanilla. Cook on 100% power (high) 6 to 10 minutes, stirring briskly after each minute until smooth. Stir in ¼ *cup* unwhipped cream. Freeze 5 minutes. Meanwhile, slice 2 bananas; dip in ReaLemon® brand and drain. Arrange on

Top to bottom: Banana Split Brownie Pie (page 170), Microwave Banana Caramel Pie

bottom of crust. Pour filling over bananas; cover. Chill at least 2 hours. In small mixer bowl, whip remaining ¾ cup cream. Spread on top of pie. Slice remaining banana. Dip in ReaLemon® brand; drain. Garnish pie with banana slices. Refrigerate leftovers.

Makes 1 (8-inch) pie

Ginger Cream Banana Pie

1½ cups gingersnap cookie crumbs
¼ cup *plus* 1 tablespoon margarine, softened
½ cup sugar
3 tablespoons cornstarch
⅛ teaspoon salt
2 cups milk
1 tablespoon crystallized ginger
1 tablespoon grated orange peel
3 tablespoons orange-flavored liqueur
4 firm, medium DOLE® Bananas, peeled
   Thawed frozen non-dairy whipped topping for garnish

• Preheat oven to 375°F. Combine crumbs and ¼ cup margarine. Press mixture onto bottom and up side of 8-inch pie plate. Bake 8 minutes; cool.

• Combine sugar, cornstarch and salt in saucepan. Stir in milk, ginger and orange peel. Cook over medium heat, stirring, until mixture boils and thickens. Remove from heat. Add liqueur and remaining 1 tablespoon margarine; stir until margarine is melted. Cool.

• Slice 2 bananas into pie shell. Cover with half of the filling. Repeat with remaining bananas and filling. Cover; chill 3 hours.

• Garnish with dollops of whipped topping, if desired. Top with remaining bananas, sliced.   *Makes 1 (8-inch) pie*

Prep time: 25 minutes
Cook time: 15 minutes
Chill time: 3 hours

Pineapple Mai Tai Pie

1 can (20 ounces) DOLE® Pineapple
    Tidbits in Juice, undrained
1 package (10 ounces) miniature
    marshmallows
1½ cups graham cracker crumbs
⅓ cup margarine, melted
¼ cup almond-flavored liqueur
1 tablespoon lime juice
1 tablespoon light rum
2 cups thawed frozen whipped topping

- **Microwave Directions:** Drain
  pineapple, reserving ½ cup juice.

- Add pineapple juice and marshmallows
  to 3-quart casserole. Cover; microwave
  on HIGH 2 to 3 minutes or until mixture
  is smooth when stirred. Refrigerate 30
  minutes or until completely cool.

- In deep-dish 9-inch pie plate, stir
  together 1½ cups graham cracker crumbs
  and margarine. Reserve ¼ cup crumb
  mixture for garnish. With back of spoon,
  press remaining crumb mixture firmly
  onto bottom and up side of pie plate.

- Beat marshmallow mixture until smooth.
  Stir in liqueur, lime juice and rum. Reserve
  ¼ cup pineapple for garnish. Gently stir
  remaining pineapple into marshmallow
  mixture. Fold in whipped topping.

- Spoon filling into prepared crust.
  Decorate top with reserved pineapple
  and graham cracker crumb mixture.
  Refrigerate until set.
  Makes 1 (9-inch) deep-dish pie

Prep time: 20 minutes
Cook time: 3 minutes
Chill time: 2 hours

Cherry Vanilla Ribbon Pie

Cherry Vanilla Ribbon Pie

1 (8-ounce) package cream cheese,
    softened
1 (14-ounce) can EAGLE® Brand
    Sweetened Condensed Milk
    (NOT evaporated milk)
¾ cup cold water
1 (4-serving size) package *instant*
    vanilla flavor pudding mix
1 cup (½ pint) BORDEN® or
    MEADOW GOLD® Whipping
    Cream, whipped
1 baked (9- or 10-inch) pie crust
1 (21-ounce) can cherry pie filling,
    chilled

In large mixer bowl, beat cheese until
fluffy; gradually beat in sweetened
condensed milk until smooth. On low
speed, beat in water and pudding mix
until smooth. Fold in whipped cream.
Spread half of the pudding mixture into
prepared pie crust; top with half of the
cherry pie filling. Repeat layers. Chill 2
hours or until set. Refrigerate leftovers.
Makes 1 (9- or 10-inch) pie

FRUIT FAVORITES

Mixed Berry Pie

Crust
9-inch Classic Crisco® Double Crust
(pages 6 and 7)

Filling
2 cups canned or frozen blackberries,
thawed and well drained
1½ cups canned or frozen blueberries,
thawed and well drained
½ cup canned or frozen gooseberries,
thawed and well drained
⅛ teaspoon almond extract
¼ cup sugar
3 tablespoons cornstarch

1. Prepare 9-inch Classic Crisco® Double
Crust; press bottom crust into 9-inch pie
plate. *Do not bake.* Heat oven to 425°F.

2. For Filling, combine blackberries,
blueberries, gooseberries and almond
extract in large bowl. Combine sugar and
cornstarch. Add to berries. Toss well to
mix. Spoon into unbaked pie crust.

3. Cut top crust into leaf shapes and
arrange on top of pie, or cover pie with
top crust. Flute edge. Cut slits into top
crust, if using, to allow steam to escape.

4. Bake at 425°F for 40 minutes or until
filling in center is bubbly and crust is
golden brown. Cool until barely warm or
at room temperature before serving.

Makes 1 (9-inch) pie

Ritz® Mock Apple Pie

Pastry for 2-crust 9-inch pie
36 RITZ® Crackers, coarsely broken
(about 1¾ cups crumbs)*
2 cups water
2 cups sugar
2 teaspoons cream of tartar
2 tablespoons lemon juice
Grated peel of one lemon
2 tablespoons BLUE BONNET®
Margarine
½ teaspoon ground cinnamon

Preheat oven to 425°F. Roll out half of the
pastry and line 9-inch pie plate. Place
cracker crumbs in prepared crust. In
saucepan, over high heat, bring water,
sugar and cream of tartar to a boil; simmer
15 minutes. Add lemon juice and peel;
cool. Pour syrup over cracker crumbs. Dot
with margarine; sprinkle with cinnamon.
Roll out remaining pastry; place over pie.
Trim, seal and flute edges. Slit top crust to
allow steam to escape.

Bake 30 to 35 minutes or until crust is
crisp and golden. Serve warm.

Makes 1 (9-inch) pie

*Substitute 2¼ cups RITZ® Bits for the
crackers, if desired. Let pie cool
completely before serving.

Mixed Berry Pie

California Apricot Frangipane Tart

California Apricot Frangipane Tart

½ cup blanched slivered almonds
¼ cup unsalted butter, at room
    temperature
¼ cup sugar
1 large egg
⅛ teaspoon almond extract
½ (15-ounce package) refrigerated pie
    shells
½ (17-ounce) can California apricot
    halves, well drained

In food processor or blender, process
almonds until finely ground, being careful
not to overprocess to a paste. Add butter
and sugar; process 15 seconds until just
combined. Add egg and almond extract;
process until creamy. Remove almond
mixture to shallow bowl; refrigerate 1
hour or until firm. Line 8-inch tart pan
with pie shell. Partially pre-bake shell as
package directs; let cool completely.

Heat oven to 350°F. Cut apricot halves
carefully into ⅛-inch slices; set aside.
Spread almond mixture into cooled tart
shell. Place 6 sliced apricot halves on top
of filling, setting them close to edge of
crust. Working from crust toward center of
tart, fan each apricot half by pressing
gently with forefinger. Place 1 sliced
apricot half in center of tart; fan as
directed. Bake 30 minutes or until tart is
golden brown. Cool tart on rack; serve at
room temperature. Refrigerate leftovers.
Makes 1 (8-inch) tart

Favorite recipe from **California Apricot Advisory Board**

Cranberry Peach Cobbler

1 can (16 ounces) whole berry
    cranberry sauce
1 can (21 ounces) peach pie filling*
¼ teaspoon ground cinnamon
1 cup unsifted all-purpose flour
2 tablespoons *plus* ½ teaspoon sugar
1½ teaspoons baking powder
¼ teaspoon salt
¼ cup BUTTER FLAVOR CRISCO®
1 egg, slightly beaten
¼ cup milk

1. Heat oven to 400°F. Combine cranberry
sauce, pie filling and cinnamon in
ungreased 8-inch square or round glass
baking dish. Stir until well mixed. Bake 15
minutes or until mixture bubbles around
edges.

2. Combine flour, 2 tablespoons sugar,
baking powder and salt. Cut in Butter
Flavor Crisco® until mixture resembles
coarse crumbs. Combine egg and milk.
Add to flour mixture; stir just until
moistened.

3. Spoon dough in nine equal portions on
top of hot fruit (3 across and 3 down).
Sprinkle remaining ½ teaspoon sugar over
top of dough.

4. Bake at 400°F for 20 minutes. Serve
warm. *Makes 9 servings*

*Substitute apple or cherry pie filling for
the peach filling, if desired.

Pineapple Meringue Pie

2 cups vanilla wafer crumbs (60 wafers)
⅓ cup margarine, melted
1 teaspoon ground cinnamon
**1 can (20 ounces) DOLE® Crushed
    Pineapple in Juice, undrained**
1 carton (8 ounces) dairy sour cream
4 eggs, separated
¼ cup all-purpose flour
¼ cup *plus* 2 tablespoons sugar
1 tablespoon fresh lime juice
1 teaspoon vanilla extract

- Preheat oven to 350°F.

- Combine crumbs, margarine and cinnamon. Press onto bottom and up side of 9-inch pie plate. Bake 10 to 12 minutes. Cool.

- Combine undrained pineapple, sour cream, egg *yolks*, flour, 2 tablespoons sugar and lime juice in large saucepan. Cook over medium heat 8 to 10 minutes or until mixture boils and thickens, stirring constantly. Cover and let cool.

- Beat egg *whites* and vanilla until soft peaks form. Add remaining ¼ cup sugar, one tablespoon at a time, beating until stiff peaks form.

- Pour cooled filling into baked crust. Cover with meringue, spreading to cover edges completely. Bake 12 to 15 minutes or until lightly browned.

Makes 1 (9-inch) pie

Prep time: 20 minutes
Cook time: 10 minutes
Bake time: 15 minutes

Freestyle Apple Pie

Crumb Topping (recipe follows)
½ cup granulated sugar
**1 tablespoon ARGO® or
    KINGSFORD'S® Corn Starch**
½ teaspoon ground cinnamon
**4 cups sliced, peeled apples (about
    4 medium)**
1 tablespoon lemon juice
**½ (15-ounce) package refrigerated pie
    shells**

Preheat oven to 425°F. Prepare Crumb Topping; set aside. In large bowl, combine granulated sugar, corn starch and cinnamon. Add apples and lemon juice; toss to coat well. Unfold pie shell; place on foil-lined cookie sheet. Spoon apples into center of pie shell, leaving 2-inch edge. Sprinkle Crumb Topping over apples. Fold up edge of pie shell, pinching at 2-inch intervals. Bake 15 minutes. *Reduce oven temperature to 350°F;* bake 35 minutes longer or until apples are tender.

Makes 1 (9-inch) pie

Crumb Topping: In small bowl, combine ⅔ cup flour and ⅓ cup packed brown sugar. With pastry blender, fork or two knives, cut in ¼ cup cold MAZOLA® Margarine just until coarse crumbs form. If desired, stir in ½ cup coarsely chopped nuts.

Freestyle Apple Pie

Classic Rhubarb Pie

Classic Rhubarb Pie

Crust
  **9-inch Classic Crisco® Double Crust
  (pages 6 and 7)**

Filling
  **4 cups red rhubarb cut into ½- to
    ¾-inch pieces**
  1⅓ to 1½ cups sugar
  ⅓ cup all-purpose flour
  2 tablespoons butter or margarine

Glaze
  1 tablespoon milk
  Sugar

1. Prepare 9-inch Classic Crisco® Double Crust; press bottom crust into 9-inch pie plate, leaving overhang. *Do not bake.* Heat oven to 400°F.

2. For Filling, combine rhubarb and 1⅓ cups sugar in large bowl; add additional sugar, if necessary, according to tartness of rhubarb. Mix well. Stir in flour. Spoon into unbaked pie crust. Dot with butter. Moisten pastry edge with water.

4. For Glaze, brush crust with milk; sprinkle with sugar. Cover edge with foil to prevent overbrowning. Bake at 400°F for 20 minutes. *Reduce oven temperature to 325°F.* Remove foil. Bake 30 minutes or until filling in center is bubbly and crust is golden brown (if using frozen rhubarb bake 60 to 70 minutes). Cool until barely warm or at room temperature before serving.   *Makes 1 (9-inch) pie*

Blueberry Slump or Grunt

Blueberry Sauce
  3 cups fresh or thawed frozen
       blueberries
  1 cup water
  ½ cup sugar
  1½ teaspoons lemon juice
  ¼ teaspoon ground cinnamon

Dumplings
  1 cup all-purpose flour
  ¼ cup sugar
  1 teaspoon baking powder
  ¼ teaspoon salt
  ¼ teaspoon grated lemon peel
  ¼ cup CRISCO® Shortening
  ⅓ cup milk

1. For Blueberry Sauce, combine blueberries, water, ½ cup sugar, lemon juice and cinnamon in large saucepan. Bring to a boil. Cover; reduce heat to low. Simmer 5 minutes.

2. For Dumplings, combine flour, ¼ cup sugar, baking powder, salt and lemon peel in medium bowl. Cut in Crisco® using pastry blender or two knives until coarse crumbs form. Stir in milk just until flour is moistened. Drop 6 heaping tablespoonfuls of dough onto simmering Blueberry Sauce. Cover pan tightly. Simmer 15 minutes without lifting cover.

3. Spoon Dumplings into six individual serving dishes. Spoon equal portions hot Blueberry Sauce over Dumplings. Serve with cream, whipped cream or ice cream, if desired.   *Makes 6 servings*

Almond Crunch Peach Pie

Filling
  5 cups sliced, peeled fresh yellow cling
       peaches (4 large peaches)
  ½ cup sugar
  2 tablespoons lemon juice
  ½ cup canned or packaged almond
       paste*
  ¼ cup all-purpose flour
  ¼ cup non-dairy powdered creamer

Crust
  9-inch Classic Crisco® Double Crust
       (pages 6 and 7)

Topping
  1 egg white, slightly beaten
  ½ cup coarsely chopped or crushed
       almonds
  3 tablespoons sugar

1. For Filling, combine peaches, ½ cup sugar and lemon juice in large bowl. Combine almond paste, flour and creamer in small bowl; mix until crumbly. Add to peaches; mix well. Refrigerate while preparing crust.

2. Prepare 9-inch Classic Crisco® Double Crust; press bottom crust into 9-inch pie plate. Heat oven to 375°F. Spoon in filling. Cover pie with top crust. Cut slits into top crust to allow steam to escape.

3. For Topping, brush top with egg white. Sprinkle with almonds and 3 tablespoons sugar. Bake at 375°F for 1 hour or until filling in center is bubbly and crust is golden brown. Cool until barely warm or at room temperature before serving.
                    Makes 1 (9-inch) pie

*Use ½ cup very finely crushed or ground almonds mixed with ½ teaspoon almond extract if almond paste is not available.

Brandied Fruit Pie

2 packages (8 ounces *each*) mixed pitted
   dried fruit
¾ cup *plus* 1 tablespoon water
¼ cup *plus* 1 tablespoon brandy or
   cognac
5 thin lemon slices
¾ cup packed brown sugar
1 teaspoon ground cinnamon
¼ teaspoon ground nutmeg
¼ teaspoon ground cloves
¼ teaspoon salt
1 KEEBLER® Ready-Crust® Graham
   Cracker Pie Crust
½ cup graham cracker crumbs
¼ cup butter or margarine, melted
   Hard sauce *or* whipped cream
   (optional)
   Lemon slices for garnish

Preheat oven to 350°F. In medium
saucepan, combine dried fruit, ¾ cup
water, ¼ cup brandy and 5 lemon slices.
Simmer over low heat 10 minutes or until
liquid is absorbed. Remove and discard
lemon slices. Stir in brown sugar, spices,
salt, remaining 1 tablespoon water and

Brandied Fruit Pie

remaining 1 tablespoon brandy; pour into
pie crust. Sprinkle graham cracker crumbs
evenly over top of pie. Drizzle melted
butter over crumbs. Bake 30 minutes. Cool
on wire rack. Serve warm or at room
temperature. Serve with hard sauce, if
desired; garnish with lemon slices.

Makes 8 servings

Whole Wheat Pear Pie

Whole Wheat Pie Shell (recipe
   follows)
4 to 5 Western winter pears
⅔ cup whole-wheat flour, divided
½ cup granulated sugar
1 teaspoon ground cinnamon, divided
2 tablespoons lemon juice
¼ cup packed brown sugar
¼ cup butter or margarine, softened
   Additional pear slices (optional)

Preheat oven to 350°F. Prepare Whole
Wheat Pie Shell. Core and slice unpeeled
pears. In large bowl, toss pear slices with
2 tablespoons flour, granulated sugar, ¾
teaspoon cinnamon and lemon juice.
Spoon into unbaked pie shell. In small
bowl, combine brown sugar, butter,
remaining flour and remaining ¼
teaspoon cinnamon; sprinkle over top of
pie. Bake 50 minutes. Garnish with
additional pear slices.

Makes 1 (9-inch) pie

Whole Wheat Pie Shell: In medium bowl,
combine 1¼ cups whole-wheat flour, 2
tablespoons granulated sugar, ⅓ cup
vegetable oil and 3 tablespoons milk; mix
well. (Mixture will be crumbly.) Press onto
bottom and up side of 9-inch pie plate.

Favorite recipe from **Oregon Washington California**
Pear Bureau

Apple Crisp

Fruit
  **4 cups sliced, peeled cooking apples
     (about 1⅓ pounds *or* 3 to 4 medium)**
  3 tablespoons apple juice

Crumb Mixture
  ⅔ cup packed brown sugar
  ½ cup all-purpose flour
  **½ cup quick oats (*not* instant or old
     fashioned)**
  ½ teaspoon ground cinnamon
  ¼ teaspoon salt
  ⅓ cup BUTTER FLAVOR CRISCO®
  1 tablespoon milk
  1 teaspoon vanilla extract

1. For Fruit, toss apples with apple juice. Spoon into 8-inch square glass baking dish. Heat oven to 375°F.

2. For Crumb Mixture, combine brown sugar, flour, oats, cinnamon and salt in large bowl. Cut in Butter Flavor Crisco® until coarse crumbs form. Combine milk and vanilla; drizzle over crumbs while tossing with fork. Sprinkle Crumb Mixture over apples.

3. Bake at 375°F for 35 to 40 minutes or until fruit is tender, center is bubbly and crumbs are browned. Serve warm with cream, whipped cream or ice cream, if desired.   *Makes 8 servings*

Blueberry Crisp: Prepare recipe as directed *except* substitute 3 cups blueberries for 4 cups apples and substitute 1 tablespoon lemon juice for 3 tablespoons apple juice.

Peach or Pear Crisp: Prepare recipe as directed *except* substitute peaches or pears for apples and substitute 1 tablespoon lemon juice for 3 tablespoons apple juice.

Lemony Peach Tart

Lemony Peach Tart

  Pastry for 1-crust 10-inch pie
  ⅓ cup margarine or butter, melted
  ¾ cup sugar
  3 eggs
  **4 tablespoons REALEMON® Lemon
     Juice from Concentrate**
  2 tablespoons flour
  **1 (16-ounce) can sliced peaches,
     drained**
  3 tablespoons BAMA® Apple Jelly

Preheat oven to 375°F. Line 10-inch tart pan with pastry; lightly prick with fork. Bake 10 to 12 minutes or until lightly browned. In large mixer bowl, combine margarine and sugar; beat well. Add eggs, one at a time, beating well after each addition. Beat in *3 tablespoons* ReaLemon® brand, then flour; pour into prepared tart shell. Arrange peach slices over egg mixture. Bake 20 to 25 minutes or until set. Meanwhile, in small saucepan, melt jelly with remaining *1 tablespoon* ReaLemon® brand, stirring until smooth. Spoon over tart; cool. Chill. Refrigerate leftovers.   *Makes 1 (10-inch) tart*

Rice Pudding Pear Tart

½ (15-ounce) package refrigerated pie
    shells
2 cups dry red wine
1 teaspoon ground cinnamon
2 large pears, peeled, halved and cored
2 cups cooked rice
2 cups half-and-half
½ cup *plus* 1 tablespoon sugar, divided
2 tablespoons butter or margarine
¼ teaspoon salt
2 eggs, beaten
1 teaspoon vanilla extract

Preheat oven to 450°F. Prepare pie crust as
package directs; place in 10-inch tart pan.
Bake 8 to 10 minutes or until lightly
browned; set aside. *Reduce oven temperature
to 350°F.*

Place wine and cinnamon in 10-inch
skillet; bring to a boil over medium heat.
Add pears; reduce heat, cover and poach
10 minutes. Carefully turn pears in liquid;
poach 5 to 10 minutes or until tender.
Remove from wine; set aside.

Combine rice, half-and-half, ½ cup sugar,
butter, and salt in 3-quart saucepan. Cook
over medium heat 12 to 15 minutes or
until slightly thickened. Gradually stir one
fourth of the hot rice pudding mixture into
eggs; return mixture to saucepan, stirring
constantly. Continue to cook 1 to 2
minutes. Stir in vanilla. Pour rice pudding
mixture into prepared crust. Place pears,
cut sides down, on cutting surface. Cut
thin lengthwise slices into each pear one
third of the way down from stem end.
Arrange pears over pudding mixture; fan
out slices.

Bake 30 minutes or until pudding is set.
Remove from oven; sprinkle with
remaining 1 tablespoon sugar. Switch
oven setting to broil. Place tart in oven
about 4 to 5 inches from heat; broil 1 to
2 minutes or until top is browned. Cool
before serving.   *Makes 1 (10-inch) tart*

Favorite recipe from **USA Rice Council**

Black Raspberry Pie

Crust
  **9-inch Classic Crisco® Double Crust
    (pages 6 and 7)**
Filling
  4 cups fresh or partially thawed frozen
    black or red raspberries
1¼ cups sugar
¼ cup cornstarch
  2 tablespoons butter or margarine,
    softened
  Dash salt

1. Prepare 9-inch Classic Crisco® Double
Crust. Roll and press bottom crust into 9-
inch pie plate. *Do not bake.* Heat oven to
350°F.

2. For Filling, combine raspberries, sugar,
cornstarch, butter and salt. Toss gently.
Spoon into unbaked pie crust. Moisten
pastry edge with water.

3. Roll out top crust; lift onto filled pie.
Trim crust ½ inch beyond edge of pie
plate. Fold top edge under bottom crust;
flute. Cut slits into top crust to allow
steam to escape.

4. Bake at 350°F for 1 hour or until filling
in center is bubbly and crust is golden
brown. Cool to room temperature before
serving.   *Makes 1 (9-inch) pie*

Rice Pudding Pear Tart

Elegant Country Fruit-Cheese Tart

Tart

  Pastry for 1-crust 9-inch pie
  1 package (8 ounces) Neufchâtel cheese
    or light cream cheese, softened
  ¼ cup sugar
  ¼ teaspoon ground nutmeg
  1 tablespoon finely grated orange peel
  1 egg
  2 fresh California nectarines, sliced
  1 fresh California peach, thinly sliced

Blush Sauce
  ⅓ cup blush wine
  1 teaspoon cornstarch

For Tart, preheat oven to 325°F. Fit crust into 9-inch tart pan with removable bottom. Bake 10 minutes. In medium bowl, beat cheese, sugar, nutmeg, orange peel and egg until smooth. Spread over crust. Bake 20 to 25 minutes or until set. Refrigerate until chilled. Fan nectarine slices around outer edge. Overlap peach slices in a swirl in center.

For Blush Sauce, in small saucepan heat wine and cornstarch until thickened, stirring constantly. Spoon over tart to glaze. Refrigerate tart until chilled; remove from pan.   *Makes 1 (9-inch) tart*

Elegant Country Fruit-Cheese Tart

Tips:
- To keep fruit colors bright and prevent browning, dip cut fruit into mixture of 1 tablespoon lemon juice and 1 cup water.
- Tart may be prepared up to 8 hours ahead of time.

Favorite recipe from California Tree Fruit Agreement

Apple Custard Tart

  1 pound WASHINGTON apples,*
    peeled, cored and sliced
  1 baked (9-inch) tart or pie crust
  ¾ cup milk
  2 eggs, beaten
  ¼ cup sugar
  1 teaspoon vanilla extract
    Dash ground cinnamon
    Dash salt

Preheat oven to 325°F. Arrange apple slices in tart crust. Combine remaining ingredients; pour into tart crust. Bake 35 minutes or until knife blade inserted near center comes out clean.
Makes 1 (9-inch) tart

Poached Apple Custard Tart: Reserve apple slices. Prepare custard filling as directed; pour into tart shell and bake as directed. Combine ¾ cup *each*: rosé or blush wine, apple juice and water in medium saucepan. Add 1 cinnamon stick and 2 tablespoons sugar. Bring mixture to a boil; simmer 10 to 15 minutes. Add half of the reserved apple slices; return to a boil and simmer about 15 minutes or until tender. Repeat with remaining apples. Drain apples well; arrange on baked custard tart.

*WASHINGTON Golden Delicious, Granny Smith, Newtown Pippin, Rome Beauty or Winesap apples, or any combination, may be used.

Favorite recipe from Washington Apple Commission

Fruit Pizza

6 cups KELLOGG'S® FROSTED
    FLAKES® Cereal, crushed to
    2¼ cups
½ cup margarine, melted
1 jar (7 ounces) marshmallow creme
2 packages (8 ounces *each*) cream
    cheese, softened
2 to 3 cups sliced fruit, fresh or canned
    (peaches, apricots, bananas,
    strawberries, kiwi and pineapple)
    Whipped topping (optional)

1. Preheat oven to 325°F. Stir together
Kellogg's® Frosted Flakes® Cereal and
margarine. Spread in 12-inch pizza pan;
press firmly with back of spoon.

2. Bake 7 minutes or until slightly golden
brown. Cool.

3. Combine marshmallow creme and
cream cheese. Spread over crust. Arrange
fruit in circles over topping. Chill. Garnish
with whipped topping.

Makes 1 (12-inch) pizza

Luscious Cranberry and Blueberry Pie

Crust
  9-inch Classic Crisco® Double Crust
    (pages 6 and 7)
 ½ teaspoon ground mace

Filling
  1 can (16 ounces) whole berry
    cranberry sauce
 ⅓ cup packed brown sugar
 ¼ cup granulated sugar
  2 tablespoons all-purpose flour
  2 tablespoons cornstarch
  2 tablespoons orange juice
 ½ teaspoon dried grated orange peel
 ⅛ teaspoon salt
  2 cups fresh or frozen blueberries
  2 tablespoons butter or margarine

Glaze
  1 egg, beaten

Luscious Cranberry and Blueberry Pie

1. Prepare 9-inch Classic Crisco® Double
Crust, adding mace to flour mixture. Roll
and press bottom crust into 9-inch pie
plate. *Do not bake.* Reserve dough scraps for
decorations. Heat oven to 425°F.

2. For Filling, combine cranberry sauce,
brown sugar, granulated sugar, flour,
cornstarch, orange juice, orange peel and
salt in large bowl. Stir in blueberries.
Spoon into unbaked pie crust; dot with
butter. Moisten pastry edge with water.

3. Roll out top crust; lift crust onto filled
pie. Trim ½ inch beyond edge of pie plate.
Fold top edge under bottom crust; flute.
Cut blossom-shaped holes in top crust to
allow steam to escape.

4. Cut flowers or other shapes from
reserved dough. Place on top of pie.

5. For Glaze, brush with egg.

6. Bake at 425°F for 40 minutes or until
filling in center is bubbly and crust is
golden brown. Cover edge with foil
during last 10 minutes to prevent
overbrowning. Cool to room temperature
before serving.   *Makes 1 (9-inch) pie*

Tropical Banana Date Pie

1½ cups graham cracker crumbs
¼ cup DOLE® Chopped Almonds, toasted
2 tablespoons sugar
½ teaspoon ground cinnamon
⅛ teaspoon ground nutmeg
6 tablespoons melted margarine
1 package (8 ounces) DOLE® Chopped Dates
½ cup water
5 medium, firm DOLE® Bananas, peeled, sliced (4 cups)
3 tablespoons frozen DOLE® Pine-Orange Banana Juice concentrate, thawed

- Preheat oven to 375°F.

- Combine graham cracker crumbs, almonds, sugar, cinnamon, nutmeg and margarine. Press into bottom and up side of 9-inch pie plate.

- Bake 8 to 10 minutes or until lightly browned. Cool.

- Combine dates and water in saucepan; bring to a boil. Cook, stirring occasionally, about 5 minutes or until thickened. Cool.

- Place sliced bananas in bowl; drizzle with juice concentrate. Fold gently to coat. With slotted spoon, lift bananas from bowl into pie crust. Pack into solid, even layer. Mix any leftover juices with date mixture.

- Spread date mixture over bananas.

- Cover; chill 30 minutes to 1 hour.

Makes 1 (9-inch) pie

Prep time: 25 minutes
Cook time: 15 minutes
Chill time: 30 minutes

Raspberry-Peach Cobbler

2 cups flour
1 teaspoon salt
1 tablespoon baking powder
½ cup *plus* 1 tablespoon granulated sugar
7 tablespoons unsalted butter or margarine, chilled, divided
1 cup low-fat milk
2 pounds peaches, pitted, peeled and cut into ½-inch slices
4 cups raspberries
Grated peel and juice of 1 lemon
Powdered sugar

Combine flour, salt, baking powder and 1 tablespoon granulated sugar in food processor or blender (or medium mixing bowl). Add 4 tablespoons butter; process 5 seconds or until well blended (or use pastry blender, fork or two knives). While processing, add milk; process 20 seconds more or until dough forms ball. *Do not overmix.* Use dough immediately or wrap in plastic wrap and store in refrigerator.

Preheat oven to 400°F. In 2½- to 3-quart baking dish, combine peaches and raspberries with remaining ½ cup granulated sugar. Sprinkle with lemon peel, juice and remaining 3 tablespoons butter. Roll out dough to ¼-inch-thickness; trim to size slightly smaller than top of baking dish. Crimp edges with fingers. Lay crust on top of fruit in dish (edges should not quite touch sides of dish). Cut several steam vents in crust. Bake 30 minutes or until crust is browned and fruit is tender. Allow cobbler to cool at least 30 minutes before serving. Sprinkle with powdered sugar.

Makes 8 to 10 servings

*Favorite recipe from **Chilean Fresh Fruit Association***

Blueberry Crisp

Blueberry Crisp

3 cups cooked brown rice
   (1 cup uncooked)
3 cups fresh blueberries*
¼ cup *plus* 3 tablespoons packed brown
   sugar, divided
   Nonstick cooking spray
⅓ cup rice bran
¼ cup whole-wheat flour
¼ cup chopped walnuts
1 teaspoon ground cinnamon
3 tablespoons margarine

Preheat oven to 375°F. Combine rice, blueberries, and 3 tablespoons sugar. Coat 8 individual custard cups or 2-quart baking dish with cooking spray. Place rice mixture in cups or baking dish; set aside.

Combine bran, flour, walnuts, remaining ¼ cup sugar, and cinnamon in bowl. Cut in margarine with pastry blender, fork or two knives until mixture resembles coarse meal. Sprinkle over rice mixture. Bake 15 to 20 minutes or until thoroughly heated. Serve warm. *Makes 8 servings*

*Substitute frozen unsweetened blueberries for fresh blueberries, if desired. Thaw and drain before using. Or, substitute your choice of fresh fruit or combinations of fruit.

Microwave: Prepare as directed using 2-quart microproof baking dish. Microwave, uncovered, on HIGH 4 to 5 minutes or until thoroughly heated, rotating dish once during cooking time. Let stand 5 minutes. Serve warm.

*Favorite recipe from **USA Rice Council***

Winter Fruit Cobbler

¾ cup *plus* 2 tablespoons sugar
1 tablespoon cornstarch
1 teaspoon ground cinnamon
½ teaspoon ground nutmeg
1 cup water
4 cups Chilean winter fruits (sliced peaches, plums, nectarines, peeled Granny Smith apples,* seedless or halved, seeded grapes)
1 cup all-purpose flour
1½ teaspoons baking powder
Dash salt
¼ cup cold butter or margarine, cut into pieces
⅓ cup cold milk
Additional sugar for garnish

Preheat oven to 425°F. In large saucepan, combine ¾ cup sugar, cornstarch and spices. Gradually stir in water to blend. Cook and stir over medium heat 2 to 3 minutes or until mixture thickens and boils. Combine with desired fruits in buttered 9-inch square baking dish; set aside.

In bowl, combine flour, remaining 2 tablespoons sugar, baking powder and salt. Cut in butter to resemble coarse meal.

Winter Fruit Cobbler

Stir in milk to form dough. Knead on floured surface several times, then pat out to ½-inch thickness. Cut into desired shapes using 2-inch cookie cutters (simple designs such as stars, circles, diamonds, or hearts work best). Arrange cut-outs over filling; sprinkle lightly with additional sugar. Bake 20 minutes or until fruit is tender and topping is golden. Serve warm with cream or ice cream.

Makes 6 servings

*If using apples, reduce oven temperature to 400°F and bake 30 to 35 minutes.

*Favorite recipe from **Chilean Fresh Fruit Association***

Dessert Fruit Pizza

1 (12-inch-square) sheet thawed frozen puff pastry
¼ cup (1 ounce) shredded mozzarella cheese
½ cup ricotta cheese
¼ cup golden raisins
2 tablespoons chopped walnuts
½ teaspoon ground cinnamon
½ teaspoon ground nutmeg
2 fresh California nectarines, sliced
1 fresh California Bartlett pear, cored and sliced
3 tablespoons orange marmalade, warmed

Preheat oven to 400°F. Place pastry on large baking pan; fold edges under to form rim. Sprinkle with mozzarella. Top with small dollops of ricotta. Sprinkle with raisins, nuts and spices. Arrange fruit on top. Drizzle with marmalade. Bake 20 to 25 minutes or until pastry is puffed and golden brown. *Makes 1 (12-inch) pizza*

*Favorite recipe from **California Tree Fruit Agreement***

Peach Mince Cobbler

Pastry for 2-crust pie
1 (27-ounce) jar NONE SUCH®
   Ready-to-Use Mincemeat (Regular
   or Brandy & Rum)
¾ cup chopped walnuts
2 (21-ounce) cans peach pie filling

Place rack in lowest position in oven; preheat oven to 425°F. Divide dough in half; roll *each* half 1½ inches larger than 2-quart shallow baking dish. Line dish with half of the pastry. Combine mincemeat and nuts; pour into prepared dish. Top with pie filling, then remaining pastry. Cut slits near center; seal and flute. Bake 30 to 35 minutes or until golden. Serve warm.   *Makes 10 to 12 servings*

French Apple Pie

French Apple Pie

Crust
   9-inch Classic Crisco® Double Crust
      (pages 6 and 7)

Nut Filling
   ¾ cup ground walnuts
   2 tablespoons packed brown sugar
   2 tablespoons beaten egg
   1 tablespoon milk
   1 tablespoon butter or margarine,
      softened
   ¼ teaspoon vanilla extract
   ¼ teaspoon lemon juice

Apple Filling
   5 cups sliced, peeled Granny Smith
      apples (about 1¾ pounds *or*
      5 medium)
   1 teaspoon lemon juice
   ¾ cup granulated sugar
   2 tablespoons all-purpose flour
   1 teaspoon ground cinnamon
   1 teaspoon ground nutmeg
   ¼ teaspoon salt
   2 tablespoons butter or margarine

1. Prepare 9-inch Classic Crisco® Double Crust; press bottom crust into 9-inch pie plate. *Do not bake.* Heat oven to 425°F.

2. For Nut Filling, combine nuts, brown sugar, egg, milk, 1 tablespoon butter, vanilla and ¼ teaspoon lemon juice. Spread over bottom of unbaked pie crust.

3. For Apple Filling, place apples in large bowl. Sprinkle with 1 teaspoon lemon juice. Combine granulated sugar, flour, cinnamon, nutmeg and salt. Sprinkle over apples. Toss to mix. Spoon over Nut Filling. Dot with 2 tablespoons butter. Moisten pastry edge with water.

4. Cover pie with top crust. Cut slits into top crust to allow steam to escape. Bake at 425°F for 50 minutes or until filling in center is bubbly and crust is golden brown. Cover crust edge with foil, if necessary, to prevent overbrowning. Cool until barely warm or at room temperature before serving.   *Makes 1 (9-inch) pie*

Chocolate and Pear Tart

1 cup milk
2 egg yolks, beaten
2 tablespoons granulated sugar
⅛ teaspoon salt
1 cup HERSHEY⭑S Semi-Sweet
   Chocolate Chips
   Chocolate Tart Crust (recipe follows)
3 large fresh pears
   Apricot Glaze (recipe follows)

In top of double boiler over hot, not boiling, water, scald milk; gradually stir in combined egg yolks, 2 tablespoons granulated sugar and salt. Cook over hot water, stirring constantly, until slightly thickened; *do not boil*. Remove from heat; immediately add chocolate chips, stirring until chips are melted and mixture is smooth. Pour into Chocolate Tart Crust. Refrigerate several hours or until firm. Core and peel pears; cut into thin slices. Place in circular pattern on top of filling. Immediately prepare Apricot Glaze. Spoon over top of fruit, covering completely. Refrigerate several hours or until firm; remove side of pan. Serve cold. Cover; refrigerate leftovers.

Makes 1 (9-inch) tart

Chocolate Tart Crust: Heat oven to 325°F. Grease and flour 9-inch round tart pan with removable bottom. In small mixer bowl, stir together ¾ cup all-purpose flour, ¾ cup confectioners' sugar and 1 tablespoon HERSHEY⭑S Cocoa. At low speed of electric mixer, blend in 6 tablespoons chilled margarine until blended and smooth. Press evenly with fingers onto bottom and up side of prepared pan. Bake 10 to 15 minutes; cool.

Apricot Glaze: In small cup, sprinkle ¾ teaspoon unflavored gelatin over 2 teaspoons cold water; let stand several minutes to soften. In small saucepan, combine 1 tablespoon arrowroot powder, ½ cup apricot nectar, ¼ cup granulated sugar and 1 teaspoon lemon juice; cook over medium heat, stirring constantly, until mixture is thickened. Remove from heat; immediately add gelatin mixture. Stir until smooth.

Rosy Raspberry Pie

Crust
9-inch Classic Crisco® Double Crust
   (pages 6 and 7)

Filling
1¼ cups sugar
3 tablespoons cornstarch
⅛ teaspoon salt
5 cups fresh raspberries
2 tablespoons butter or margarine

1. Prepare 9-inch Classic Crisco® Double Crust; press bottom crust into 9-inch pie plate. *Do not bake.* Heat oven to 375°F.

2. For Filling, combine sugar, cornstarch and salt in large bowl. Add raspberries. Toss gently to mix. Spoon into unbaked pie crust. Dot with butter. Moisten pastry edge with water.

3. Cover pie with top crust. Cut slits or designs into top crust to allow steam to escape. Cover edge with foil to prevent overbrowning.

4. Bake at 375°F for 35 minutes. Remove foil. Bake 15 minutes or until filling in center is bubbly and crust is golden brown. Cool until barely warm or at room temperature before serving.

Makes 1 (9-inch) pie

Chocolate and Pear Tart

Sumptuous Strawberry Rhubarb Pie

Sumptuous Strawberry Rhubarb Pie

Crust
   9-inch Classic Crisco® Double Crust
   (pages 6 and 7)

Filling
   4 cups fresh cut rhubarb (½-inch
      pieces)
   3 cups sliced strawberries
   1⅓ cups sugar
   ⅓ cup *plus* ¼ cup all-purpose flour
   2 tablespoons *plus* 1½ teaspoons quick-
      cooking tapioca
   ½ teaspoon grated orange peel
   ½ teaspoon ground cinnamon
   ¼ teaspoon ground nutmeg
   2 tablespoons butter or margarine

Glaze
   1 egg, beaten
   1 tablespoon sugar

1. Prepare 9-inch Classic Crisco® Double
Crust; roll and press bottom crust into 9-
inch pie plate. *Do not bake.* Heat oven to
425°F.

2. For Filling, combine rhubarb and
strawberries in large bowl. Combine 1⅓
cups sugar, flour, tapioca, orange peel,
cinnamon and nutmeg in medium bowl;
stir well. Add to fruit. Toss to coat. Spoon
filling into unbaked pie crust. Dot with
butter. Moisten pastry edge with water.

3. Roll out top crust. Lift onto filled pie.
Trim ½ inch beyond edge of pie plate. Fold
top edge under bottom crust; flute. Cut
desired shapes into top crust to allow
steam to escape.

4. For Glaze, brush with egg. Sprinkle
with 1 tablespoon sugar.

5. Bake at 425°F for 40 to 50 minutes or
until filling in center is bubbly and crust is
golden brown. Cover edge with foil, if
necessary, to prevent overbrowning. Cool
until barely warm or at room temperature
before serving.   *Makes 1 (9-inch) pie*

Love Apple Pie

   ⅓ cup HEINZ® Tomato Ketchup
   2 teaspoons lemon juice
   5 cups thinly sliced peeled cooking
      apples (2 to 2½ pounds)
   ¾ cup sugar
   ¾ cup all-purpose flour
   ½ teaspoon ground cinnamon
   ⅓ cup butter or margarine, softened
   1 unbaked (9-inch) pie shell

Preheat oven to 375°F. Blend ketchup and
lemon juice;* combine with apples.
Combine sugar, flour and cinnamon; cut
in butter until thoroughly mixed. Fill pie
shell with apple mixture; top with sugar
mixture. Bake 40 to 45 minutes or until
apples are tender. Serve warm with ice
cream, if desired.   *Makes 1 (9-inch) pie*
*If apples are very tart, add 1 to 2
tablespoons sugar to ketchup mixture.

Door County Cherry Pie

Crust
  **9-inch Classic Crisco® Single Crust
  (pages 6 and 7)**

Filling
  **1 package (8 ounces) cream cheese,
    softened**
  ¾ cup confectioners sugar
  ½ teaspoon vanilla extract
  ½ teaspoon almond extract
  1 cup whipping cream, whipped
  **2 tablespoons chopped, slivered
    almonds**

Topping
**2½ cups pitted Door County (or other
    variety) cherries (fresh or frozen)***
  ½ cup cherry juice**
  **2 tablespoons granulated sugar (tart
    cherries will require more sugar)**
1½ tablespoons cornstarch
  1 tablespoon quick-cooking tapioca
  ½ teaspoon vanilla extract
  ½ teaspoon almond extract
  **3 or 4 drops red food color
    Whipped cream (optional)**

1. Prepare and bake 9-inch Classic Crisco® Single Crust. Cool.

2. For Filling, combine cream cheese and confectioners sugar in large bowl. Beat at medium speed of electric mixer until smooth. Beat in ½ teaspoon vanilla and ½ teaspoon almond extract. Fold in 1 cup whipped cream and nuts. Spoon into cooled baked pie crust. Refrigerate until firm.

3. For Topping, combine cherries, cherry juice, granulated sugar, cornstarch, tapioca, ½ teaspoon vanilla, ½ teaspoon almond extract and food color in medium saucepan. Cook and stir on medium heat until mixture comes to a boil. Boil 6

minutes. Remove from heat. Cool until thickened. Spread over filling. Garnish with whipped cream. Refrigerate leftovers.

Makes 1 (9-inch) pie

*Thaw cherries, if frozen.

**Mash and press additional cherries through large strainer over bowl to obtain ½ cup juice.

Country Fruit Pie

  Pastry for 2-crust 8-inch pie
  **5 fresh California peaches or
    nectarines, cut into eighths
    (about 3 cups)**
  3 plums, cut into sixths (about 1 cup)
  ⅓ cup honey
  3 tablespoons all-purpose flour
  ½ teaspoon almond extract

Preheat oven to 400°F. Press bottom crust into 8-inch pie plate. Cut out 35 leaf or other desired shapes from top crust; set aside. In large bowl, lightly toss fruit with remaining ingredients. Spoon fruit into crust. Place 8 crust cut-outs on top of fruit. Press remaining crust cut-outs onto rim with small amount of water. Bake 25 to 30 minutes or until crust is browned and fruit is easily pierced with knife.

Makes 1 (8-inch) pie

*Favorite recipe from **California Tree Fruit Agreement***

Country Fruit Pie

Fruit Flan

Pastry for 1 crust 10-inch pie
1 package (3 ounces) cream cheese
1 egg, slightly beaten
3 tablespoons sugar
½ teaspoon lemon juice
2 cans (16 ounces *each*) or 1 can (29-ounces) sliced fruit (peaches, pears, pineapple, apricots or whole figs), drained, ¾ cup liquid reserved
2 teaspoons cornstarch
¼ cup currant or strawberry jelly

Preheat oven to 400°F. Fit pastry into 10-inch flan pan or pie plate. Bake 13 to 15 minutes. Cool. *Reduce oven temperature to 350°F.* Beat together cream cheese, egg, sugar and lemon juice; spread over baked crust. Bake 5 to 7 minutes. Cool 5 minutes. Arrange drained fruit atop cheese mixture. Combine reserved liquid and cornstarch in saucepan. Cook over medium heat until mixture boils and thickens; add jelly and stir until melted. Spoon jelly mixture over fruit. Refrigerate.   *Makes 1 (10-inch) flan*

*Favorite recipe from **Canned Food Information Council***

Fruit Flan

Desert Cooler Green Tomato Cheese Pie

Crust
10-inch Classic Crisco® Double Crust
    (pages 6 and 7)
  1 teaspoon grated lemon peel
  1 teaspoon grated orange peel
  1 teaspoon ground allspice

Cheese Layer
  1 package (8 ounces) cream cheese,
    softened
  1 can (14 ounces) sweetened condensed
    milk
  1 teaspoon vanilla extract
  ⅓ cup lemon juice

Filling
1½ cups sugar
  1 teaspoon ground allspice
  ¼ teaspoon salt
  ⅓ cup all-purpose flour
  3 tablespoons cornstarch
1½ cups orange juice
  ½ cup honey
  2 tablespoons lemon juice
  3 egg yolks, beaten
  2 tablespoons butter or margarine
  2 teaspoons grated orange peel
  1 cup pecans, quartered
20 to 25 unpeeled small (1- to 2-inch
    diameter) fresh green tomatoes
    (2 to 2¼ pounds), sliced ¼ inch
    thick

Topping
  Baked pastry squares
  3 tablespoons sugar
  1 teaspoon ground cinnamon

Garnish
  Additional green tomatoes
  Pecans

1. Prepare 10-inch Classic Crisco® Double Crust, adding lemon peel, 1 teaspoon orange peel and 1 teaspoon allspice to flour mixture. Roll and press bottom crust into 10-inch pie plate. Bake and cool. Heat oven to 425°F.

2. Roll remaining dough to ¼-inch thickness. Cut into 2-inch squares. Place on ungreased baking sheet.

3. Bake at 425°F for 10 minutes or until browned. Cool completely.

4. For Cheese Layer, beat cream cheese in medium bowl at high speed of electric mixer until light and fluffy. Gradually beat in sweetened condensed milk and vanilla until smooth. Gradually blend in ⅓ cup lemon juice. Pour into baked pie crust. Refrigerate several hours.

5. For Filling, combine 1½ cups sugar, 1 teaspoon allspice and salt in medium saucepan. Combine flour, cornstarch, orange juice, honey and 2 tablespoons lemon juice in food processor or blender; process until smooth. Stir into sugar mixture. Cook and stir on medium heat until thickened and smooth. Remove from heat. Stir small amount of hot mixture into egg yolks, mixing thoroughly. Return mixture to saucepan; cook and stir 3 minutes. Remove from heat. Stir in butter, 2 teaspoons orange peel and nuts.

6. Steam tomatoes over simmering water until tender; drain well. Add to warm filling; cool. Refrigerate several hours or until very cold. Remove tomatoes from filling using slotted spoon. Arrange over cheese layer. Refrigerate until firm. Discard remaining filling.

7. For Topping, crumble baked pastry pieces. Sprinkle over top. Combine 3 tablespoons sugar and cinnamon. Sprinkle over crumbs.

8. For Garnish, decorate with tomatoes, sliced or whole, and nuts. Refrigerate leftovers.   *Makes 1 (10-inch) pie*

Fresh Apricot Lattice Pie

Fresh Apricot Lattice Pie

1 (15-ounce) package refrigerated pie
   shells
5½ cups sliced fresh California apricots
   (about 2 pounds)
1 cup sugar
¼ cup all-purpose flour

Preheat oven to 400°F. On lightly floured
surface, roll out pie shells to 2 (12-inch)
rounds. Transfer one pie shell to 10-inch
pie plate; let extra dough hang over edge.
In large bowl, combine apricots, sugar and
flour; toss gently. Pour fruit into pie shell;
spread fruit evenly. Cut remaining pie
shell into long strips, ½ inch wide, with
fluted pastry wheel or knife. Arrange half
of the strips in one direction across pie;
arrange remaining strips in opposite
direction.* Fold outer edges of crust; crimp
edges to seal. Place pie on baking sheet;
reduce oven temperature to 375°F. Bake 50 to
60 minutes or until crust is golden and
juices are bubbly.   *Makes 1 (10-inch) pie*

*For twisted lattice crust, twist pastry
before placing on apricot mixture.

Favorite recipe from **California Apricot Advisory Board**

Pandowdy

Filling
   5 cups sliced, peeled cooking apples,
      pears or peaches
½ cup pure maple syrup or maple-
      flavored pancake syrup
   2 tablespoons lemon juice
½ teaspoon ground cinnamon
¼ teaspoon ground nutmeg
   2 tablespoons BUTTER FLAVOR
      CRISCO®

Crust and Glaze
   9-inch Classic Crisco® Single Crust
      (pages 6 and 7)
   2 teaspoons milk
   1 teaspoon sugar

1. For Filling, toss apples with maple
syrup, lemon juice, cinnamon and nutmeg
in large bowl. Spoon into 8-inch square
glass baking dish. Dot with Butter Flavor
Crisco®. Heat oven to 400°F.

2. Prepare 9-inch Classic Crisco® Single
Crust; roll dough into 9-inch square
between lightly floured sheets of waxed
paper on dampened countertop. Peel off
top sheet of waxed paper. Flip dough over
on top of apples. Remove other sheet of
waxed paper. Press dough down along
insides of dish. Trim pastry along inside
edge. Cut large vents to allow steam to
escape.

3. For Glaze, brush with milk. Sprinkle
with sugar. Bake at 400°F for 25 to 30
minutes or until crust is light golden
brown. Remove from oven.

4. Cut pastry into 2-inch squares.
Carefully lift up squares and spoon juice
from bottom of dish over entire top of
pastry. Return to oven. Bake 20 to 25
minutes or until top is deep golden brown.
Serve warm with cream, whipped cream
or ice cream, if desired.
                                    Makes 8 servings

Strawberry Glazed Pie

Crust
9-inch Classic Crisco® Single Crust
   (pages 6 and 7)

Filling
3½ cups fresh strawberry halves (1 quart)
 ½ cup sugar
  2 tablespoons cornstarch
 ⅛ teaspoon salt
  6 tablespoons cold water
  2 packages (3 ounces *each*) cream
     cheese, softened
  2 tablespoons orange juice

Garnish
Sweetened whipped cream (optional)

1. Prepare and bake 9-inch Classic Crisco® Single Crust. Cool completely.

2. For Filling, set aside 2 cups strawberry halves. Mash remaining 1½ cups strawberries with fork.

3. Combine sugar, cornstarch and salt in small saucepan. Gradually add cold water; stir until smooth. Add mashed strawberries. Cook and stir on medium heat until mixture comes to a boil. Cook and stir 1 minute. Remove from heat. Cool by setting pan in bowl of ice water.

4. Beat cream cheese at medium speed of electric mixer until fluffy. Gradually add orange juice. Beat until smooth. Spread in bottom of baked pie crust. Arrange reserved strawberry halves over cheese layer. Pour cooled strawberry mixture over strawberry halves. Refrigerate. Top each serving with a dollop of whipped cream.
Makes 1 (9-inch) pie

Dutch Apple Cobbler

2 (21-ounce) cans apple pie filling
2 eggs
1 (14-ounce) can EAGLE® Brand
   Sweetened Condensed Milk
   (NOT evaporated milk)
¼ cup margarine or butter, melted
½ teaspoon ground cinnamon
¼ teaspoon ground nutmeg
½ cup packed light brown sugar
½ cup unsifted flour
¼ cup cold margarine or butter
½ cup chopped nuts
½ cup oats

Preheat oven to 375°F. Spread pie filling in buttered 9-inch square baking pan. In medium bowl, beat eggs. Add sweetened condensed milk, *melted* margarine, cinnamon and nutmeg; mix well. Pour over pie filling. In medium bowl, combine brown sugar and flour; cut in cold margarine until crumbly. Add nuts and oats. Sprinkle over custard. Bake 50 to 55 minutes or until set. Serve warm with ice cream, if desired. Refrigerate leftovers.
Makes 9 to 12 servings

Dutch Apple Cobbler

Celia's Flat Fruit Pie

2 packages (8 ounces *each*) mixed dried
    fruit (pitted prunes, pears, apples,
    apricots and peaches)
3 cups water
½ cup sugar
½ teaspoon ground cinnamon
¼ teaspoon ground cloves
1 teaspoon lemon juice
    Flaky Pastry (recipe follows)

Combine fruit, water, sugar, cinnamon
and cloves in 3-quart pan. Cook, stirring
occasionally, over medium heat until sugar
is dissolved. Cover; reduce heat and
simmer 45 minutes or until fruit is tender.
Pour fruit and liquid into food processor
or blender; process to make coarse fruit
mixture. (Fruit mixture should measure
3 cups. If fruit mixture measures more,
return to pan and cook, stirring frequently,
to reduce to 3 cups.) Stir in lemon juice.
Let cool. While fruit is cooling, prepare
Flaky Pastry.

Preheat oven to 400°F. Roll one pastry ball
on lightly floured board to 13-inch circle
about ⅛ inch thick. Fold pastry circle into
quarters. Place in 12-inch pizza pan;
unfold. Trim edge of pastry to leave ½-
inch overhang. Spread fruit mixture in
even layer over pastry. Roll out second ball
to 13-inch circle; place over filling. Cut
slits or design into center of crust. Fold
edge of top crust under edge of bottom
crust; flute edge. Bake 35 to 40 minutes or
until pastry is golden brown. Place pie on
rack. Let cool 1 hour before cutting into
thin wedges.　　　　*Makes 1 (12-inch) flat pie*

Flaky Pastry

⅓ cup all-purpose flour
¾ teaspoon salt
1 cup shortening or lard
6 to 8 tablespoons cold water

Combine flour and salt in medium bowl.
With fingers, pastry blender, fork or two
knives, rub or cut shortening into flour
mixture until it resembles fine crumbs.
Gradually add water; stir with fork until
mixture forms dough. Shape into two
balls. Wrap in plastic wrap; refrigerate
30 minutes.

Humble Huckleberry Pie

Crust
  9-inch Classic Crisco® Double Crust
    (pages 6 and 7)

Filling
3½ cups Montana huckleberries *or*
    blueberries
  1 cup *minus* 1 tablespoon sugar
  ¼ cup all-purpose flour
  1 tablespoon *plus* 1 teaspoon quick-
    cooking tapioca
  1 tablespoon butter or margarine

1. Prepare 9-inch Classic Crisco® Double
Crust; press bottom crust into 9-inch pie
plate leaving overhang. *Do not bake.* Heat
oven to 375°F.

2. For Filling, gently combine
huckleberries with sugar, flour and
tapioca in large bowl; let stand 15
minutes. Spoon filling into unbaked pie
crust. Dot with butter. Moisten pastry
edge with water.

3. Cover pie with woven lattice top. Cover
with foil. Bake at 375°F for 25 minutes.
Remove foil. Bake 25 to 30 minutes.
Sprinkle lightly with granulated sugar, if
desired. Cool until barely warm or at room
temperature before serving.
　　　　Makes 1 (9-inch) pie

Celia's Flat Fruit Pie

Peach Delight Pie

Peach Delight Pie

Filling
2½ cups sliced, peeled peaches (about
    1¼ pounds *or* 2 to 3 large)
¾ cup granulated sugar
¼ cup quick-cooking tapioca
1 teaspoon lemon juice
1 teaspoon peach-flavored brandy

Crumb Mixture
¼ cup all-purpose flour
¼ cup packed brown sugar
¼ cup chopped almonds
3 tablespoons butter or margarine,
    melted

Crust
9-inch Classic Crisco® Double Crust
    (pages 6 and 7)

Glaze
1 egg white, slightly beaten
    Granulated sugar

1. For Filling, combine peaches, ¾ cup granulated sugar, tapioca, lemon juice and brandy in medium bowl. Stir well. Set aside.

2. For Crumb Mixture, mix flour, brown sugar, nuts and butter until crumbly.

3. Heat oven to 425°F.

4. Prepare 9-inch Classic Crisco® Double Crust; press bottom crust into 9-inch pie plate. *Do not bake.* Sprinkle half of the crumb mixture over unbaked pie crust. Add filling. Top with remaining crumb mixture.

5. Roll out top crust. Cut out desired shapes with cookie cutter. Place on filling around edge of pie.

6. For Glaze, brush cutouts with egg white. Sprinkle with granulated sugar. Cover edge of pie with foil to prevent overbrowning.

7. Bake at 425°F for 10 minutes. *Reduce oven temperature to 350°F.* Bake 25 minutes. Remove foil. Bake 5 minutes. Cool until barely warm or at room temperature before serving.   *Makes 1 (9-inch) pie*

Cherry Mince Pie

1 (9-ounce) package NONE SUCH®
    Condensed Mincemeat,
    reconstituted as package directs
¾ cup chopped walnuts
    Pastry for 2-crust 9-inch pie
1 (21-ounce) can cherry pie filling

Place rack in lowest position in oven; preheat oven to 425°F. Combine mincemeat and nuts; turn into pastry-lined pie plate. Top with pie filling. Cover with top crust; cut slits near center. Seal and flute. Bake 25 minutes or until golden.
   Makes 1 (9-inch) pie

Basic Margarine Double Pie Crust

2 cups *minus* 2 tablespoons unsifted
    flour
¼ teaspoon salt
⅔ cup MAZOLA® Margarine
3 tablespoons cold water

In large bowl, mix flour and salt. With
pastry blender, fork or two knives, cut in
margarine until mixture resembles fine
crumbs. (*Do not worry about overmixing.*)
Sprinkle water over mixture while tossing
with fork to blend well. Press dough
firmly into ball. (If mixture seems
crumbly, work with hands until it holds
together.) Divide dough in half. On lightly
floured surface, roll out each dough half
to 12-inch circle. Fit one circle loosely into
9-inch pie plate. Trim dough ½ inch
beyond rim. Fill as desired. Cut slits into
other dough circle to allow steam to
escape during baking; place over filling.
Trim ½ inch beyond rim. Fold edges
under; seal and flute. Bake according to
recipe.   *Makes 1 (9-inch) double pie crust*

Cinnamon Fruit Tart with Sour Cream Filling

1 envelope KNOX® Unflavored
    Gelatine
¼ cup cold water
1 cup (8 ounces) cottage cheese
½ cup canned pineapple juice
½ cup sour cream
½ cup milk
¼ cup sugar
1 teaspoon lemon juice
    Cinnamon Graham Cracker Crust
    (recipe follows)
    Fresh fruit*
2 tablespoons orange *or* apricot
    marmalade, melted

Microwave Directions: In 1-cup glass
measure, sprinkle unflavored gelatine over
cold water; let stand 2 minutes. Microwave
at HIGH (Full Power) 40 seconds. Stir
thoroughly; let stand 2 minutes or until
gelatine is completely dissolved.

In food processor or blender, process
cottage cheese, pineapple juice, sour
cream, milk, sugar and lemon juice until
blended. While processing, through feed
cap, gradually add gelatine mixture;
process until blended. Pour into
Cinnamon Graham Cracker Crust; chill
until firm, about 3 hours. To serve, top
with fresh fruit; brush with marmalade.
    Makes 1 (10-inch) tart

Cinnamon Graham Cracker Crust: In
10-inch microwave-safe quiche dish or
pie plate, microwave ½ cup IMPERIAL®
Margarine at HIGH (Full Power) 45
seconds or until melted. Stir in 2 cups
graham cracker crumbs, 1 tablespoon
sugar and ½ teaspoon ground cinnamon.
Press firmly onto bottom and up side of
dish. Microwave 1½ minutes; cool.

*Use any combination of the following to
equal 2 cups: Sliced strawberries, kiwi or
oranges; blueberries or raspberries.

Cinnamon Fruit Tart with Sour Cream Filling

Lattice Pineapple Pie

1 can (20 ounces) DOLE® Crushed
    Pineapple in Juice, undrained
½ cup sugar
2 tablespoons cornstarch
¼ teaspoon salt (optional)
1 tablespoon margarine
    Juice from 1 DOLE® Lemon
    Pastry for 2-crust 9-inch pie

- Preheat oven to 400°F.

- Combine undrained pineapple with
  sugar, cornstarch and salt in saucepan.
  Cook, stirring, until thickened and clear.

- Stir in margarine and 1 tablespoon
  lemon juice. Cool. Press 1 crust into
  bottom and up side of 9-inch pie plate.
  Pour filling into crust.

- Cut remaining crust into 1-inch-wide
  strips. Weave strips crisscross over pie to
  make lattice top; pinch edges to seal.

- Bake 25 to 30 minutes.

Makes 1 (9-inch) pie

Prep time: 20 minutes
Cook time: 35 minutes

Easy-As-Pie Crust

1¼ cups flour
⅛ teaspoon salt
½ cup MAZOLA® Margarine
2 tablespoons cold water

In medium bowl, mix flour and salt. With
pastry blender, fork or two knives, cut in
margarine until mixture resembles fine
crumbs. Sprinkle water over flour mixture
while tossing with fork to blend well.
Press dough firmly into ball. On lightly
floured surface, roll dough out to 12-inch
circle. Fit loosely into 9-inch pie plate.
Trim and flute edge. Fill and bake
according to recipe.

Makes 1 (9-inch) pie crust

Carameled Apple Pie

Crust
  9-inch Classic Crisco® Double Crust
    (pages 6 and 7)
  1 teaspoon cornstarch

Filling
  6 cups sliced, peeled apples (about
    2 pounds or 6 medium)
  ¼ cup apple juice
  2 teaspoons lemon juice
  ½ cup packed brown sugar
  1 tablespoon quick-cooking tapioca
  1 tablespoon cornstarch
  1 tablespoon all-purpose flour
  ½ teaspoon ground cinnamon
  ¼ teaspoon salt
  ½ cup caramel ice cream topping
  2 tablespoons butter or margarine

Glaze
  1 egg white, slightly beaten
  1 tablespoon cold water
  2 tablespoons granulated sugar
  1 teaspoon brown sugar

Decorations
  Reserved dough scraps
  Reserved egg white mixture
  Red and green food color
  Granulated sugar
  Caramel ice cream topping

1. Prepare 9-inch Classic Crisco® Double
Crust. Roll and press bottom crust into
9-inch pie plate, leaving overhang. *Do not
bake.* Reserve dough scraps for
Decorations. Sprinkle 1 teaspoon
cornstarch in pie crust.

2. For Filling, toss apples with juices in
large microwave-safe bowl.

3. Combine ½ cup brown sugar, tapioca,
1 tablespoon cornstarch, flour, cinnamon
and salt. Add to apples. Stir. Let stand 20
minutes, stirring several times.

4. Cover bowl with plastic wrap; vent. Microwave at 100% (HIGH) 7 to 15 minutes or until apples are partially cooked and mixture starts to thicken, stirring every 4 minutes. Stir in ½ cup caramel topping. Refrigerate until cold, or place bowl in ice water.

5. Heat oven to 425°F.

6. Spoon filling into crust. Dot with butter. Moisten pastry edge with water.

7. Cover pie with woven lattice top.

8. For Glaze, combine egg white and water; brush over lattice. Reserve extra egg white mixture. Combine 2 tablespoons granulated sugar and 1 teaspoon brown sugar. Sprinkle over lattice.

9. Bake at 425°F for 10 minutes. *Reduce oven temperature to 375°F.* Cover with foil, if necessary, to prevent overbrowning. Bake 40 minutes or until apples are tender and filling in center is bubbly.

10. For Decorations, roll out reserved dough scraps. Cut out 6 to 8 apple and leaf shapes. Divide reserved egg white mixture. Add red food color to one half and green to other half. Brush apples with red mixture and leaves with green mixture; allow to dry. Brush again. Sprinkle with additional granulated sugar. Place on greased baking sheet. Bake at 375°F for 6 to 8 minutes; cool. Spread backs with caramel topping. Arrange on pie. Cool to room temperature before serving.   *Makes 1 (9-inch) pie*

Carameled Apple Pie

Cherry Cheesecake Pie

Cherry Cheesecake Pie

Crust
9-inch Classic Crisco® Single Crust
(pages 6 and 7)

Filling
2 cans (16 ounces *each*) pitted red tart
    cherries packed in water
¼ cup reserved cherry liquid
½ cup sugar
1 tablespoon cornstarch
1 teaspoon lemon juice
⅛ teaspoon almond extract

Topping
1½ packages (8 ounces *each*) cream
    cheese, softened
½ cup sugar
2 eggs
½ teaspoon vanilla extract
    Baked pastry cutouts (optional)

1. Heat oven to 425°F. Prepare 9-inch
Classic Crisco® Single Crust. *Do not bake.*
Reserve dough scraps for decoration; roll
out and cut into desired shapes using
cookie cutter. Arrange pastry cutouts on
baking sheet; set aside.

2. For Filling, drain cherries in large
strainer over bowl, reserving ¼ cup liquid.
Combine ½ cup sugar and cornstarch in
large bowl. Stir in reserved ¼ cup cherry
liquid, lemon juice and almond extract.
Stir in cherries. Spoon into unbaked pie
crust. Bake at 425°F for 15 minutes.

3. Remove pie from oven. *Reduce oven
temperature to 350°F.*

4. For Topping, combine cream cheese,
½ cup sugar, eggs and vanilla in medium
bowl. Beat at medium speed of electric
mixer until smooth. Spoon over filling.

5. Return pie to oven with pastry cutouts.
Bake at 350°F for 25 minutes or until
topping is set. Cool to room temperature
before serving. Garnish with baked pastry
cutouts, if desired. Refrigerate leftovers.
Makes 1 (9-inch) pie

Grapefruit Rhubarb Cobbler

3 tablespoons cornstarch
¼ cup water
¾ cup *plus* 1 tablespoon sugar, divided
¾ cup light corn syrup
1 tablespoon butter or margarine
¼ teaspoon ground mace
4 cups Florida grapefruit sections, well
    drained
1 cup diced fresh rhubarb
1¼ cups biscuit baking mix
½ cup milk

Preheat oven to 425°F. In small saucepan,
combine cornstarch and water. Stir in ¾
cup sugar and corn syrup. Cook, stirring
constantly, over medium heat until
mixture boils. Boil 1 minute. Stir in butter
and mace. Combine fruit in buttered
shallow 1½-quart baking dish; pour
cornstarch mixture over fruit.

In small bowl, combine biscuit mix,
remaining 1 tablespoon sugar and milk;
drop by spoonfuls onto grapefruit
mixture. Bake 20 to 25 minutes or until
biscuit topping is golden brown.
Makes 4 to 6 servings

*Favorite recipe from **Florida Department of Citrus***

Lattice-Topped Raisin Pie

3 cups DOLE® Raisins
2¼ cups water, divided
¼ cup packed brown sugar
2 tablespoons cornstarch
1 DOLE® Orange
1 DOLE® Lemon
2 tablespoons margarine
1½ teaspoons ground cinnamon
    Pastry for 2-crust 9-inch pie

- Preheat oven to 425°F.

- In saucepan, bring raisins, 2 cups water and brown sugar to a boil. Cover; simmer 5 minutes. Mix cornstarch with remaining ¼ cup water; stir into raisin mixture. Cook, stirring, until mixture boils and thickens. Remove from heat.

- Grate 1 teaspoon peel *each* from orange and lemon. Squeeze 1 tablespoon juice *each* from orange and lemon. Add peel, juice, margarine and cinnamon to raisin mixture.

- Press 1 crust into bottom and up side of 9-inch pie plate. Pour filling into crust.

- Cut remaining crust into 1-inch-wide strips. Weave strips over pie to make lattice top; pinch edges to seal.

- Bake 30 to 35 minutes until filling begins to bubble and crust is golden. Cool 1 hour before cutting.

Makes 1 (9-inch) pie

Prep time: 15 minutes
Cook time: 45 minutes
Cool time: 1 hour

Apple Cheddar Pie

2⅓ cups all-purpose flour, divided
½ cup AUNT JEMIMA® or QUAKER® Enriched Corn Meal
1 teaspoon salt (optional)
⅓ cup *plus* 2 tablespoons margarine or butter
⅓ cup vegetable shortening
1½ cups (6 ounces) shredded Cheddar cheese
½ cup ice water
8 cups peeled, sliced apples (about 8 medium apples)
⅔ cup sugar
¾ teaspoon ground cinnamon

Combine 2 cups flour, corn meal and salt. Cut in ⅓ cup margarine and shortening until mixture resembles coarse crumbs. Stir in cheese. Add water, one tablespoon at a time, stirring lightly until mixture forms a ball. Divide dough into two parts, one slightly larger than the other. Shape each to form a ball. Wrap securely in plastic wrap or waxed paper; chill about 30 minutes. Roll large ball on lightly floured surface to form 11-inch circle. Fit loosely into 9-inch pie plate; trim. Roll remaining dough to form 12-inch square. Cut into 12×¾-inch strips.

Heat oven to 400°F. Combine remaining ⅓ cup flour, apples, sugar and cinnamon; spoon into crust. Dot with remaining 2 tablespoons margarine. Weave strips over filling to make lattice crust. Trim even with outer rim of pie plate. Fold lower crust over strips; seal and flute. Bake 30 to 35 minutes or until crust is light golden brown, covering edges with foil, if necessary, to prevent overbrowning.

Makes 1 (9-inch) pie

Note: To make double-crust pie, roll remaining dough to form 10-inch circle. Prepare filling as directed. Place top crust over filling; trim. Turn edges under; flute. Cut slits into top crust to allow steam to escape.

CHOCK FULL O' CHOCOLATE

Chocolate Truffle Tart

Crust
- ⅔ cup all-purpose flour
- ½ cup sugar
- ½ cup walnuts, ground
- 6 tablespoons (¾ stick) butter or margarine, softened
- ⅓ cup NESTLÉ® Cocoa

Filling
- 1 cup heavy or whipping cream
- ¼ cup sugar
- 4 foil-wrapped bars (8-ounce package) NESTLÉ® Semi-Sweet Chocolate Baking Bars, broken up
- 2 tablespoons seedless raspberry jam
- Additional whipped cream for garnish
- Fresh raspberries for garnish

Crust: Preheat oven to 350°F. In small mixer bowl, beat flour, ½ cup sugar, walnuts, butter, and Nestlé® Cocoa until soft dough forms. Press dough into 9-inch fluted tart pan with removable bottom. Bake 12 to 14 minutes or until puffed. Cool completely.

Filling: In medium saucepan, bring heavy cream and ¼ cup sugar just to a boil, stirring occasionally. Remove from heat. Stir in Nestlé® Semi-Sweet Chocolate Baking Bars and jam; cool 5 minutes. Whisk until chocolate is melted and mixture is smooth. Transfer to small mixer bowl. Cover; refrigerate 45 to 60 minutes or until mixture is cool and slightly thickened. Beat Filling just until color lightens slightly. Pour into Crust. Refrigerate. Garnish with whipped cream and raspberries. *Makes 1 (9-inch) tart*

Chocolate Truffle Tart

Cocoa Cloud Pie

Preheat oven to 350°F. In medium bowl, mix coconut, chocolate chips and pecans; sprinkle over bottom of pie crust. In same bowl, combine corn syrup, sugars, margarine and eggs until well blended. Pour over coconut mixture. Bake 50 to 55 minutes or until puffed and set. Cool on wire rack. *Makes 1 (9-inch) pie*

Prep Time: 15 minutes
Bake Time: 55 minutes, plus cooling

Cocoa Cloud Pie

2 packages (3 ounces *each*) cream cheese, softened
1 cup confectioners' sugar
2 teaspoons vanilla extract
½ cup HERSHEY⨾S Cocoa
¼ cup milk
2 cups (1 pint) cold whipping cream
1 (8-inch) prepared graham cracker or other flavor crumb crust

In large mixer bowl, beat cream cheese, confectioners' sugar and vanilla until well blended. Add cocoa alternately with milk, beating until smooth. Gradually add whipping cream, beating until stiff. Spoon into crust. Cover; refrigerate several hours or overnight. *Makes 1 (8-inch) pie*

Jackpot Pie

1 cup flaked coconut
1 cup (6 ounces) semisweet chocolate chips
1 cup coarsely chopped pecans
Easy-As-Pie Crust (page 116)
⅔ cup KARO® Light or Dark Corn Syrup
½ cup granulated sugar
½ cup packed brown sugar
2 tablespoons MAZOLA® Margarine, melted
4 eggs

Chocolate Caramel Ooze Pie

½ cup caramel or butterscotch-flavored ice cream topping
1 (8-inch) prepared chocolate cookie crumb crust
1 envelope KNOX® Unflavored Gelatine
⅓ cup cold water
1½ cups whipping or heavy cream, divided
1 package (6 ounces) semisweet chocolate chips
1 teaspoon vanilla extract
Additional whipped cream (optional)

Pour caramel topping into prepared crust; set aside. In small saucepan, sprinkle unflavored gelatine over cold water; let stand 1 minute. Stir over low heat until gelatine is completely dissolved, about 3 minutes. Stir in 1 cup cream. Bring just to a boil; stir in chocolate. Reduce heat to low; stir until chocolate is completely melted, about 3 minutes. Stir in remaining ½ cup cream and vanilla. Pour into prepared crust. Chill until firm, about 3 hours. Garnish with additional whipped cream. *Makes 1 (8-inch) pie*

Rocky Road Pie

1 (14-ounce) can EAGLE® Brand
    Sweetened Condensed Milk
    (NOT evaporated milk)
¾ cup water
1 (4-serving size) package chocolate
    flavor pudding mix (*not instant*)
2 cups CAMPFIRE® Miniature
    Marshmallows
¾ cup chopped peanuts
1 cup (½ pint) BORDEN® or
    MEADOW GOLD® Whipping
    Cream, whipped
1 (9-inch) prepared graham cracker
    crumb crust

In medium saucepan, combine sweetened
condensed milk, water and pudding mix;
mix well. Over medium heat, cook and stir
until thickened. Place in large bowl; chill
thoroughly, about 45 minutes, stirring
occasionally. Stir in marshmallows and
peanuts. Fold in whipped cream. Pour into
prepared crust. Chill thoroughly. Garnish
as desired. Refrigerate leftovers.

Makes 1 (9-inch) pie

Rocky Road Peanut Butter Pie: Add ½
cup peanut butter to chocolate mixture
before cooking. Proceed as directed.

Chocolate Brownie Pie

1 package (4 ounces) BAKER'S®
    GERMAN'S® Sweet Chocolate
¼ cup (½ stick) margarine or butter
¾ cup sugar
2 eggs
1 teaspoon vanilla extract
½ cup all-purpose flour
½ cup chopped nuts
    Ice cream, any flavor
    Regal Chocolate Sauce (page 156)
    Strawberries (optional)

- Heat oven to 350°F.
- Microwave chocolate and margarine in
  large microwavable bowl on HIGH 2
  minutes or until margarine is melted.
  Stir until chocolate is completely melted.
- Stir sugar into melted chocolate mixture.
  Mix in eggs and vanilla until well
  blended. Stir in flour and nuts. Spread in
  greased and floured 9-inch pie plate.
- Bake 25 minutes or until toothpick
  inserted into center comes out with
  fudgy crumbs. *Do not overbake.* Cool in
  pie plate.
- Serve with ice cream and Regal
  Chocolate Sauce. Garnish with
  strawberries, if desired.

Makes 1 (9-inch) pie

Prep time: 20 minutes
Baking time: 25 minutes

Chocolate Brownie Pie

Chocolate Marble Cheesepie

Chocolate Marble Cheesepie

¼ cup HERSHEY᾿S Cocoa
1 can (14 ounces) sweetened condensed milk, divided
3 teaspoons vanilla extract, divided
4 packages (3 ounces *each*) cream cheese, softened
2 tablespoons lemon juice
   Chocolate Crumb Crust (recipe follows)
   Chocolate curls (optional)

In small saucepan, stir together cocoa and ⅔ cup sweetened condensed milk. Cook over low heat, stirring constantly, until mixture is smooth and very thick. Remove from heat; stir in 1 teaspoon vanilla. In small mixer bowl, beat 2 packages cream cheese until light and fluffy; add cocoa mixture. Cool thoroughly. In large mixer bowl, beat remaining 2 packages cream cheese until light and fluffy. Gradually beat in remaining sweetened condensed milk, lemon juice and remaining 2 teaspoons vanilla. Alternately spoon vanilla and chocolate mixtures into prepared pie crust; gently swirl with knife or spatula for marbled effect. Refrigerate 8 hours or until firm. Garnish with chocolate curls, if desired.

Makes 1 (9-inch) pie

Chocolate Crumb Crust: In medium bowl, stir together 1¼ cups graham cracker crumbs, ¼ cup HERSHEY᾿S Cocoa and ¼ cup sugar. Blend in 6 tablespoons melted butter or margarine. Press mixture firmly onto bottom and up side of 9-inch pie plate; refrigerate about 2 hours before filling.

Mocha Cheese Pie

1 cup (6-ounce package) NESTLÉ® Toll House® Semi-Sweet Chocolate Morsels
1 tablespoon TASTER'S CHOICE® Freeze-Dried Coffee
1 tablespoon boiling water
2 packages (8 ounces *each*) cream cheese, softened
⅓ cup sugar
3 eggs
¼ cup heavy cream
1 unbaked (9-inch) pie shell*
   Sweetened whipped cream (optional)

Preheat oven to 350°F. Melt Nestlé® Toll House® Semi-Sweet Chocolate Morsels over hot, not boiling, water; stir until smooth. Set aside. In cup, dissolve Taster's Choice® Freeze-Dried Coffee in boiling water. In large bowl, combine cream cheese and sugar; beat until smooth. Add eggs, one at a time, beating well after each addition. Add melted morsels and coffee; mix well. Blend in heavy cream. Pour into pie shell. Bake 35 to 40 minutes. Turn oven off. Let pie stand in oven with door ajar 15 minutes. Remove. Cool completely; chill. Garnish with sweetened whipped cream. *Makes 1 (9-inch) pie*

*If using frozen pie shell, use deep dish style, thawed. Place on cookie sheet and bake additional 10 minutes.

Chocolate Silk Pie

1 envelope unflavored gelatin
¼ cup cold water
1 cup DANNON® Plain Nonfat or
    Lowfat Yogurt
1 cup skim milk
2 teaspoons vanilla extract
1 package (4-serving size) instant
    chocolate pudding and pie
    filling mix
⅓ cup sugar
1 (8-inch) prepared graham cracker
    crumb crust
Reduced-calorie whipped topping

In small saucepan, sprinkle gelatin over water; let stand 3 minutes to soften. Stir over low heat until gelatin is completely dissolved. In food processor or blender, combine gelatin mixture with yogurt, milk, vanilla, pudding mix and sugar. Process until well blended. Pour into prepared crust. Cover; chill several hours. Top with whipped topping.

Makes 1 (8-inch) pie

Hot Chocolate Pie

1 KEEBLER® Ready-Crust® Chocolate
    Flavored Pie Crust
1 egg yolk, slightly beaten
¾ cup granulated sugar, divided
½ cup all-purpose flour, divided
3 tablespoons unsweetened cocoa
1 teaspoon baking powder
¼ teaspoon salt
½ cup chopped nuts (optional)
¼ cup milk
2 tablespoons butter or margarine,
    melted
½ teaspoon vanilla extract
¼ cup packed brown sugar
½ cup cold water
Whipping cream, whipped (optional)

Preheat oven to 350°F. Brush bottom and side of pie crust with egg yolk. Bake 5 minutes. Cool on wire rack. In medium bowl, combine ½ cup granulated sugar, flour, 1½ tablespoons cocoa, baking powder and salt. Stir in nuts, milk, butter and vanilla. (If mixture seems too stiff, add a few more drops milk.) Spread mixture in pie crust. In small bowl, combine brown sugar, water, remaining ¼ cup granulated sugar and remaining 1½ tablespoons cocoa. Pour over top of pie. Bake 30 to 35 minutes. Cool on wire rack. Serve warm with whipped cream.

Makes 8 servings

Chocolate Chip Cookie Pie à la Mode

1 cup packed brown sugar
⅓ cup margarine
1 egg
1 teaspoon vanilla extract
1¼ cups all-purpose flour
1 cup QUAKER® Oats (quick or old
    fashioned, uncooked)
½ cup semisweet chocolate pieces
¼ teaspoon baking soda
¼ teaspoon salt
Prepared frosting
Ice cream
Chocolate, hot fudge or caramel ice
    cream topping

Preheat oven to 350°F. Beat brown sugar and margarine until fluffy. Add egg and vanilla; beat well. Add flour, oats, chocolate pieces, baking soda and salt. Spread dough evenly into well-greased 9-inch pie plate. Bake 23 to 28 minutes or until golden brown. Cool completely in pie plate on wire rack. Decorate with prepared frosting. Cut pie into wedges. Serve with ice cream; garnish with ice cream topping.

Makes 1 (9-inch) pie

Chocolate Turtle Pie

¼ cup caramel or butterscotch-flavored dessert topping
1 baked (8- or 9-inch) pie crust, cooled
¾ cup pecan halves
1 package (4-serving size) JELL-O® Chocolate Flavor Pudding and Pie Filling or Sugar Free Pudding and Pie Filling*
1¾ cups milk
1¾ cups (4 ounces) thawed COOL WHIP® Non-Dairy Whipped Topping

- Bring caramel topping to a boil in small saucepan, stirring constantly. Pour into pie crust. Arrange pecans on top and chill.

- Combine pie filling mix with milk in saucepan. Cook and stir over medium heat until mixture comes to a boil. Cool 5 minutes, stirring twice.

- Pour into pie shell; place plastic wrap on surface of filling. Chill 3 hours.

- Remove plastic wrap. Garnish with whipped topping. Drizzle with additional caramel and garnish with additional pecans, if desired.

Makes 1 (8- or 9-inch) pie

*Or, use JELL-O® Chocolate Flavor Instant Pudding and Pie Filling or Sugar Free Instant Pudding and Pie Filling; prepare as package directs, using 1½ cups cold milk.

Chocolate Turtle Pie

Chocolate Sweetheart Pie

1 package (8 ounces) BAKER'S® Semi-Sweet Chocolate
⅓ cup corn syrup
1 cup (½ pint) heavy cream
3 eggs
1 unbaked (9-inch) pie shell
2 tablespoons sugar
½ teaspoon vanilla extract
1 pint strawberries, sliced

- Heat oven to 350°F.

- Melt 6 squares chocolate in heavy saucepan over very low heat. Stir in corn syrup and ½ cup cream. Add eggs, one at a time, beating well after each addition. Pour into pie shell.

- Bake 45 minutes or until knife inserted 1 inch from center comes out clean. Cool on wire rack. (Center of pie will sink after cooling.)

- Whip remaining ½ cup cream, sugar and vanilla until soft peaks form; spoon into center of cooled pie. Top with strawberries. Melt remaining 2 squares chocolate and drizzle over strawberries.

Makes 1 (9-inch) pie

Prep time: 30 minutes
Baking time: 45 minutes

Tip: To avoid spoilage, refrigerate pies with cream or custard fillings as soon as they have cooled. Refrigerate leftovers immediately.

Mocha-Almond Pie

2 squares BAKER'S® Unsweetened
    Chocolate
2 squares BAKER'S® Semi-Sweet
    Chocolate
½ cup (1 stick) margarine or butter
1 tablespoon instant coffee
1 cup sugar
¼ cup corn syrup
3 eggs
2 tablespoons sour cream *or* plain
    yogurt
1 teaspoon vanilla extract
1 unbaked (9-inch) pie shell
½ cup sliced almonds

- Heat oven to 350°F.

- Microwave chocolates, margarine and instant coffee in large microwavable bowl on HIGH 2 minutes or until margarine is melted. *Stir until chocolate is completely melted.*

- Stir in sugar and corn syrup. Beat in eggs, sour cream and vanilla. Pour into pie shell; sprinkle with almonds.

- Bake 45 minutes or until knife inserted 1 inch from center comes out clean. Cool on wire rack.   *Makes 1 (9-inch) pie*

Prep time: 15 minutes
Baking time: 45 minutes

Chocolate Peanut Butter Pie

    Chocolate Nut Crust (page 148)
¾ cup (1½ sticks) margarine or butter
¾ cup peanut butter
½ cup packed brown sugar
5¼ cups (12 ounces) thawed COOL
      WHIP® Whipped Topping
  Peanuts (optional)
2 squares BAKER'S® Semi-Sweet
    Chocolate (optional)

*Top to bottom: Chocolate Sweetheart Pie,
Mocha-Almond Pie, Chocolate Peanut Butter Pie*

- Prepare Chocolate Nut Crust.

- Beat margarine, peanut butter and brown sugar until well blended. Reserve ¼ cup whipped topping for garnish. Gently stir in remaining 5 cups whipped topping until mixture is smooth and creamy. Spoon into Chocolate Nut Crust.

- Refrigerate until firm, about 4 hours. Garnish with reserved whipped topping. Sprinkle with peanuts; drizzle with melted chocolate.   *Makes 1 (9-inch) pie*

Prep time: 20 minutes
Chill time: 4 hours

Cookies & Cream Pudding Pie

26 chocolate sandwich cookies
1½ cups cold milk
1 cup (½ pint) vanilla ice cream, softened
1 package (4-serving size) JELL-O® Instant Pudding, Chocolate Flavor COOL WHIP® Whipped Topping, thawed, for garnish

- Place cookies on bottom and side of 9-inch pie plate. Cookies should cover plate evenly.

- Pour cold milk into bowl. Add ice cream. Beat with wire whisk until well blended. Add pudding mix. Beat with wire whisk until well blended, about 2 minutes. Let pudding stand 3 minutes.

- Pour pudding into cookie-lined pie plate. Refrigerate until set, about 3 hours. To decorate, pipe with whipped topping. Chill until serving time.

Makes 1 (9-inch) pie

Minty Mousse Pie au Chocolat

6 tablespoons sugar, divided
2 tablespoons *plus* 2 teaspoons cornstarch
1 cup (⅔ of 10-ounce package) NESTLÉ® Toll House® Mint Flavored Semi-Sweet Chocolate Morsels
1½ cups milk
1 cup heavy cream
1 (9-inch) prepared graham cracker crumb crust

In heavy medium saucepan, combine 4 tablespoons sugar, cornstarch, and Nestlé® Toll House® Mint Flavored Semi-Sweet Chocolate Morsels. Gradually stir in milk. Cook, stirring constantly, over medium heat until mixture *boils. Boil 1 minute*; remove from heat. Transfer to large bowl; cover surface of chocolate mixture with plastic wrap. Cool to room temperature, 20 to 30 minutes. In medium bowl, combine heavy cream with remaining 2 tablespoons sugar; beat until stiff. Remove plastic wrap from chocolate mixture; beat chocolate mixture well. Fold in whipped cream mixture. Spoon into prepared crust. Chill until firm, about 2 to 3 hours.

Makes 1 (9-inch) pie

Chocolate Crumb Crust

3 squares BAKER'S® Semi-Sweet Chocolate
3 tablespoons margarine or butter
1 cup graham cracker crumbs

- Heat oven to 375°F.

- Microwave chocolate and margarine in microwavable bowl on HIGH 2 minutes or until margarine is melted. *Stir until chocolate is completely melted.*

- Stir in crumbs. Press mixture onto bottom and up side of 9-inch tart pan or pie plate. Freeze 10 minutes. Bake 8 minutes. Cool on wire rack.

Makes 1 (9-inch) crust

Prep time: 5 minutes
Freezing time: 10 minutes
Baking time: 8 minutes

Tip: To serve crumb crust pie, dip pie plate just to rim in hot water 30 seconds. Cut; serve.

Cookies & Cream Pudding Pie

Nestlé® Candy Shop Pizza

Nestlé® Candy Shop Pizza

1½ cups all-purpose flour
½ teaspoon baking soda
½ teaspoon salt
10 tablespoons (1¼ sticks) butter, softened
½ cup granulated sugar
½ cup packed brown sugar
1 egg
½ teaspoon vanilla extract
2 cups (12-ounce package) NESTLÉ® Toll House® Semi-Sweet Chocolate Morsels, divided
½ cup peanut butter
1 cup coarsely chopped candy such as NESTLÉ® Crunch Bars, Alpine White Bars, Butterfinger Bars, Baby Ruth Bars, Goobers and Raisinets

Preheat oven to 375°F. Lightly grease 12- to 14-inch pizza pan or 15½×10½×1-inch baking pan. In small bowl, combine flour, baking soda, and salt; set aside.

In large mixer bowl, beat butter and sugars until creamy. Beat in egg and vanilla. Gradually beat in flour mixture. Stir in 1 cup Nestlé® Toll House® Semi-Sweet Chocolate Morsels. Spread in prepared pan. Bake 20 to 24 minutes or until lightly browned.

Immediately sprinkle remaining 1 cup Nestlé® Toll House® Semi-Sweet Chocolate Morsels over crust; drop peanut butter by spoonfuls over crust. Let stand 5 minutes or until morsels become shiny and soft. Gently spread chocolate and peanut butter evenly over crust. Decorate pizza with Nestlé® candy. Cut into wedges; serve warm.

Makes about 12 servings

Luscious Brownie Chip Pie

25 CHIPS AHOY!® Chocolate Chip Cookies
½ cup BLUE BONNET® Margarine, melted
½ cup light corn syrup
3 eggs
½ cup sugar
⅓ cup unsweetened cocoa
2 teaspoons vanilla extract
Whipped cream for garnish
Chocolate curls for garnish

Preheat oven to 350°F. Cut 5 cookies in half; set aside. Finely roll remaining cookies into crumbs using rolling pin. Combine cookie crumbs and ¼ cup melted margarine; press onto bottom and up side of 9-inch pie plate.

In saucepan, heat remaining ¼ cup margarine and corn syrup until warm; remove from heat. Beat in eggs, sugar, cocoa and vanilla; pour into crust. Bake 15 minutes; insert cookie halves around edge of pie crust. Bake 15 to 20 minutes more or until set, tenting with foil during last 5 to 10 minutes if excessive browning occurs. Cool. Garnish with whipped cream and chocolate curls.   *Makes 1 (9-inch) pie*

Fudge Surprise Key Lime Pie

Crust
9-inch Classic Crisco® Single Crust
(pages 6 and 7)

Filling
½ cup chocolate fudge topping
⅔ cup chopped macadamia nuts
1 teaspoon unflavored gelatin
¼ cup water
1 cup granulated sugar
¼ cup cornstarch
1 cup milk
3 egg yolks, slightly beaten
⅓ cup Key lime juice
¼ cup BUTTER FLAVOR CRISCO®
1 cup dairy sour cream

Topping
2 cups whipping cream
¼ cup confectioners sugar
Chocolate shavings

1. Prepare and bake 9-inch Classic Crisco® Single Crust. Cool.

2. For Filling, spread fudge topping over bottom of cooled baked pie crust. (Heat topping slightly if too thick to spread.) Sprinkle with nuts. Soften gelatin in water in top of double boiler. Place over boiling water. Stir until gelatin is dissolved. Combine granulated sugar and cornstarch in medium saucepan. Stir in milk until smooth. Stir in egg yolks and lime juice. Add Butter Flavor Crisco®. Cook and stir on medium heat until mixture comes to a boil; boil 1 minute. Remove from heat. Stir in gelatin mixture slowly. Pour into large bowl. Chill 40 to 50 minutes. Gently stir in sour cream. Pour into baked pie crust. Chill 2 hours.

3. For Topping, combine whipping cream and confectioners sugar. Beat until stiff. Spoon on top of pie. Garnish with chocolate shavings.   *Makes 1 (9-inch) pie*

Chocolate Raspberry Tart

1 package (4-serving size) JELL-O®
    Pudding and Pie Filling, Vanilla
    Flavor
1¾ cups half and half or milk
1 Chocolate Crumb Crust (page 129),
    baked in 9-inch tart pan and cooled
1 pint raspberries
2 squares BAKER'S® Semi-Sweet
    Chocolate, melted

• **Microwave Directions:** Microwave pie filling mix and half and half in large microwavable bowl on HIGH 3 minutes; stir well. Microwave 3 minutes longer; stir again. Microwave 1 minute or until mixture comes to a boil. Cover surface with plastic wrap. Refrigerate at least 4 hours.

• Spoon filling into Chocolate Crumb Crust just before serving. Arrange raspberries on top of filling. Drizzle with melted chocolate.   *Makes 1 (9-inch) tart*

Prep time: 30 minutes
Chill time: 4 hours

Chocolate Raspberry Tart

Chocolate Bourbon Pie

1 cup BLUE DIAMOND® Blanched Whole Almonds, toasted
1½ cups flour, divided
1 cup *plus* 2 tablespoons sugar
Salt
6 tablespoons cold butter
4 to 5 tablespoons cold water
½ teaspoon baking soda
½ cup BLUE DIAMOND® Blanched Whole Almonds, toasted and ground
¾ cup strong coffee
¼ cup bourbon
2 ounces unsweetened chocolate
½ cup butter, softened
1 egg, slightly beaten
½ teaspoon vanilla extract
Whipped cream

Finely grind whole almonds with ½ cup flour in food processor. Add ½ cup flour, 2 tablespoons sugar and ⅛ teaspoon salt. Add cold butter; mix with on-off pulses until mixture resembles coarse cornmeal. (To prepare by hand, finely grind whole almonds with ½ cup flour in blender. Transfer to large bowl. Add ½ cup flour, 2 tablespoons sugar and ⅛ teaspoon salt. With fingertips, work cold butter into flour mixture until mixture resembles coarse cornmeal.) *Do not overmix.* Add just enough water to form dough. Shape dough into a ball; chill 30 minutes.

Preheat oven to 275°F. Roll out dough on lightly floured board. Fit into 9-inch pie plate; trim edges. Prick bottom of pastry shell with fork. Chill 10 minutes. Sift together remaining ½ cup flour, baking soda and pinch of salt. Stir in ground almonds; reserve. In double boiler over simmering water, heat coffee and bourbon. Add chocolate and softened butter, stirring until smooth and melted. Remove from heat; stir in remaining 1 cup sugar. Cool 3 minutes. Beat in flour mixture. Add egg and vanilla, beating until smooth. Pour into prepared pastry shell. Bake 1½ hours. Serve with whipped cream. *Makes 1 (9-inch) pie*

Cappuccino Cheese Pie

1 unbaked (9-inch) pie shell, pricked
2 to 3 tablespoons coffee-flavored liqueur
1 tablespoon instant coffee or espresso powder
1 (8-ounce) package cream cheese, softened
1 (14-ounce) can EAGLE® Brand Sweetened Condensed Milk (NOT evaporated milk)
2 eggs
2 tablespoons cocoa
Whipped cream or whipped topping

Preheat oven to 375°F. Bake pie shell 15 minutes; remove from oven. *Reduce oven temperature to 325°F.* Combine liqueur and coffee, stirring until coffee dissolves. In large mixer bowl, beat cheese until fluffy. Gradually beat in sweetened condensed milk until smooth. Add eggs, liqueur mixture and cocoa; mix well. Pour into baked pie shell. Bake 40 minutes or until set. Cool. Chill thoroughly. Serve with whipped cream. Garnish as desired. Refrigerate leftovers.

Makes 1 (9-inch) pie

German Chocolate Pie

1 unbaked (9-inch) pie shell, pricked
1 (4-ounce) package sweet cooking
   chocolate
4 tablespoons margarine or butter
1 (14-ounce) can EAGLE® Brand
   Sweetened Condensed Milk
   (NOT evaporated milk)
1 cup (½ pint) BORDEN® or
   MEADOW GOLD® Whipping
   Cream, *unwhipped*
½ cup biscuit baking mix
2 eggs *plus* 1 egg *yolk*
1½ teaspoons vanilla extract
½ cup flaked coconut
½ cup chopped pecans, toasted

Preheat oven to 375°F. Bake pie shell 10 minutes; remove from oven. *Reduce oven temperature to 325°F.* In small saucepan, melt chocolate with *2 tablespoons* margarine. In large mixer bowl, beat chocolate mixture, ⅔ *cup* sweetened condensed milk, cream, biscuit mix, 2 eggs and *1 teaspoon* vanilla until well blended. Pour into prepared pie shell. Bake 40 minutes or until center is set. In small saucepan, combine remaining sweetened condensed milk, egg *yolk*, 2 tablespoons margarine and ½ *teaspoon* vanilla. Over medium heat, cook and stir until thickened and bubbly, about 5 minutes. Add coconut and pecans; spread over top of pie. Serve warm or chilled. Refrigerate leftovers.

Makes 1 (9-inch) pie

Left to right: German Chocolate Pie, Cappuccino Cheese Pie

Hershey's Syrup Pie

Hershey's Syrup Pie

1 baked (9-inch) pie crust or
    1 (8-inch) prepared graham cracker
    crumb crust
2 egg yolks
⅓ cup cornstarch
¼ teaspoon salt
1¾ cups milk
1 cup HERSHEY'S Syrup
1 teaspoon vanilla extract
    Syrup Whipped Topping (recipe
    follows)
    Fresh fruit

Microwave Directions: In medium microwave-safe bowl, beat egg yolks. Add cornstarch, salt, milk and syrup; blend well. Microwave at MEDIUM-HIGH (70%) 6 to 8 minutes, stirring every 2 minutes with whisk, until mixture is smooth and very thick. Stir in vanilla. Pour into crust. Press plastic wrap directly onto surface; refrigerate several hours or overnight. Garnish with Syrup Whipped Topping and fresh fruit.

Makes 1 (9-inch) pie

Syrup Whipped Topping: In small mixer bowl, combine 1 cup cold whipping cream, ½ cup HERSHEY'S Syrup, 2 tablespoons confectioners' sugar and ½ teaspoon vanilla extract. Beat just until cream holds definite shape; *do not overbeat*. Makes about 2¼ cups topping.

Fudgy Pecan Pie

⅓ cup butter or margarine
⅔ cup sugar
⅓ cup unsweetened cocoa
1 teaspoon instant coffee
1 teaspoon hot water
3 eggs
1 cup light corn syrup
¼ teaspoon salt
1 cup chopped pecans
1 unbaked (9-inch) pie shell
1 cup pecan halves
    Sweetened whipped cream (optional)
    Additional pecan halves (optional)

Preheat oven to 375°F. In medium saucepan over low heat, melt butter; add sugar and cocoa, stirring until well blended. Remove from heat; set aside. In custard cup, combine instant coffee and hot water, stirring until coffee is dissolved; set aside. In medium mixing bowl, beat eggs slightly. Stir in corn syrup and salt. Add cocoa mixture and coffee mixture; blend well. Stir in chopped pecans. Pour into pie shell. Arrange 1 cup pecan halves over top. Bake 45 to 50 minutes or until set. Cool. Cover; refrigerate about 8 hours before serving. Garnish with whipped cream and additional pecan halves.

Makes 1 (9-inch) pie

*Favorite recipe from **Pecan Marketing Board***

Chocolate Linzer Tart

2 unbaked (9-inch) pie shells
6 squares BAKER'S® Semi-Sweet
   Chocolate
½ cup (1 stick) margarine or butter,
   softened
½ cup sugar
2 eggs (1 separated)
1 cup toasted ground almonds
1 cup seedless raspberry preserves

- Heat oven to 425°F.

- Fit one pie shell into 9-inch tart pan. Bake 5 to 8 minutes or until pie shell begins to brown.

- Microwave chocolate and 2 tablespoons margarine in large microwavable bowl on HIGH 2 minutes or until margarine is melted. *Stir until chocolate is completely melted.*

- Beat remaining 6 tablespoons margarine and sugar in large bowl until light and fluffy. Beat in 1 egg, 1 egg yolk and almonds. Stir in melted chocolate mixture. Spread mixture evenly over baked crust. Top with preserves.

- Cut remaining pie shell into ½-inch strips. Arrange in lattice design over preserves. Beat remaining egg white until foamy; brush over pastry strips.

- Bake 10 minutes. *Reduce oven temperature to 350°F; bake 30 minutes longer or until crust is golden brown. Cool on wire rack.*
  Makes 1 (9-inch) tart

Prep time: 30 minutes
Baking time: 40 minutes

Chocolate Mint Dream Pie

2 envelopes DREAM WHIP® Whipped
   Topping Mix
2½ cups cold milk
2 packages (4-serving size) JELL-O®
   Instant Pudding and Pie Filling,
   Chocolate Flavor
3 tablespoons white creme de menthe
   liqueur*
1 (8- or 9-inch) prepared chocolate
   cookie crumb crust
   Additional whipped topping
   Fresh mint leaves (optional)

- Combine whipped topping mix with 1 cup milk in large bowl. Beat at high speed of electric mixer until topping thickens and forms stiff peaks, about 6 minutes. Add remaining 1½ cups milk, pudding mix and liqueur; blend at low speed. Beat at high speed 2 minutes, scraping side of bowl occasionally.

- Spoon filling mixture into prepared crust. Chill at least 4 hours or overnight. Garnish with additional whipped topping and mint leaves.
  Makes 1 (8- or 9-inch) pie

Prep time: 10 minutes
Chill time: 4 hours

*Substitute ¼ teaspoon peppermint extract for creme de menthe liqueur, if desired.

Chocolate Mint Dream Pie

M.V.P. Pie

Crust
1¼ cups all-purpose flour
½ cup unsalted peanuts, ground
3 tablespoons sugar
¾ teaspoon salt
⅓ cup shortening
3 to 4 tablespoons ice water

Chocolate Layer
¼ cup (½ stick) butter or margarine
2 cups (11½-ounce package) NESTLÉ®
   Toll House® Milk Chocolate
   Morsels, divided

Filling
1 package (8 ounces) cream cheese,
   softened
¾ cup creamy peanut butter
¾ cup sugar
1 cup heavy or whipping cream,
   divided

Crust: Preheat oven to 400°F. In medium bowl, combine flour, peanuts, 3 tablespoons sugar, and salt. With pastry blender, fork or two knives, cut in shortening until mixture resembles coarse crumbs. Sprinkle 3 tablespoons ice water over flour mixture. Stir with fork until mixture forms a ball, adding additional 1 tablespoon ice water if necessary. Flatten into circle. Between two sheets of waxed paper, roll dough to ⅛-inch thickness. Remove top sheet of waxed paper. Invert pastry into 9-inch pie plate; remove waxed paper. Flute edge. Prick Crust with fork. Bake 15 to 17 minutes until lightly browned. Cool completely.

Chocolate Layer: In small saucepan, melt butter. Remove from heat. Stir 1½ cups Nestlé® Toll House® Milk Chocolate Morsels into butter until smooth. Reserve remaining ½ cup milk chocolate morsels for garnish. Spread Chocolate Layer on bottom and side of prepared Crust. Refrigerate while making Filling.

Filling: In large mixer bowl, beat cream cheese, peanut butter, and ¾ cup sugar until creamy. Beat in ¼ cup heavy cream until light and fluffy. Set aside. In small mixer bowl, beat remaining ¾ cup heavy cream until soft peaks form. Fold into Filling. Spoon over Chocolate Layer. Sprinkle with reserved ½ cup Nestlé® Toll House® Milk Chocolate Morsels. Refrigerate at least 3 hours until filling is set.   *Makes 1 (9-inch) pie*

Black Forest Pie

4 (1-ounce) squares unsweetened
   chocolate
1 (14-ounce) can EAGLE® Brand
   Sweetened Condensed Milk
   (NOT evaporated milk)
1 teaspoon almond extract
1½ cups BORDEN® or MEADOW
   GOLD® Whipping Cream,
   whipped
1 baked (9- or 10-inch) pie crust
1 (21-ounce) can cherry pie filling,
   chilled
Toasted almonds (optional)

In heavy saucepan over medium-low heat, melt chocolate with sweetened condensed milk. Remove from heat; stir in extract. Pour into large bowl; cool or chill thoroughly. Beat until smooth. Gradually fold in whipped cream. Pour into prepared pie crust; chill 4 hours or until set. Top with pie filling. Garnish with almonds. Refrigerate leftovers.
        Makes 1 (9- or 10-inch) pie

Microwave Tip: In l-quart glass measure with handle, combine chocolate and sweetened condensed milk. Cook on 100% power (high) 2 to 4 minutes, stirring after each minute until smooth. Proceed as directed.

Chocolate Amaretto Pie

1 (3-ounce) package cream cheese, softened
2 (1-ounce) bars unsweetened baking chocolate, melted
⅛ teaspoon salt
1 (14-ounce) can EAGLE® Brand Sweetened Condensed Milk (NOT evaporated milk)
2 eggs
¼ to ⅓ cup amaretto liqueur
1 cup sliced almonds, toasted (optional)
1 unbaked (9-inch) pie shell

Preheat oven to 350°F. In large mixer bowl, beat cheese, chocolate and salt until well blended. Gradually beat in sweetened condensed milk until smooth. Add eggs; mix well. Stir in liqueur and almonds. Pour into pie shell. Bake 30 to 35 minutes or until center is set. Cool. Serve warm or chilled. Garnish as desired. Refrigerate leftovers. *Makes 1 (9-inch) pie*

Chocolate Amaretto Pie

Chocolate & Peanut Butter Cup Pie

1 envelope KNOX® Unflavored Gelatine
¼ cup cold water
¾ cup creamy or chunky peanut butter
1½ cups milk
½ cup sugar
1 (8-inch) prepared chocolate cookie crumb crust
¼ cup whipping or heavy cream
½ cup (3 ounces) semisweet chocolate chips

In small saucepan, sprinkle unflavored gelatine over cold water; let stand 1 minute. Stir over low heat until gelatine is completely dissolved, about 3 minutes.

In food processor or blender, process peanut butter, milk and sugar. While processing, through feed cap, gradually add gelatine mixture; process until blended. Pour into prepared crust; chill until almost set, about 45 minutes.

Meanwhile, in small saucepan, bring cream just to a boil; remove from heat. Stir in chocolate until completely melted. Let stand 5 minutes. Slowly pour over prepared pie and spread to edges; chill until firm, about 3 hours.

Makes 1 (8-inch) pie

Hint: For easy cutting, slice pie with wet, hot knife.

Chocolate Almond
Caramel Tart

½ cup (1 stick) butter or margarine,
    softened
¾ cup sugar, divided
4 eggs, divided
1¼ cups all-purpose flour
½ cup ground toasted almonds
28 caramel candies, unwrapped
2 tablespoons water
½ cup (1 stick) butter or margarine,
    melted
¼ cup HERSHEY'S European Style
    Cocoa or HERSHEY'S Cocoa
¾ cup light corn syrup
½ teaspoon vanilla extract
½ teaspoon salt
1 cup sliced almonds
    Sweetened whipped cream or
    whipped topping (optional)

Heat oven to 350°F. In small mixer bowl,
beat ½ cup softened butter and ¼ cup
sugar until light and fluffy; blend in 1 egg.
Gradually beat in flour until smooth; stir
in ground almonds. Press mixture onto
bottom and up side of 11-inch round tart
pan with removable bottom. In small
saucepan over low heat, melt caramels
with water until completely smooth;
immediately spread onto bottom of crust.
In small mixer bowl, beat together ½ cup
melted butter, remaining ½ cup sugar and
cocoa. Blend in corn syrup, remaining
3 eggs, vanilla and salt. Pour into tart.
Sprinkle almonds over tart surface,
leaving 1 inch from outer edge uncovered.
Bake 55 to 60 minutes or until center has
started to firm and cracks begin to form
along outer edges. (Tart will puff and then
fall as it cools.) Cool completely. Cover;
refrigerate. Serve with sweetened
whipped cream, if desired.
Makes 1 (11-inch) tart

To toast almonds: Spread almonds on
cookie sheet. Bake at 350°F, stirring
occasionally, until lightly browned, 8 to
10 minutes; cool.

Microwave Peanutty Chocolate Pie

Microwave Peanutty
Chocolate Pie

½ cup sugar
3 tablespoons ARGO® or
    KINGSFORD'S® Corn Starch
2 cups milk
½ cup SKIPPY® Creamy Peanut Butter
⅔ cup semisweet chocolate chips
1 (8-inch) prepared graham cracker
    crumb crust
1 cup heavy cream
⅓ cup chopped peanuts

In large microwavable bowl, combine
sugar and corn starch. Gradually stir in
milk until smooth. Microwave on High
(100%), stirring three times with fork or
wire whisk, 7 to 9 minutes or until mixture
boils; boil 1 minute. Stir in peanut butter.
In medium bowl, combine 2 cups warmed
peanut butter mixture and chocolate chips
until chocolate melts. Spread in prepared
crust. Chill pie and remaining peanut
butter mixture 45 minutes or until cool.
Whip cream until stiff peaks form; gently
fold into peanut butter mixture. Spoon
over chocolate layer in crust. Refrigerate
several hours or overnight. Just before
serving, garnish with peanuts.
Makes 1 (8-inch) pie

Left to right: Two-Tone Cream Pie, Chocolate Chip Walnut Pie, Double Chocolate Mocha Pie

Two-Tone Cream Pie

1 package (4¾ ounces) vanilla pudding
   and pie filling
3½ cups milk
1 cup REESE'S® Peanut Butter Chips
1 cup HERSHEY'S Semi-Sweet
   Chocolate Chips or MINI CHIPS®
   Semi-Sweet Chocolate
1 baked (9-inch) pie crust
   Whipped topping

In medium saucepan, combine pudding mix and milk. Stir constantly over medium heat until mixture comes to a full boil; remove from heat. Pour 2 cups hot pudding into small bowl and add peanut butter chips; stir until melted and smooth. To remaining hot pudding, add chocolate chips; stir until melted and smooth. Pour chocolate mixture into baked pie crust. Gently pour and spread peanut butter mixture over top. Press plastic wrap directly onto surface. Refrigerate several hours or overnight. Garnish with whipped topping.   *Makes 1 (9-inch) pie*

Double Chocolate Mocha Pie

1 package (6 ounces) instant chocolate
   pudding and pie filling
2⅔ cups HERSHEY'S Chocolate Milk
1 (8-inch) prepared graham cracker or
   other flavor crumb crust
   Coffee Whipped Cream (recipe
   follows) or whipped cream

In large mixer bowl, beat pudding mix and chocolate milk until blended. Pour into crust. Cover; refrigerate several hours or overnight. Serve with Coffee Whipped Cream.   *Makes 1 (8-inch) pie*

Coffee Whipped Cream: In small mixer bowl, combine 1 cup cold whipping cream, ¼ cup confectioners' sugar, 1 tablespoon powdered instant coffee and ½ teaspoon vanilla extract. Beat just until cream holds definite shape; *do not overbeat*. Makes about 2 cups.

Chocolate Chip Walnut Pie

¾ cup packed light brown sugar
½ cup all-purpose flour
½ teaspoon baking powder
¼ teaspoon ground cinnamon
2 eggs, slightly beaten
1 cup HERSHEY'S Semi-Sweet
    Chocolate Chips, HERSHEY'S
    MINI CHIPS® Semi-Sweet
    Chocolate or HERSHEY'S Milk
    Chocolate Chips
1 cup coarsely chopped walnuts
1 baked (9-inch) pie crust, cooled
    Spiced Cream (recipe follows)

Heat oven to 350°F. In bowl, stir together brown sugar, flour, baking powder and cinnamon. Add eggs; stir until well blended. Stir in chocolate chips and walnuts. Pour into baked pie crust. Bake 25 to 30 minutes or until lightly browned and set. Serve slightly warm or at room temperature with Spiced Cream.

Makes 1 (9-inch) pie

Spiced Cream: In small mixer bowl, combine ½ cup cold whipping cream, 1 tablespoon confectioners' sugar, ¼ teaspoon vanilla extract, ¼ teaspoon ground cinnamon and dash ground nutmeg; beat until stiff. Makes about 1 cup.

Oreo® Fudge Pie

1 (15- to 16-ounce) package
    brownie mix
1 (7-ounce) package Mini OREO® Bite
    Size Chocolate Sandwich Cookies
1 unbaked (9-inch) pie shell
1 pint ice cream, any flavor
    Chocolate-flavored syrup

Preheat oven to 350°F. Prepare brownie mix batter as package directs. Carefully stir in cookies; pour into pie shell. Bake 30 to 35 minutes or just until set. (*Do not overbake.*) Cool slightly on wire rack. Cut into wedges; serve with scoop of ice cream and syrup.
Makes 1 (9-inch) pie

Chocolate Truffle Pie

1 envelope KNOX® Unflavored
    Gelatine
¼ cup cold orange juice
⅓ cup sugar
1 teaspoon instant coffee
1 package (6 ounces) semisweet
    chocolate chips
1 teaspoon vanilla extract
1½ cups whipping or heavy cream,
    whipped*
½ cup coarsely chopped walnuts *or*
    pecans (optional)
1 (8- or 9-inch) prepared chocolate
    cookie crumb crust
    Additional whipped cream (optional)

In medium saucepan, sprinkle unflavored gelatine over cold juice; let stand 1 minute. Stir over low heat until gelatine is completely dissolved, about 5 minutes. Add sugar, instant coffee and chocolate; cook, stirring constantly, until sugar and chocolate are melted. Remove from heat; stir in vanilla. Let stand 10 minutes or until lukewarm.

In large bowl, fold whipped cream into chocolate mixture. Sprinkle walnuts into prepared crust; add gelatine mixture and chill until firm, about 3 hours. Garnish with additional whipped cream.
Makes 1 (8- or 9-inch) pie

*Substitute 2 cups thawed frozen whipped topping for whipped cream, if desired.

Banana Chocolate Cream Pie

2 packages (3½ ounces *each*) chocolate-flavored pudding and pie filling mix (not instant)
2 cups low-fat milk
2 ounces unsweetened chocolate, melted
2 cups chocolate wafer crumbs
½ cup margarine, melted
2 firm, large DOLE® Bananas, peeled, sliced
½ cup thawed frozen whipped topping
Additional sliced DOLE® Bananas for garnish

- Combine pudding mix with milk in saucepan; prepare as package directs. Stir in melted chocolate. Remove from heat. Cool.

- Combine crumbs and margarine; blend well. Press evenly onto bottom and up side of 8- or 9-inch pie plate. Chill.

- Alternately layer pudding and bananas in prepared crust. Chill.

- Garnish with dollops of whipped topping and additional banana slices.

Makes 1 (8- or 9-inch) pie

Prep time: 20 minutes
Cook time: 5 minutes
Chill time: 2 hours

Banana Chocolate Cream Pie

Chocolate Ribbon Peanut Butter Pie

4 cups Rice CHEX® Brand Cereal, crushed to 1½ cups
6 tablespoons margarine or butter, melted
¾ cup sugar, divided
8 ounces cream cheese, softened
½ cup peanut butter
1 container (8 ounces) frozen non-dairy whipped topping, thawed and divided
2 tablespoons chocolate ice cream topping
2 tablespoons chopped peanuts

Preheat oven to 350°F. In medium bowl, combine cereal, margarine and ¼ cup sugar; mix well. Press onto bottom and up side of ungreased 9-inch pie plate. Bake 8 to 10 minutes or until lightly browned. Cool completely.

In medium bowl, beat cream cheese, peanut butter, remaining ½ cup sugar and ½ cup whipped topping until smooth. Fold in remaining whipped topping until well blended. Pour into cooled crust. Spoon chocolate topping over filling; swirl with knife. Sprinkle with nuts. Chill 2 hours or until set.   *Makes 1 (9-inch) pie*

Microwave: Prepare crust as directed *except* press cereal mixture onto bottom and up side of ungreased microwave-safe 9-inch pie plate. Microwave on HIGH 2 to 2½ minutes, turning pie plate ¼-turn after 1 minute. Cool completely. Prepare remaining pie as directed.

Chocolate Cream Pie

6 squares BAKER'S® Semi-Sweet Chocolate
½ cup corn syrup
1½ cups heavy cream
1 teaspoon vanilla
   Chocolate Nut Crust (page 148)
   Chocolate shavings (optional)
   Sliced strawberries (optional)

- Microwave chocolate, corn syrup and ½ cup of the cream in large microwavable bowl on HIGH 2 minutes. *Stir until chocolate is completely melted.* Stir in vanilla. Cool to room temperature.

- Beat the remaining 1 cup cream until soft peaks form. Gently stir in chocolate mixture. Spoon into Chocolate Nut Crust. Refrigerate until firm, about 4 hours. Garnish with additional whipped cream, chocolate shavings and strawberries, if desired.

Makes 8 servings

Prep time: 30 minutes
Chill time: 4 hours

Chocolate Cream Strawberry Tart

Tart Shell
   Pastry for 1-crust 9-inch pie

Pastry Cream
   ¼ cup sugar
   3 tablespoons all-purpose flour
   ¼ teaspoon salt
   1 cup milk
   4 egg yolks
   1 cup (6-ounce package) NESTLÉ® Toll House® Semi-Sweet Chocolate Morsels
   2 tablespoons butter
   2 teaspoons vanilla extract
   2 pints strawberries, washed and hulled
   2 tablespoons strawberry jelly

Chocolate Cream Strawberry Tart

Tart Shell: Preheat oven to 425°F. Fit pastry into 9-inch tart pan with removable bottom. Press pastry firmly into bottom and side of pan; trim edges. Line with foil; weight with dried beans. Bake 10 minutes. Remove foil and beans; bake additional 2 to 3 minutes. Cool completely. Remove tart shell from pan.

Pastry Cream: In medium saucepan, combine sugar, flour, and salt. Gradually add milk. Cook over low heat, stirring constantly, until mixture *boils. Boil 2 minutes*, stirring constantly; remove from heat. Beat in egg yolks; return to heat and cook 1 minute longer. Remove from heat. Add Nestlé® Toll House® Semi-Sweet Chocolate Morsels, butter, and vanilla. Stir until morsels are melted and mixture is smooth. Place plastic wrap on surface of Pastry Cream. Chill 30 minutes. Stir; spread evenly into baked Tart Shell. Arrange strawberries on top. In small saucepan over low heat, melt strawberry jelly. Brush over strawberries. Chill several hours. Let stand at room temperature 15 minutes before serving.

Makes 1 (9-inch) tart

Decadent Pie

¾ cup packed brown sugar
¾ cup corn syrup
4 squares BAKER'S® Semi-Sweet
    Chocolate
6 tablespoons margarine or butter
3 eggs
1⅓ cups BAKER'S® ANGEL FLAKE®
    Coconut
1 cup chopped pecans
1 unbaked (9-inch) pie shell
1¾ cups (4 ounces) thawed COOL
    WHIP® Whipped Topping
1 tablespoon bourbon (optional)
    Chocolate shavings (optional)

- Heat oven to 350°F.

- Microwave brown sugar and corn syrup in large microwavable bowl on HIGH 4 minutes or until boiling. Add chocolate and margarine. *Stir until chocolate is completely melted.* Cool slightly.

- Add eggs, one at a time, beating well after each addition. Stir in coconut and pecans. Pour into pie shell.

- Bake 1 hour or until knife inserted 1 inch from center comes out clean. Cool on wire rack.

- Combine whipped topping and bourbon; spoon or pipe onto pie. Garnish with chocolate shavings.

Makes 1 (9-inch) pie

Prep time: 20 minutes
Baking time: 1 hour

Chocolate Coconut Marshmallow Pie

Crust
2 cups BAKER'S® ANGEL FLAKE®
    Coconut
½ cup chopped pecans
¼ cup (½ stick) margarine or butter,
    melted

Filling
4 squares BAKER'S® Semi-Sweet
    Chocolate
2 cups KRAFT® Miniature
    Marshmallows
½ cup milk
1 package (3 ounces) PHILADELPHIA
    BRAND® Cream Cheese, softened
3½ cups (8 ounces) thawed COOL
    WHIP® Whipped Topping
    Chocolate curls (optional)

- Heat oven to 350°F.

- Mix coconut, pecans and margarine in 9-inch pie plate; press onto bottom and up side of pie plate. Bake 20 minutes or until lightly browned. Cool.

- Microwave chocolate, marshmallows and milk in large microwavable bowl on HIGH 3 minutes or until marshmallows are melted. *Stir until chocolate is completely melted.*

- Beat in cream cheese until smooth. Refrigerate until slightly thickened. Gently stir in whipped topping. Spoon into crust. Refrigerate until firm, about 3 hours. Garnish with chocolate curls. Before cutting, dip bottom of pie plate briefly in hot water to loosen crust.

Makes 1 (9-inch) pie

Prep time: 30 minutes
Baking time: 20 minutes
Chill time: 3 hours

Top to bottom: Decadent Pie, Chocolate Coconut Marshmallow Pie, Chocolate Cream Pie (page 143)

Jubilee Pie

3 eggs
1 cup milk
½ cup buttermilk baking mix
½ cup KARO® Light or Dark Corn
   Syrup
¼ cup MAZOLA® Margarine, softened
1 cup (6 ounces) semisweet chocolate
   chips, melted
1 can (21 ounces) cherry pie filling
¼ teaspoon almond extract
1 cup heavy cream, whipped
   Chocolate curls (optional)

Preheat oven to 350°F. Grease 9-inch pie
plate. In food processor or blender, beat
eggs, milk, baking mix, corn syrup,
margarine and melted chocolate 1 minute.
Pour into prepared pie plate; let stand 5
minutes. Bake 35 to 40 minutes or until
filling is puffed and set. Cool on wire rack
1 hour; center will fall, forming a well.
While pie bakes, mix cherry pie filling and
almond extract; refrigerate. Fill center of
cooled pie with cherry mixture. Refrigerate
at least 1 hour. Before serving, pipe or
swirl whipped cream around edge.
Garnish with chocolate curls.

Makes 1 (9-inch) pie

Prep Time: 20 minutes
Bake Time: 40 minutes, plus cooling and
chilling

Jubilee Pie

Chocolate On Chocolate Pie

Chocolate Crumb Crust
   (recipe follows)
⅓ cup granulated sugar
⅓ cup ARGO® or KINGSFORD'S®
   Corn Starch
⅛ teaspoon salt
3 cups half-and-half
8 squares (1 ounce *each*) semisweet
   chocolate, divided
1½ teaspoons vanilla extract, divided
1 cup heavy cream, divided
3 tablespoons powdered sugar
   Chocolate curls (optional)

Prepare Chocolate Crumb Crust. In
2-quart saucepan, combine granulated
sugar, corn starch and salt. Gradually
stir in half-and-half until smooth. Add
6 squares chocolate. Stirring constantly,
bring to a boil over medium heat; boil 1
minute. Remove from heat. Stir in 1
teaspoon vanilla. Pour into chilled
Chocolate Crumb Crust. Cover with
plastic wrap; refrigerate at least 2 hours or
until set. In small saucepan, melt
remaining 2 squares chocolate with ¼ cup
heavy cream. Pour into small bowl; stir in
remaining ¾ cup heavy cream, powdered
sugar and remaining ½ teaspoon vanilla
until smooth. Chill at least 2 hours. Beat
chilled chocolate cream mixture until stiff;
spread over filling. Top with chocolate
curls.   *Makes 1 (9-inch) pie*

Chocolate Crumb Crust: In small bowl,
combine 1¾ cups chocolate cookie
crumbs, 3 tablespoons granulated sugar
and ½ cup melted MAZOLA® Margarine
until well mixed. Press evenly into 9-inch
pie plate; chill until firm.

Chocolate Mudslide Pie

4 foil-wrapped bars (8-ounce package)
　　NESTLÉ® Semi-Sweet Chocolate
　　Baking Bars, broken up
1 teaspoon TASTER'S CHOICE®
　　Freeze-Dried Instant Coffee
1 teaspoon water
¾ cup sour cream
½ cup granulated sugar
1 teaspoon vanilla extract
1 (9-inch) prepared chocolate cookie
　　crumb crust
1 cup confectioners' sugar
¼ cup NESTLÉ® Cocoa
1½ cups heavy or whipping cream
2 tablespoons NESTLÉ® Toll House®
　　Semi-Sweet Chocolate Mini
　　Morsels

In small saucepan over low heat, melt
Nestlé® Semi-Sweet Chocolate Baking
Bars; cool 10 minutes. In small bowl,
dissolve instant coffee in water. Add sour
cream, granulated sugar, and vanilla; stir
until sugar dissolves. Blend in melted
chocolate. Spread in prepared crust;
set aside.

In small mixer bowl, beat confectioners'
sugar, Nestlé® Cocoa, and heavy cream
until stiff peaks form. Spoon cream
mixture into pastry bag fitted with star tip;
pipe onto pie. Sprinkle with Nestlé® Toll
House® Semi-Sweet Chocolate Mini
Morsels. Cover; refrigerate at least 4 hours
until firm.　　　　　*Makes 1 (9-inch) pie*

Chocolate Velvet Pie

Chocolate Velvet Pie

1 unbaked (9-inch) pie shell, pricked
2 (1-ounce) bars unsweetened baking
　　chocolate
1 (14-ounce) can EAGLE® Brand
　　Sweetened Condensed Milk
　　(NOT evaporated milk)
2 eggs, well beaten
1 cup water
2 teaspoons vanilla extract
　　Whipped cream or whipped topping

Preheat oven to 400°F. Bake pie shell 15
minutes. Meanwhile, in heavy saucepan
over medium heat, melt chocolate with
sweetened condensed milk; remove from
heat. Stir in eggs. Add water and vanilla;
mix well. Pour into *hot* pastry shell. Bake
10 minutes. *Reduce oven temperature to
300°F;* bake 20 minutes longer or until
center is set. Cool. Chill thoroughly. Top
with whipped cream. Garnish as desired.
Refrigerate leftovers.

Makes 1 (9-inch) pie

Chocolate Peanut Crunch Pie

4 cups Corn CHEX® Brand Cereal,
    crushed to 1 cup
¼ cup packed brown sugar
⅓ cup chopped salted peanuts
⅓ cup margarine or butter, melted
1½ cups milk
1 package (4½ ounces) chocolate instant
    pudding and pie filling
1 cup dairy sour cream

Preheat oven to 300°F. Grease 9-inch pie plate. Combine cereal, brown sugar and peanuts. Add margarine; mix thoroughly. Press evenly onto bottom and up side of prepared pie plate. Bake 10 minutes. Cool completely. In large mixing bowl, combine milk and pudding. Beat slowly on low speed of electric mixer about 1 minute. Beat in sour cream just until blended. Pour filling into crust. Chill about 1 hour or until set. Garnish as desired.

Makes 1 (9-inch) pie

Chocolate Nut Crust

6 squares BAKER'S® Semi-Sweet
    Chocolate
1 tablespoon margarine or butter
1½ cups toasted finely chopped nuts

- **Microwave Directions:** Line 9-inch pie plate with foil.

- Microwave chocolate and margarine in large microwavable bowl on HIGH 2 minutes or until margarine is melted. *Stir until chocolate is completely melted.*

- Stir in nuts. Press mixture onto bottom and up side of prepared pie plate. Refrigerate until firm, about 1 hour.

Remove crust from pie plate; peel off foil. Return crust to pie plate or place on serving plate. Refrigerate.

Makes 1 (9-inch) crust

Prep time: 15 minutes
Chill time: 1 hour

Toll House® Derby Pie

2 eggs
½ cup all-purpose flour
½ cup granulated sugar
½ cup packed brown sugar
1 cup butter, melted and cooled to
    room temperature
1 cup (6-ounce package) NESTLÉ®
    Toll House® Semi-Sweet Chocolate
    Morsels
1 cup chopped walnuts
1 unbaked (9-inch) pie shell*
    Whipped cream *or* ice cream
    (optional)

Preheat oven to 325°F. In large bowl, beat eggs until foamy. Add flour and sugars; beat until well blended. Blend in melted butter. Stir in Nestlé® Toll House® Semi-Sweet Chocolate Morsels and walnuts. Pour into pie shell. Bake 1 hour. Serve warm with whipped cream.

Makes 1 (9-inch) pie

*If using frozen pie shell, use deep dish style, thawed. Place on cookie sheet and bake additional 10 minutes.

Tip: Recipe may be doubled. Bake two pies; freeze one for later use.

Brownie Pudding Pizza

Brownie Pudding Pizza

1 package (10½ ounces) microwave
    brownie mix (*plus* ingredients to
    prepare mix)
1¼ cups cold milk
1 package (4-serving size) JELL-O®
    Instant Pudding, any flavor
1 cup thawed COOL WHIP® Whipped
    Topping
2 cups cut-up fruit

- **Microwave Directions:** Prepare brownie mix in medium bowl as package directs. Pour mixture into 9-inch microwavable pie plate. Microwave as package directs for 9-inch square pan. Cool.

- Pour cold milk into small bowl. Add pudding mix. Beat with wire whisk until well blended, about 2 minutes. Let pudding stand 5 minutes.

- Gently stir whipped topping into pudding with rubber spatula until mixture is blended. Refrigerate until serving time. Just before serving, spoon pudding mixture over brownie crust, spreading with back of spoon to cover evenly.

- Cut into wedges. Top each wedge with fruit.   *Makes 1 (9-inch) pie*

Top to bottom: Microwave Hershey® Bar Pie, Creme de Cacao Pie

Creme de Cacao Pie

1 envelope unflavored gelatin
½ cup cold milk
¼ cup butter or margarine
⅔ cup sugar, divided
6 tablespoons HERSHEY'S Cocoa
3 eggs, separated
¼ cup creme de cacao
1 baked (9-inch) pie crust

In small bowl, sprinkle gelatin over milk; let stand 5 minutes to soften. In medium saucepan over low heat, melt butter; remove from heat. Stir in ⅓ cup sugar and cocoa. Add gelatin mixture; blend well. Slightly beat egg yolks; stir into chocolate mixture. Cook over medium heat, stirring constantly, until mixture is hot and gelatin is dissolved. *Do not boil.* Remove from heat; stir in creme de cacao. Cool to room temperature, stirring occasionally. In large mixer bowl, beat egg whites until foamy; gradually add remaining ⅓ cup sugar, beating until stiff peaks form. Fold in chocolate mixture; pour into pie crust. Cover; chill about 4 hours or until set.

Makes 1 (9-inch) pie

Microwave Hershey® Bar Pie

Chocolate Crumb Crust
(recipe follows)
1 HERSHEY'S Milk Chocolate Bar
(8 ounces), broken into pieces
⅓ cup milk
1½ cups miniature marshmallows
1 cup heavy or whipping cream
Sweetened whipped cream
Chilled cherry pie filling

Prepare Chocolate Crumb Crust; set aside. Combine chocolate bar pieces, milk and miniature marshmallows in medium micro-proof bowl. Microwave at HIGH (100%) 1½ to 2½ minutes or until chocolate is softened and mixture is melted and smooth when stirred. Cool completely.

Whip cream until stiff; fold into chocolate mixture. Spoon into crust. Cover; chill several hours or until firm. Garnish with sweetened whipped cream; serve with chilled cherry pie filling.

Makes 1 (9-inch) pie

Chocolate Crumb Crust: Grease micro-proof 9-inch pie plate. In small micro-proof bowl, microwave ½ cup butter or margarine at HIGH (100%) 1 minute or until melted. Stir in 1½ cups graham cracker crumbs, 6 tablespoons HERSHEY'S Cocoa and ⅓ cup confectioners' sugar. Press onto bottom and up side of prepared pie plate. Microwave an additional 1 to 1½ minutes until bubbly. *Do not overcook.* Cool completely before filling.

Sweet'sa Pizza

¼ cup (½ stick) margarine or butter
4½ cups miniature marshmallows
5 cups Rice CHEX® Brand Cereal
½ cup semisweet chocolate pieces, melted
½ cup peanut butter pieces
½ cup chopped walnuts
6 maraschino cherries, halved

Line baking sheet with waxed paper. In large saucepan, melt margarine over low heat. Add marshmallows and heat, stirring constantly, until marshmallows are melted. Gradually add cereal, stirring until cereal pieces are evenly coated. With buttered hands, press mixture into 12-inch circle on waxed paper. Spread chocolate onto crust to within 1 inch of edge. Top with peanut butter pieces, nuts and cherries. When cooled, cut into wedges.

Makes 1 (12-inch) pizza

Mocha Walnut Tart

2 (1-ounce) squares unsweetened chocolate
¼ cup margarine or butter
1 (14-ounce) can EAGLE® Brand Sweetened Condensed Milk (NOT evaporated milk)
¼ cup water
2 eggs, well beaten
¼ cup coffee-flavored liqueur
1 teaspoon vanilla extract
⅛ teaspoon salt
1 unbaked (9-inch) pie shell
1 cup walnuts, toasted and chopped

Preheat oven to 350°F. In medium saucepan over low heat, melt chocolate and margarine. Stir in sweetened condensed milk, water and eggs; *mix well.*

Remove from heat; stir in liqueur, vanilla and salt. Pour into pie shell; top with walnuts. Bake 40 to 45 minutes or until center is set. Cool. Serve warm or chilled. Garnish as desired. Refrigerate leftovers.

Makes 1 (9-inch) pie

Elegant Raspberry Chocolate Pie

1 package (4-serving size) JELL-O® Brand Gelatin, Raspberry Flavor
1¼ cups boiling water
1 pint vanilla ice cream, softened
1 (8- or 9-inch) prepared chocolate cookie crumb crust
3 tablespoons PARKAY® Margarine
2 squares BAKER'S® Semi-Sweet Chocolate
Thawed COOL WHIP® Whipped Topping (optional)
Raspberries (optional)

- Dissolve gelatin in boiling water. Spoon in ice cream, stirring until melted and smooth. Chill until slightly thickened, about 10 minutes. Pour into prepared crust. Chill until firm, about 2 hours.

- Melt margarine with chocolate; cool. Spread over pie. Chill until chocolate mixture hardens. Garnish with whipped topping and raspberries.

Makes 1 (8- or 9-inch) pie

Prep time: 15 minutes
Chill time: 2½ hours

Note: For ease in serving, let pie stand 5 minutes after spreading on chocolate. With knife, lightly score pie into serving-size pieces. Chill as directed.

FROM THE FREEZER

◆

Ice Cream Shop Pies

1½ cups cold half and half or milk
1 package (4-serving size) JELL-O®
    Instant Pudding and Pie Filling,
    any flavor
3½ cups (8 ounces) thawed COOL
    WHIP® Non-Dairy Whipped
    Topping
    Ice Cream Shop Ingredients*
1 packaged chocolate cookie, graham
    cracker or vanilla wafer crumb
    crust

- Pour half and half into large bowl. Add pudding mix. Beat with wire whisk until well blended, 1 to 2 minutes. Let stand 5 minutes or until slightly thickened.

- Fold whipped topping and desired Ice Cream Shop ingredients into pudding mixture. Spoon into crust.

- Freeze pie until firm, about 6 hours or overnight. Remove from freezer. Let stand at room temperature about 10 minutes before serving. Store any leftover pie in freezer.

Makes 1 (8-inch) pie

Prep time: 15 minutes
Freezing time: 6 hours

*Rocky Road Pie: Use chocolate flavor pudding mix and chocolate cookie crumb crust. Fold ½ cup *each* BAKER'S® Semi-Sweet Real Chocolate Chips, KRAFT® Miniature Marshmallows and chopped nuts into whipped topping. Serve with chocolate sauce, if desired.

*Toffee Bar Crunch Pie: Use French vanilla or vanilla flavor pudding mix and graham cracker crumb crust, spreading ⅓ cup butterscotch sauce onto bottom of crust before filling. Fold 1 cup chopped chocolate-covered English toffee bars (about 6 bars) into whipped topping. Garnish with additional chopped toffee bars, if desired.

*Strawberry Banana Split Pie: Use French vanilla or vanilla flavor pudding mix. Reduce half and half to ¾ cup and add with ¾ cup pureed BIRDS EYE® Quick Thaw Strawberries. Use vanilla wafer crumb crust; line bottom with banana slices. Garnish with whipped topping, maraschino cherries and chopped nuts. Serve with remaining strawberries, pureed, if desired.

*Chocolate Cookie Pie: Use French vanilla or vanilla flavor pudding mix and chocolate cookie crumb crust. Fold 1 cup chopped chocolate sandwich cookies into whipped topping.

Top to bottom: Rocky Road Pie, Toffee Bar Crunch Pie, Strawberry Banana Split Pie

Kahlúa® Cappuccino Almond Pie

Kahlúa® Cappuccino Almond Pie

1 (9-inch) prepared chocolate cookie or graham cracker crumb crust
1 teaspoon espresso instant coffee powder
6 tablespoons KAHLÚA®, divided
2 cups French vanilla or vanilla ice cream, softened
2 cups mocha almond fudge ice cream, softened
3 cups dairy whipped topping
¼ cup toasted sliced almonds
Heavenly Kahlúa® Fudge Sauce (recipe follows) (optional)

Place crust in freezer. Stir coffee powder and 2 tablespoons Kahlúa® into vanilla ice cream until well blended. Remove crust from freezer. Spoon ice cream

mixture into crust; freeze until firm. Stir 2 tablespoons Kahlúa® into mocha almond fudge ice cream; spoon over vanilla layer. Freeze until firm. When ready to serve, stir remaining 2 tablespoons Kahlúa® into whipped topping until blended; spread over top of pie. Sprinkle pie with almonds. Serve with Heavenly Kahlúa® Fudge Sauce. Freeze leftovers. *Makes 1 (9-inch) pie*

Heavenly Kahlúa® Fudge Sauce

1 (16-ounce) can chocolate fudge topping
¼ cup KAHLÚA®

In saucepan (or microwave-proof bowl), heat fudge topping (or microwave on High) until melted; stir in Kahlúa®. Serve warm. To store, cover and refrigerate; reheat as needed. Makes 1⅔ cups.

Blackberry Ice Cream Pie

Crust
9-inch Classic Crisco® Single Crust (pages 6 and 7)
Filling
1 package (3 ounces) peach or berry flavor gelatin (not sugar free)
1 cup boiling water
1 pint vanilla ice cream, softened
1¾ cups fresh or frozen dry pack blackberries, partially thawed

1. For Crust, prepare and bake 9-inch Classic Crisco® Single Crust; cool.

2. For Filling, combine gelatin and water in large bowl. Stir until dissolved. Cut ice cream into small chunks. Add to gelatin mixture, one spoonful at a time. Blend with wire whisk after each addition.

3. Carefully dry blackberries between paper towels. Fold into gelatin mixture. Spoon into cooled baked pie crust. Refrigerate or freeze several hours before serving. *Makes 1 (9-inch) pie*

White Chocolate Mousse Pie

1¼ cups chocolate wafer crumbs
    (about 32 chocolate wafers)
¼ cup ground pecans
5 tablespoons butter or margarine,
    melted
9 ounces white chocolate, coarsely
    chopped
⅓ cup milk
1 cup heavy cream
1 tablespoon white crème de cacao
2 egg whites
1 can SOLO® *or* 1 jar BAKER®
    Raspberry Filling
Grated white or dark chocolate *or*
    chocolate leaves or curls for
    garnish

Preheat oven to 350°F. Grease 9-inch pie plate and set aside. Combine chocolate wafer crumbs and ground pecans in bowl. Add melted butter; stir until well blended. Press crumb mixture onto bottom and up side of prepared pie plate. Bake 8 to 10 minutes. Cool completely on wire rack.

Place chocolate and milk in top of double boiler set over (not in) pan of barely simmering water. Cook, stirring constantly, until chocolate is melted and mixture is smooth. Pour chocolate into large bowl; set aside to cool to room temperature. Whip cream with electric mixer until soft peaks form. Add crème de cacao; whip until firm. Spoon 2 to 3 tablespoons whipped cream mixture over cooled chocolate; stir well to lighten chocolate. Fold in remaining whipped cream. Beat egg whites in clean bowl with electric mixer until stiff peaks form. Fold beaten egg whites into chocolate mixture.

Spoon three fourths of the raspberry filling into cooled crust. Spoon chocolate mousse over filling. Refrigerate 30 minutes. Spoon remaining raspberry filling around edge of pie. Decorate top of pie with desired chocolate garnish. Freeze 2 hours or overnight.

Makes 1 (9-inch) pie

Rapid Raspberry Pie

1 quart premium vanilla ice cream,
    slightly softened
1 pint premium raspberry sherbet,
    slightly softened
¼ cup raspberry liqueur (framboise) *or*
    thawed, undiluted raspberry-juice
    concentrate *or* thawed, undiluted
    cranberry-raspberry juice
    concentrate
1 KEEBLER® Ready-Crust
    Chocolate Flavored Pie Crust
    (reserve plastic lid)
1 cup fresh or frozen dry-pack
    raspberries, fresh mint leaves or
    chocolate curls for garnish

In large bowl (preferably with an electric mixer), mix ice cream, sherbet and liqueur until blended.

Scrape into pie crust. Smooth top with spatula; cover pie with reserved lid and freeze at least 1 hour or until firm *or* wrap airtight, then label and freeze up to 1 month.

Remove from freezer 15 minutes before serving to soften slightly. Garnish with raspberries, mint leaves or chocolate curls.

Makes 1 (8-inch) pie

Rapid Raspberry Pie

Frozen Black Bottom Pie

1 cup Regal Chocolate Sauce (recipe
   follows)
1 baked Chocolate Crumb Crust
   (page 129)
1 quart ice cream, any flavor, softened

- Pour ¾ cup Regal Chocolate Sauce into
Chocolate Crumb Crust, spreading
lightly to cover bottom and side of crust.
Refrigerate until set. Fill crust with ice
cream. Freeze until firm, about 2 hours.
Let stand at room temperature about 10
minutes before serving. Top with
remaining ¼ cup Regal Chocolate Sauce.
Makes 1 (9-inch) pie

Total prep time: 30 minutes
Freezing time: 2 hours

Regal Chocolate Sauce

2 squares BAKER'S® Unsweetened
   Chocolate
⅓ cup water
½ cup sugar
3 tablespoons margarine or butter
¼ teaspoon vanilla extract

Frozen Black Bottom Pie

Microwave Directions: Microwave
chocolate and water in microwavable bowl
on HIGH 1½ minutes. *Stir until chocolate is
completely melted.* Stir in sugar. Microwave
1 minute. Stir. Microwave 2 minutes
longer; stir in margarine and vanilla.
Makes about 1 cup.

Saucepan preparation: Heat chocolate
and water in saucepan over low heat,
stirring constantly, until chocolate is
melted and mixture is smooth. Add sugar;
bring to a boil. Boil 2 to 3 minutes or until
slightly thickened, stirring constantly.
Remove from heat; stir in margarine and
vanilla.

Orange-Chocolate Sauce: Prepare Regal
Chocolate Sauce as directed, substituting
1 tablespoon orange liqueur for vanilla
extract.

Chocolate Fudge Mint Pie

5 cups vanilla ice cream, softened
1 cup MRS. RICHARDSON'S® Hot
   Fudge Topping
36 chocolate-covered thin mint cookies,
   coarsely crushed
½ cup MRS. RICHARDSON'S® Hot
   Fudge Topping, warmed
1 (9-inch) prepared graham cracker
   crumb crust
   Whipped cream and additional
   chocolate-covered thin mint
   cookies (optional)

In mixing bowl on low speed, combine
softened ice cream, 1 cup hot fudge
topping and crushed cookies until
blended. Freeze until slushy, about 1 hour.
Spread ½ cup *warmed* hot fudge topping
evenly onto bottom of crumb crust. Spoon
slushy ice cream mixture into pie shell,
mounding mixture in center. Freeze at
least 3 hours. To serve, let pie stand at
room temperature 10 minutes before
cutting into wedges. Garnish with
whipped cream and additional cookies.
Makes 1 (9-inch) pie

Oreo® Mud Pie

26 OREO® Chocolate Sandwich
    Cookies, finely rolled
    (about 2 cups crumbs)
¼ cup BLUE BONNET® Margarine,
    melted
1 quart coffee ice cream, softened
1½ cups chocolate fudge sauce
    Prepared whipped topping for
    garnish

In small bowl, combine cookie crumbs
and margarine. Press onto bottom and up
side of 9-inch pie plate.

Spread softened ice cream into prepared
crust. Top with fudge sauce. Freeze 6
hours or until firm.

To serve, garnish pie with whipped
topping; cut into wedges.

Makes 1 (9-inch) pie

Frosty Pumpkin Pie

1 (12-ounce) container non-dairy
    whipped topping, thawed, divided
1 cup canned solid-pack pumpkin
½ cup KRETSCHMER® Wheat Germ
½ cup packed brown sugar
½ teaspoon ground cinnamon
½ teaspoon ground nutmeg
¼ teaspoon ground ginger
1 (9-inch) prepared graham cracker
    crumb crust

Combine 3½ cups whipped topping,
pumpkin, wheat germ, sugar and spices;
mix well. Pour into crumb crust. Freeze 2
hours or until firm. Let stand 10 to 15
minutes before cutting into wedges. Serve
with remaining whipped topping; sprinkle
with additional Kretschmer Wheat Germ,
if desired.   *Makes 1 (9-inch) pie*

Green Mountain Pie in Chewy Crust

Crust
1¾ cups soft macaroon crumbs (about
    seven 2-inch macaroons crumbled
    with fingers)
¼ cup BUTTER FLAVOR CRISCO®,
    melted

Filling
2 pints lime sherbet, softened, divided
1 quart vanilla ice cream, softened
1½ cups soft macaroon crumbs

1. For Crust, preheat oven to 350°F.
Lightly grease 9-inch pie plate.

2. Combine 1¾ cups crumbs and melted
Butter Flavor Crisco®. Press into greased
pie plate.

3. Bake at 350°F for 10 minutes. Cool
completely before filling.

4. For Filling, spread 1 pint sherbet in
cooled Crust. Freeze about 1 hour or until
firm.

5. Combine ice cream and 1½ cups
crumbs. Spread evenly over sherbet.
Freeze about 1 hour or until firm.

6. Spread remaining 1 pint sherbet over
ice cream mixture. Freeze several hours.
Remove from freezer 10 to 15 minutes
before cutting into wedges.

Makes 1 (9-inch) pie

Patriotic Pie

Crust
    1 package DUNCAN HINES®
        Blueberry Muffin Mix, separated
¼ cup butter or margarine

Filling
    1 quart vanilla ice cream, softened*
½ cup crumb mixture, reserved from
        Crust

Topping
    Can of blueberries from Mix
    1 pint fresh strawberries, rinsed,
        drained and sliced
    2 tablespoons sugar (optional)

1. Preheat oven to 400°F. Grease 9-inch pie plate.

2. For Crust, place muffin mix and butter in medium bowl. Cut in butter with pastry blender or two knives until mixture is crumbly. Spread evenly in ungreased 9-inch square baking pan. *Do not press.* Bake at 400°F for 10 to 12 minutes. Stir with fork to break into small crumbs. Cool slightly. Reserve ½ cup crumbs for Filling. Press remaining crumbs onto bottom and up side of prepared pie plate to form crust. Cool completely.

3. For Filling, spread softened ice cream over crust. Sprinkle with reserved crumbs. Freeze several hours or until firm.

4. For Topping, rinse blueberries from Mix with cold water and drain. Combine strawberries and sugar, if desired.

5. To serve, let pie stand 5 minutes at room temperature. Top with blueberries and strawberries. Cut into 8 wedges using sharp knife.   *Makes 8 servings*

*Ice cream can be softened by allowing to stand at room temperature 15 minutes or placing in refrigerator 30 minutes.

Lemonade Stand Pie

    1 can (6 ounces) frozen concentrated
        lemonade or pink lemonade,
        partially thawed
    1 pint vanilla ice cream, softened
3½ cups (8 ounces) thawed COOL
        WHIP® Non-Dairy Whipped
        Topping
    1 (9-inch) prepared graham cracker
        crumb crust
    Strawberries

- Place concentrate in large mixer bowl; beat about 30 seconds. Gradually spoon in ice cream and blend. Fold in whipped topping until smooth. Freeze, if necessary, until mixture mounds. Spoon into crust. Freeze until firm, at least 4 hours.

- Let stand at room temperature or in refrigerator until pie can be easily cut, about 30 minutes. Garnish with strawberries.   *Makes 1 (9-inch) pie*

Frozen Pumpkin Cream Pie

    1 cup canned pumpkin
⅔ cup KARO® Light or Dark Corn
        Syrup
½ cup coarsely chopped walnuts
½ teaspoon ground cinnamon
¼ teaspoon ground nutmeg
¼ teaspoon ground cloves
    2 cups thawed frozen whipped topping
    1 (8- or 9-inch) prepared graham
        cracker crumb crust

In medium bowl, combine pumpkin, corn syrup, nuts, cinnamon, nutmeg and cloves. Fold in whipped topping. Spoon into prepared crust. Cover; freeze 3 to 4 hours or until firm. Let stand 15 minutes before serving.   *Makes 1 (8- or 9-inch) pie*

Patriotic Pie

Banana Split Pie

20 chocolate sandwich cookies
¼ cup margarine, melted
2 firm, medium DOLE® Bananas,
     peeled, sliced
1 quart strawberry ice cream, softened
1 can (20 ounces) DOLE® Crushed
     Pineapple in Juice, drained
1 cup whipping cream, whipped
¼ cup chopped nuts
     Maraschino cherry (optional)

• Preheat oven to 350°F. Pulverize cookies
  in food processor or blender. Add melted
  margarine. Process until blended. Press
  into 9-inch pie plate.

• Bake 5 minutes. Cool.

• Arrange sliced bananas over crust.
  Spread ice cream over bananas. Add
  pineapple. Cover pie with whipped
  cream. Sprinkle with nuts. Freeze 4
  hours or until firm. Remove from freezer
  30 minutes before cutting. Garnish with
  maraschino cherry.

Makes 1 (9-inch) pie

Prep time: 20 minutes
Baking time: 5 minutes
Freezing time: 4 hours

Kahlúa® Baked Alaska Pie

1 baked (9-inch) pie crust
4 tablespoons KAHLUA®, divided
1½ cups chocolate ice cream, softened
1½ cups strawberry or cherry ice cream,
     softened
1½ cups cookies 'n' cream or chocolate
     chip ice cream, softened
3 egg whites
⅛ teaspoon cream of tartar
⅓ cup sugar
     Heavenly Kahlúa® Fudge Sauce
     (page 154)

Place pie crust in freezer. Stir 2
tablespoons Kahlúa® into chocolate ice
cream until blended. Spoon into crust;
freeze until firm. Spread softened
strawberry ice cream over chocolate layer;
freeze until firm. Stir remaining 2
tablespoons Kahlúa® into cookies 'n'
cream ice cream; spoon over strawberry
layer. Freeze until firm. (Pie may be
covered and frozen up to 1 month before
serving.)

About 15 minutes before serving time,
preheat oven to 500°F. In large mixer
bowl, beat egg whites and cream of tartar
on high speed of electric mixer until soft
peaks form; gradually beat in sugar until
stiff peaks form and sugar is dissolved.
Spread over top of pie, sealing meringue
carefully to crust edge. Bake 2 to 3
minutes or until light golden brown. Serve
pie immediately with Heavenly Kahlúa®
Fudge Sauce.   *Makes 1 (9-inch) pie*

Frozen Lemon Satin Pie

1 (8-ounce) package cream cheese,
   softened
1 (14-ounce) can EAGLE® Brand
   Sweetened Condensed Milk
   (NOT evaporated milk)
½ cup cold water
¼ cup REALEMON® Lemon Juice from
   Concentrate
1 (4-serving size) package *instant*
   lemon flavor pudding mix
   Yellow food color (optional)
1 cup (½-pint) BORDEN® or
   MEADOW GOLD® Whipping
   Cream, whipped
1 (9-inch) graham cracker crumb crust
   or 1 baked (9-inch) pie crust
   Golden Lemon Sauce (recipe follows)

In large mixer bowl, beat cheese until
fluffy. Gradually beat in sweetened
condensed milk until smooth. Add water,
ReaLemon® brand, pudding mix and food
coloring; mix well. Chill 15 minutes. Fold
in whipped cream. Pour into prepared
crust. Freeze 6 hours or until firm. Serve
with Golden Lemon Sauce. Freeze leftover
pie.   *Makes 1 (9-inch) pie*

Golden Lemon Sauce: In heavy saucepan,
combine ⅓ cup sugar, 1 tablespoon
cornstarch and dash salt. Add ½ cup
water, ¼ cup ReaLemon® brand and 1 egg
yolk; mix well. Over medium heat, cook
and stir until thickened and bubbly.
Remove from heat; add 1 tablespoon
margarine or butter and yellow food
coloring. Stir until well blended. Cool
slightly. Serve warm. Makes about 1 cup.

Cool 'n Creamy Chocolate Pie

Cool 'n Creamy Chocolate Pie

1 package (3 ounces) cream cheese,
   softened
¼ cup sugar
1 teaspoon vanilla extract
½ cup HERSHEY'S Syrup
1 cup (½ pint) cold whipping cream
1 (8-inch) prepared crumb crust (any
   variety)
   Sliced fresh fruit (optional)
   Chocolate curls (optional)

In small mixer bowl, beat cream cheese,
sugar and vanilla until well blended.
Gradually add syrup, beating until
smooth. In small mixer bowl, beat
whipping cream until stiff. Carefully fold
into chocolate mixture. Pour into crust.
Cover; freeze until firm. Just before
serving, garnish with fresh fruit and
chocolate curls, if desired.

Makes 1 (8-inch) pie

Pineapple Apricot Sundae Pie

1 package (8 ounces) cream cheese, softened
1 container (8 ounces) vanilla yogurt
½ cup sugar
1 can SOLO® *or* 1 jar BAKER® Apricot Filling
1 can SOLO® *or* 1 jar BAKER® Pineapple Filling
1 container (8 ounces) frozen nondairy whipped topping, thawed, *or* 1 cup heavy cream, whipped
½ cup SOLO® Toasted Almond Crunch Topping
1 (9-inch) prepared graham cracker or chocolate cookie crumb crust
6 tablespoons chocolate syrup, divided

Beat cream cheese in large bowl with electric mixer until fluffy. Add yogurt and sugar; beat until blended. Stir in apricot and pineapple fillings until well combined. Fold in whipped topping and toasted almond crunch topping. Pour into prepared crust; spoon 4 tablespoons chocolate syrup over top. Swirl syrup lightly through filling with flat-bladed knife. Freeze pie 3 hours.

Drizzle remaining 2 tablespoons chocolate syrup over top of pie in zig-zag pattern. Return to freezer until firm, about 2 hours. Place pie in refrigerator 20 minutes to soften before serving.

Makes 1 (9-inch) pie

Lime Parfait Ice Cream Pie

Coconut Crust (recipe follows) *or* 1 baked (9-inch) pie crust
½ cup butter or margarine
1 cup sugar
½ cup REALIME® Lime Juice from Concentrate
¼ teaspoon salt
3 egg *yolks*
2 eggs
Green food coloring (optional)
1½ quarts BORDEN® or MEADOW GOLD® Vanilla Ice Cream, slightly softened

Prepare crust. In medium saucepan, melt butter. Add sugar, ReaLime® brand and salt; mix well. In small bowl, beat egg *yolks* and eggs; gradually add to lime mixture. Over low heat, cook and stir constantly until smooth and thick; add food coloring. Cool. Spoon half of the sauce into prepared crust. Scoop ice cream into prepared crust; top with remaining sauce and reserved coconut mixture from crust. Freeze 6 hours or until firm. Remove from freezer 10 minutes before serving. Freeze leftovers. *Makes 1 (9-inch) pie*

Coconut Crust: Toast 1 (7-ounce) package flaked coconut (2⅔ cups); combine with ⅓ cup butter or margarine, melted. Reserving 2 tablespoons, press remainder firmly onto bottom and up side to rim of 9-inch pie plate. Chill. Makes one 9-inch crust.

Tip: To toast coconut, spread evenly in shallow pan. Toast in preheated 350°F oven 7 to 15 minutes or until golden, stirring frequently.

Frozen Peach Melba Pie

2 cups *crushed* granola or natural cereal
3 tablespoons flour
3 tablespoons margarine or butter, melted
2 teaspoons ground cinnamon
1 (10-ounce) package frozen red raspberries in syrup, thawed and drained, reserving ⅓ cup syrup
¼ cup BAMA® Red Currant Jelly
1 tablespoon cornstarch
¼ teaspoon almond extract
½ (½-gallon) carton BORDEN® or MEADOW GOLD® Peach Premium Frozen Yogurt, slightly softened

Preheat oven to 375°F. In medium bowl, combine granola, flour, margarine and cinnamon; press onto bottom and up side to rim of 9-inch pie plate to form crust. Bake 8 to 10 minutes. Cool. In small saucepan, combine reserved raspberry syrup, jelly and cornstarch. Over medium heat, cook and stir until slightly thickened and glossy; stir in extract and raspberries. Cool. Scoop yogurt into prepared crust; top with raspberry sauce. Freeze 6 hours or until firm. Remove from freezer 8 to 10 minutes before serving. Garnish as desired. Freeze ungarnished leftovers.

Makes 1 (9-inch) pie

Left to right: Lime Parfait Ice Cream Pie, Frozen Peach Melba Pie

Peanut Candy Bar Pie

Peanut Candy Bar Pie

1 (8-ounce) package cream cheese,
   softened
1 (14-ounce) can EAGLE® Brand
   Sweetened Condensed Milk
   (NOT evaporated milk)
¾ cup creamy peanut butter
1 teaspoon vanilla extract
2 (2-ounce) chocolate-coated peanut
   candy bars, chopped into small
   pieces
1 cup (½ pint) BORDEN® or
   MEADOW GOLD® Whipping
   Cream, whipped
1 baked (9-inch) pie crust
½ to ⅔ cup Hot Fudge Sauce (recipe
   follows) *or* chocolate fudge ice
   cream topping, warmed

In large mixer bowl, beat cheese until
fluffy. Gradually beat in sweetened
condensed milk, then peanut butter and
vanilla until smooth. Stir in candy pieces.
Fold in whipped cream. Pour into
prepared pie crust. Freeze 4 hours or until
firm. Remove from freezer 10 minutes
before serving. Serve with Hot Fudge
Sauce. Garnish with additional candy
pieces, if desired. Freeze leftovers.

Makes 1 (9-inch) pie

Hot Fudge Sauce: In heavy saucepan
over medium heat, melt 1 cup (6 ounces)
semisweet chocolate chips and 2
tablespoons margarine or butter with 1
(14 ounce) can Eagle® Brand Sweetened
Condensed Milk and 2 tablespoons water.
Cook and stir constantly 5 minutes or until
thickened. Add 1 teaspoon vanilla extract.
Serve warm. Refrigerate leftovers. Makes
about 2 cups.

Maple Praline Ice Cream Pie

Crust
   2 cups QUAKER® Oats (quick or old
      fashioned, uncooked)
   ⅔ cup packed brown sugar
   ½ cup toasted chopped pecans
   ¼ cup (½ stick) margarine, melted
   2 egg whites, slightly beaten

Filling
   2 pints vanilla ice cream, softened
   ½ cup AUNT JEMIMA® Syrup, any
      flavor
   ½ cup toasted chopped pecans

Heat oven to 350°F. Lightly grease 9-inch
pie plate. Combine oats, brown sugar,
½ cup pecans, margarine and egg whites;
mix well. Press onto bottom and up side of
prepared pie plate. Bake about 15 minutes
or until light golden brown. Cool
completely. Combine ice cream, syrup and
½ cup pecans; spread into crust. Freeze
until firm. Serve with additional Aunt
Jemima Syrup, if desired.

Makes 1 (9-inch) pie

Microwave: Lightly grease 9-inch
microwave-safe pie plate. Combine crust
ingredients; mix well. Press onto bottom
and up side of prepared pie plate.
Microwave at HIGH 4½ to 5½ minutes or
until browned and slightly firm to the
touch. Cool completely. Combine filling
ingredients; spread into crust. Freeze until
firm. Serve with additional Aunt Jemima
Syrup, if desired.

Strawberry Swirl Pie

3½ cups Rice CHEX® Brand Cereal, crushed to 1 cup
¼ cup packed brown sugar
⅓ cup flaked coconut
⅓ cup margarine or butter, melted
1 pint strawberries, hulled
3 tablespoons granulated sugar
1 quart vanilla ice cream, softened

Preheat oven to 300°F. Grease 9-inch pie plate. Combine crushed cereal, brown sugar and coconut. Add margarine. Mix thoroughly. Press evenly onto bottom and up side of prepared pie plate. Bake 10 minutes. Cool completely.

Reserve 5 berries for garnish. Mash remaining berries. Combine with granulated sugar. Mix into ice cream until thoroughly blended. Spoon into crust. Freeze 4 to 5 hours or until firm. To serve, garnish with reserved berries.

Makes 1 (9-inch) pie

Cocoa Strawberry Pie

¼ cup peanut butter
¼ cup corn syrup
2 cups KELLOGG'S® COCOA KRISPIES® Cereal
1 quart strawberry-flavored frozen yogurt or ice cream, softened
Chocolate syrup (optional)
Sliced strawberries for garnish

1. Stir together peanut butter and corn syrup in medium mixing bowl. Add Kellogg's® Cocoa Krispies® Cereal, stirring until well coated. Press evenly into 9-inch pie plate. Chill in refrigerator about 15 minutes.

2. Spoon frozen yogurt into crust. Freeze until firm, about 3 hours. Remove from freezer 10 minutes before serving. Drizzle with chocolate syrup; garnish with strawberries. *Makes 1 (9-inch) pie*

Cookies and Cream Pie

1½ cups cold half and half, light cream or milk
1 package (4-serving size) JELL-O® Vanilla Flavor Instant Pudding and Pie Filling
3½ cups (8 ounces) thawed COOL WHIP® Non-Dairy Whipped Topping or COOL WHIP® Extra Creamy Dairy Recipe Whipped Topping
cookies
1 (8-inch) prepared chocolate cookie crumb crust

• Pour half and half into large mixing bowl. Add pie filling mix. Beat with wire whisk until well blended, 1 to 2 minutes. Let stand 5 minutes.

• Fold in whipped topping and chopped cookies. Spoon into crust.

• Freeze until firm, about 6 hours or overnight. Remove from freezer. Let stand about 10 minutes to soften before serving. *Makes 1 (8-inch) pie*

Note: Store any leftover pie in freezer.

Cookies and Cream Pie

Frozen Lemon Angel Pie

3 egg whites*
½ teaspoon vanilla extract
¼ teaspoon cream of tartar
1½ cups sugar
2 cups (1 pint) BORDEN® or
    MEADOW GOLD® Whipping
    Cream
½ cup REALEMON® Lemon Juice from
    Concentrate
    Yellow food coloring (optional)

Preheat oven to 275°F. In small mixer bowl, beat egg whites, vanilla and cream of tartar until soft peaks form. Gradually add ½ cup sugar, beating until stiff but not dry. Spread on bottom and up side of well-buttered 9-inch pie plate to form crust. Bake 1 hour. Turn oven off; leave crust in oven 1 hour. Cool to room temperature. In large mixer bowl, combine cream, remaining 1 cup sugar, ReaLemon® brand and food coloring; beat until stiff. Spoon into prepared crust. Freeze 3 hours or until firm. Garnish as desired. Freeze ungarnished leftovers.

Makes 1 (9-inch) pie

*Use only Grade A clean, uncracked eggs.

Mile High Strawberry Pie

2 quarts strawberry ice cream, softened
1 (8- or 9-inch) prepared graham
    cracker or chocolate cookie crumb
    crust
3½ cups (8 ounces) thawed COOL
    WHIP® Non-Dairy Whipped
    Topping

• Spoon softened ice cream into crust. Spread whipped topping over ice cream. Freeze until firm, about 4 hours.

• Let stand at room temperature 10 minutes before serving. Garnish with chocolate-dipped whole strawberries, if desired.   *Makes 1 (8- or 9-inch) pie*

Note: Store any leftover pie in freezer.

Margarita Parfait Pie

1¼ cups *finely* crushed SEYFERT'S®
    Pretzels
¼ cup sugar
½ cup *plus* 2 tablespoons margarine or
    butter, melted
1 (14-ounce) can EAGLE® Brand
    Sweetened Condensed Milk
    (NOT evaporated milk)
¼ cup REALIME® Lime Juice from
    Concentrate
¼ cup tequila
2 tablespoons triple sec or other
    orange-flavored liqueur
1 cup chopped fresh or frozen
    unsweetened strawberries,
    thawed and *well drained*
    Red food coloring (optional)
1½ cups BORDEN® or MEADOW
    GOLD® Whipping Cream,
    whipped

Combine pretzel crumbs, sugar and margarine; press firmly onto bottom and up side to rim of lightly buttered 9-inch pie plate to form crust. In large bowl, combine sweetened condensed milk, ReaLime® brand, tequila and triple sec; mix well. Divide mixture in half. Add strawberries and food coloring to one half. Divide half of the whipped cream between each mixture. Spoon mixtures alternately into prepared crust. With metal spatula, swirl through mixtures to marble. Freeze 4 hours or until firm. Remove from freezer 10 minutes before serving. Garnish as desired. Freeze ungarnished leftovers.

Makes 1 (9-inch) pie

*Top to bottom: Frozen Lemon Angel Pie,
Margarita Parfait Pie*

Kiwiberry Frozen Yogurt Pie

Kiwiberry Frozen Yogurt Pie

1½ cups finely crushed chocolate wafer
    cookies
6 tablespoons melted butter
⅓ cup toasted shredded coconut
2 pints raspberry frozen yogurt
3 New Zealand kiwifruit, peeled and
    sliced
½ cup fresh raspberries
    Chocolate syrup
    Toasted coconut for garnish (optional)

Mix together cookie crumbs, butter and
coconut until well blended. Press evenly
into bottom and up side of 9-inch pie
plate; freeze until firm. Use ice cream
scoop to fill pie shell with frozen yogurt,
piling scoops into mound in center. Freeze
until firm. Remove pie from freezer 10
minutes before serving. Garnish with
kiwifruit and raspberries; drizzle with
chocolate syrup. Sprinkle with toasted
coconut. *Makes 1 (9-inch) pie*

Favorite recipe from **New Zealand Kiwifruit Marketing
Board**

Double Chocolate Alaska Pie

Crust
⅓ cup margarine or butter, melted
¼ cup packed brown sugar
1 tablespoon cocoa
4 cups Rice CHEX® Brand Cereal,
    crushed to 1 cup

Filling-Meringue
1 quart chocolate ice cream, softened
3 egg whites
½ teaspoon vanilla extract
¼ teaspoon cream of tartar
6 tablespoons granulated sugar

Preheat oven to 300°F. Grease 9-inch pie
plate. Combine margarine, brown sugar
and cocoa in large bowl. Add crushed
cereal; mix thoroughly. Press evenly onto
bottom and up side of prepared pie plate.
Bake 10 minutes. Cool completely.

Fill crust with ice cream. Freeze until firm,
6 hours or overnight. Beat egg whites with
vanilla and cream of tartar in medium
bowl until soft peaks form. Gradually add
granulated sugar; beat until stiff and
glossy and sugar is dissolved. Spread
meringue over ice cream. Seal to edges*
and freeze. At serving time, bake in
preheated 375°F oven about 2½ minutes
or until very lightly browned; *watch closely.*
Serve immediately. *Makes 1 (9-inch) pie*

*May be baked at this point as directed.
Let stand a few minutes before serving.

Note: Best if frozen no longer than 2 days.

Layered Mocha Pie

1 tablespoon butter
1¼ cups chocolate wafer cookies
⅓ cup walnuts, finely chopped
⅓ cup unsalted butter, melted
1 quart DREYER'S®/EDY'S®
    Chocolate Ice Cream
1 quart DREYER'S®/EDY'S® Coffee
    Ice Cream
4 ounces bittersweet or semisweet
    chocolate
6 to 8 camellia or other firm *nontoxic*
    leaves*

Grease 9-inch pie plate with 1 tablespoon butter. Crush chocolate wafer cookies with rolling pin. Combine cookie crumbs with walnuts and melted butter. Press crumb mixture onto bottom and up side of greased pie plate. Chill crust in freezer 30 minutes.

Soften 1 quart Dreyer's®/Edy's® Chocolate Ice Cream 10 minutes at room temperature. Carefully spoon ice cream into chilled crust; freeze 1 hour.

Let Dreyer's®/Edy's® Coffee Ice Cream stand at room temperature 10 minutes. Turn into large bowl; stir with wooden spoon until smooth and softened. Spread coffee ice cream over chocolate layer. Freeze 6 hours or overnight.

In top of double boiler, melt chocolate until smooth. Use spoon to coat back of leaves with chocolate. Lay coated leaves, leaf side down, on waxed paper. Chill at least 30 minutes.

Allow pie to stand at room temperature 10 minutes. Before serving, peel green leaves away from chocolate. Garnish pie with chocolate leaves. Run knife blade under hot water and pat dry to ease slicing.

Makes 1 (9-inch) pie

*Nontoxic leaves can be found at most floral shops.

Frozen Strawberry Fudge Pie

2 (10-ounce) packages frozen quick
    thaw strawberries, thawed and
    drained
¼ cup corn syrup
1 (12-ounce) container frozen non-
    dairy whipped topping, thawed,
    divided
1 (9-inch) prepared chocolate cookie
    crumb crust
1 cup (6-ounce package) NESTLÉ®
    Toll House® Semi-Sweet Chocolate
    Morsels

Place drained strawberries in food processor or blender. Cover; process until blended and smooth. Transfer to large bowl. Add corn syrup; mix well. Fold in 2 cups whipped topping. Spoon mixture into crust. Freeze until firm, about 1½ hours. Combine 1 cup whipped topping and Nestlé® Toll House® Semi-Sweet Chocolate Morsels over hot (not boiling) water; stir until morsels are melted and mixture is smooth. Spread evenly over strawberry layer. Freeze until firm, about 1½ hours. Garnish with remaining whipped topping and chocolate-dipped strawberries, if desired.

Makes 1 (9-inch) pie

Frozen Strawberry Fudge Pie

German Sweet Chocolate Pie

1 package (4 ounces) BAKER'S®
    GERMAN'S® Sweet Chocolate
⅓ cup milk
1 package (3 ounces) PHILADELPHIA
    BRAND® Cream Cheese, softened
2 tablespoons sugar (optional)
3½ cups (8 ounces) COOL WHIP® Non-
    Dairy Whipped Topping, thawed
1 (9-inch) prepared crumb crust
    Chocolate shavings or curls (optional)

• **Microwave Directions:** Microwave
chocolate and 2 tablespoons milk in
large microwavable bowl on HIGH 1½ to
2 minutes or until chocolate is almost
melted, stirring after 1 minute. *Stir until
chocolate is completely melted.*

• Beat in cream cheese, sugar and
remaining milk until well blended.
Refrigerate to cool, about 10 minutes.

• Gently stir in whipped topping until
smooth. Spoon into crust. Freeze until
firm, about 4 hours. Garnish with
chocolate shavings.

Makes 1 (9-inch) pie

Prep time: 20 minutes
Freezing time: 4 hours

German Sweet Chocolate Pie

Banana Split Brownie Pie

1 (12.9- or 15-ounce) package fudge
    brownie mix
2 firm, medium bananas, sliced, dipped
    in REALEMON® Lemon Juice
    from Concentrate and well drained
BORDEN® or MEADOW GOLD®
    Vanilla, Chocolate and Strawberry
    Ice Cream, slightly softened
Hot Fudge Sauce (page 164)
Chopped toasted pecans
BORDEN® or MEADOW GOLD®
    Whipping Cream, whipped
Maraschino cherries (optional)

Preheat oven to 350°F. Prepare brownie
mix as package directs. Spoon batter into
greased 9-inch round layer cake pan; bake
25 minutes. Cool 10 minutes; remove from
pan. Place brownie on serving plate; top
with bananas, scoops of ice cream and
Hot Fudge Sauce. Garnish with nuts,
whipped cream and cherries. Serve
immediately. Freeze leftovers.

Makes 1 (9-inch) pie

Teddy Peanut Butter Swirl Pie

2 cups TEDDY GRAHAMS® Graham
    Snacks, any flavor
1 (8-inch) prepared crumb crust
½ cup creamy peanut butter
1 quart vanilla ice milk, softened
¼ cup PLANTERS® Dry Roasted
    Peanuts, chopped

Place ½ cup Teddy Grahams® in bottom
of prepared crust. Heat peanut butter over
low heat until smooth and pourable;
drizzle ¼ cup over cookies in crust. Fold 1
cup Teddy Grahams® into ice milk; spread
into crust. Drizzle remaining ¼ cup peanut
butter over pie; quickly swirl with knife to
create marbled effect. Top with remaining
½ cup Teddy Grahams® and chopped
peanuts. Cover and freeze until firm,
about 4 hours. *Makes 1 (8-inch) pie*

Triple Chocolate Dessert Cups

1 cup (6 ounces) semisweet or white
    chocolate pieces
1 tablespoon corn syrup
2 cups Rice CHEX® Brand Cereal,
    crushed to ⅔ cups
1 pint heavenly hash or chocolate ice
    cream
    Chocolate sauce

Butter 12 (2½-inch) muffin cups. In small saucepan over low heat, melt chocolate. Stir in syrup. Add cereal, stirring until cereal pieces are evenly coated. Place 1 heaping tablespoon chocolate mixture into each muffin cup. With back of spoon, spread mixture over bottoms and up sides of cups. Refrigerate or freeze 30 minutes or until chocolate is set. About 1 hour before serving, use table knife to *carefully* pry chocolate cups from muffin cups; let cups stand at room temperature. Just before serving, scoop ice cream into chocolate cups. Top with chocolate sauce.
Makes 12 (2½-inch) dessert cups

Microwave: In 1-quart microwave-safe bowl, microwave chocolate on HIGH 1 to 2 minutes, stirring every minute, until melted. Continue recipe as directed.

Mocha Brownie Pie with Chocolate-Caramel Sauce

4 (3×2-inch) unfrosted homemade or
    bakery brownies
1 quart coffee-flavored ice cream,
    softened
1 KEEBLER® Ready-Crust Chocolate
    Flavored Pie Crust
6 to 8 ounces chocolate-covered
    caramel candies
2 tablespoons milk
2 tablespoons dark rum
    Whipped cream
    Chocolate shavings

Cut brownies into ½-inch cubes; freeze. Gently fold frozen brownie cubes into softened ice cream. Spoon into crust; freeze at least 3 hours. To prepare sauce, combine candy and milk in saucepan. Heat on low until melted and smooth. Stir in rum. Remove pie from freezer 5 minutes before serving. Top each serving with warm sauce, whipped cream and chocolate shavings. *Makes 8 servings*

Pumpkin Mousse Ice Cream Pie

1½ cups crushed gingersnap cookies
    (about 30)
⅓ cup butter or margarine, melted
2 cups (1 pint) vanilla ice cream,
    softened
1 cup LIBBY'S® Solid Pack Pumpkin
¾ cup sugar
1½ teaspoons pumpkin pie spice
1 cup (8-ounce carton) whipping cream
½ teaspoon vanilla extract
    Chopped toasted pecans (optional)

Preheat oven to 350°F. In small bowl, combine gingersnap crumbs and butter. Press onto bottom and up side of buttered 9-inch pie plate. Bake 5 to 8 minutes. Cool on wire rack. Soften ice cream; spread over pie crust. Freeze until firm, about 1 hour. In medium bowl, combine pumpkin, sugar and pumpkin pie spice. In small mixer bowl, beat cream and vanilla until stiff; fold into pumpkin mixture. Spoon over ice cream. Freeze again until firm, about 2 hours. Garnish with chopped toasted pecans.
Makes 1 (9-inch) pie

FESTIVE CLASSICS

Classic Pecan Pie

3 eggs, slightly beaten
1 cup sugar
1 cup KARO® Light or Dark Corn
　　Syrup
2 tablespoons MAZOLA® Margarine,
　　melted
1 teaspoon vanilla extract
1½ cups whole pecans
1 unbaked (9-inch) pie shell*

Preheat oven to 350°F. Combine eggs, sugar, corn syrup, margarine and vanilla; stir until well blended. Stir in pecans. Pour into pie shell. Bake 50 to 55 minutes or until knife inserted halfway between center and edge comes out clean. Cool on wire rack.　　　*Makes 1 (9-inch) pie*

*If using frozen prepared crust, use 9-inch deep-dish crust. *Do not thaw.* Preheat oven and cookie sheet. Pour filling into frozen crust; place on cookie sheet and bake.

Chocolate Pecan Pie: Melt 4 ounces semisweet *or* 2 ounces unsweetened chocolate with margarine.

Sour Cream Pecan Pie: Stir ¼ cup sour cream into eggs until blended.

Kentucky Bourbon Pecan Pie: Add 2 tablespoons bourbon to filling.

Date Nut Pie: Substitute 1 cup finely chopped dates and ½ cup walnut halves for pecans.

Maple-Flavored Pecan Pie: Substitute KARO® Pancake Syrup for light or dark corn syrup.

Coconut Pecan Pie: Add 1 cup flaked coconut to filling.

Orange Pecan Pie: Add 1 tablespoon grated orange peel to filling.

Peppermint Rice Cloud

2 cups cooked rice (about ⅔ cup
　　uncooked)
1½ cups miniature marshmallows
1 cup milk
⅓ cup crushed peppermint candy
1 teaspoon vanilla extract
1 cup whipping cream, whipped
1 (8- or 9-inch) prepared chocolate
　　crumb crust
¼ cup fudge sauce

Combine rice, marshmallows, milk, and candy in 2-quart saucepan. Cook over medium heat until thick and creamy, 6 to 8 minutes, stirring constantly. Remove from heat and stir in vanilla; cool. Fold in whipped cream. Spoon into chocolate crust. Chill at least 3 hours. Drizzle with warm fudge sauce before serving.
　　　Makes 1 (8- or 9-inch) pie

*Favorite recipe from **USA Rice Council***

Classic Pecan Pie

Maple Walnut Cream Pie

Crust
  9-inch Classic Crisco® Single Crust
    (pages 6 and 7)

Filling
  1 cup pure maple syrup or maple-
    flavored pancake syrup
  ½ cup milk
  2 egg yolks, slightly beaten
  1 envelope (1 tablespoon) unflavored
    gelatin
  ¼ cup water
  1 teaspoon maple flavor or extract
  1 cup whipping cream, whipped
  ¾ cup chopped walnuts
    Sweetened whipped cream
    Baked pastry cutouts (optional)

1. Prepare and bake 9-inch Classic
Crisco® Single Crust. Reserve dough
scraps for pastry cutouts, if desired. Cool.

2. For Filling, combine syrup and milk in
small saucepan. Cook on low heat just
until hot. *Do not boil.* Stir small amount of
hot mixture gradually into egg yolks.

Maple Walnut Cream Pie

3. Return egg mixture to saucepan. Bring
to a boil on medium heat. Simmer 1
minute. Soften gelatin in water. Remove
saucepan from heat. Add gelatin and
maple flavor. Stir until gelatin dissolves.
Refrigerate until mixture begins to thicken.

4. Fold whipped cream into maple
mixture. Fold in nuts. Spoon into cooled
baked pie crust. Refrigerate 2 hours or
until firm. Garnish with whipped cream
and baked pastry cutouts, if desired.
Makes 1 (9-inch) pie

Praline Pie

  1½ cups PLANTERS® Pecans
  27 LORNA DOONE® Shortbread,
    finely crushed (about
    2 cups crumbs)
  ½ cup BLUE BONNET® Margarine,
    melted, divided
  1 cup packed light brown sugar
  ¾ cup all-purpose flour
  1 egg
  1 teaspoon DAVIS® Baking Powder
  1 teaspoon vanilla extract
    Prepared whipped topping for
    garnish

Preheat oven to 350°F. Reserve 6 pecan
halves; finely chop ½ cup pecans. In small
bowl, combine ¼ cup chopped pecans,
shortbread crumbs and ¼ cup melted
margarine. Press onto bottom and up side
of 9-inch pie plate; set aside.

In medium bowl with electric mixer at
slow speed, beat remaining ¼ cup
margarine and brown sugar until blended;
mix in flour, egg, baking powder and
vanilla until well combined. Stir in 1 cup
pecans. Spread in crust; sprinkle with
¼ cup chopped pecans. Bake 18 minutes
or until lightly browned.

Serve pie warm or cold, topped with
whipped topping. Garnish with remaining
pecan halves.
Makes 1 (9-inch) pie

Apple Strudel Macaroon Pie

Crust
   9-inch Classic Crisco® Double Crust
      (pages 6 and 7)

Filling
   2 cups diced, peeled Granny Smith
      apples (about ¾ pound *or*
      2 medium)
   2 eggs, slightly beaten
   1 cup packed brown sugar
   ½ cup crumbled soft coconut macaroon
      cookies
   ½ cup raisins
   ¼ cup apple juice or cider
   ¼ cup chopped walnuts
   ½ teaspoon ground cinnamon

Glaze
   ½ cup confectioners sugar
   ⅛ teaspoon ground cinnamon
   2 teaspoons apple juice or cider

1. Prepare 9-inch Classic Crisco® Double Crust; press bottom crust into 9-inch pie plate. *Do not bake.* Heat oven to 400°F.

2. For Filling, combine apples, eggs, brown sugar, cookies, raisins, ¼ cup apple juice, nuts and ½ teaspoon cinnamon in large bowl. Mix well. Spoon into unbaked Crust. Moisten pastry edge with water.

3. Cover pie with top crust. Cut slits into top crust to allow steam to escape.

4. Bake at 400°F for 40 to 50 minutes or until filling in center is bubbly and crust is golden brown. Cover edge with foil, if necessary, to prevent overbrowning.

5. For Glaze, combine confectioners sugar and ⅛ teaspoon cinnamon. Add 2 teaspoons apple juice. Mix well. Spoon over top of hot pie. Cool until barely warm or to room temperature before serving. *Makes 1 (9-inch) pie*

Creamy Egg Nog Pie

Creamy Egg Nog Pie

   1 (6-serving size) package vanilla flavor
      pudding mix (*not instant*)
   ¼ teaspoon ground nutmeg
   1½ cups canned BORDEN® Egg Nog
   2 tablespoons light rum *or* 1 teaspoon
      rum flavoring (optional)
   2 cups (1 pint) BORDEN® or
      MEADOW GOLD® Whipping
      Cream, whipped
   1 baked (9-inch) pie crust
      Additional ground nutmeg

In medium saucepan, combine pudding mix, ¼ *teaspoon* nutmeg and egg nog; mix well. Over medium heat, cook and stir until thickened and bubbly. Remove from heat; stir in rum. Cool or chill thoroughly. Beat until smooth. Fold in whipped cream. Spoon into prepared pie crust. Garnish with additional nutmeg. Chill 4 hours or until set. Refrigerate leftovers.
Makes 1 (9-inch) pie

Microwave: In 2-quart glass measure with handle, combine pudding mix, ¼ teaspoon nutmeg and egg nog; mix well. Cook on 100% power (high) 6 to 8 minutes or until thickened and bubbly, stirring every 1½ minutes. Proceed as directed.

Libby's® Famous Pumpkin Pie

Libby's® Famous Pumpkin Pie

Homemade Pastry (recipe follows)
2 eggs, slightly beaten
1¾ cups (16-ounce can) LIBBY'S® Solid
    Pack Pumpkin
¾ cup sugar
½ teaspoon salt
1 teaspoon ground cinnamon
½ teaspoon ground ginger
¼ teaspoon ground cloves
1½ cups (12-ounce can) *undiluted*
    CARNATION® Evaporated Milk

Preheat oven to 425°F. Prepare
Homemade Pastry. In large bowl, combine
eggs, pumpkin, sugar, salt, cinnamon,
ginger, cloves and evaporated milk. Pour
into pie crust.* Bake 15 minutes. *Reduce
oven temperature to 350°F.* Bake an
additional 40 to 50 minutes or until knife
inserted near center comes out clean. Cool
on wire rack. Top pie as desired.

Makes 1 (9-inch) pie

*When using metal or foil pie plate, bake
on preheated cookie sheet. When using
glass or ceramic pie plate, do not use
cookie sheet.

Homemade Pastry

1 cup all-purpose flour
½ teaspoon salt
6 tablespoons shortening
2 to 3 tablespoons cold water

In bowl, combine flour and salt. Using
pastry blender, fork, or two knives, cut in
shortening until mixture is crumbly.
Gradually add water, mixing until flour is
moistened. Shape dough into a ball;
flatten to 1-inch thickness. On lightly
floured surface, roll dough into circle
about 2 inches larger than inverted 9-inch
pie plate. Line pan with pastry. Turn edge
under; flute, if desired. Makes 1 (9-inch)
pie crust.

Jack-o'-Lantern Pie

1 package (4-serving size) JELL-O®
    Gelatin, Orange Flavor
1 cup boiling water
1 pint vanilla ice cream, softened
1 (9-inch) prepared chocolate cookie
    crumb crust
    Candy corn
    Black licorice, cut into 1-inch pieces
    COOL WHIP® Whipped Topping,
    thawed, for garnish

• Pour gelatin into a bowl. Add 1 cup
boiling water to gelatin. Stir until gelatin
is completely dissolved, about 2 minutes.

• Add ice cream to gelatin. Stir until ice
cream is melted and mixture is smooth.

• Refrigerate gelatin mixture until slightly
thickened, about 10 minutes. Pour
gelatin mixture into crust. Refrigerate
until firm, about 2 hours. Make jack-o'-
lantern face on pie with candy corn and
licorice.

• Pipe whipped topping over pie to
garnish. *Makes 1 (9-inch) pie*

Date Streusel Pie

1 package (8 ounces) light cream cheese, softened
1 can (14 ounces) sweetened condensed milk
  Grated peel and juice from 2 DOLE® Oranges
1 baked (9-inch) pie crust, cooled
1 package (8 ounces) DOLE® Chopped Dates
¼ cup margarine
⅓ cup all-purpose flour
½ cup chopped DOLE® Almonds, toasted

- Preheat oven to 375°F. Beat cream cheese, sweetened condensed milk, 1 teaspoon orange peel and ¼ cup orange juice until smooth. Pour into pie crust.

- Process remaining orange juice, peel and dates in food processor or blender until smooth. Spoon mixture over cheese filling.

- Cut margarine into flour until crumbly. Stir in almonds. Spoon over pie. Bake 40 to 45 minutes. Cool. Refrigerate.
  Makes 1 (9-inch) pie

Prep Time: 15 minutes
Bake Time: 45 minutes

Southern Pecan Bourbon Pie

Crust
  9-inch Classic Crisco® Single Crust (pages 6 and 7)

Filling
  3 eggs
  ½ cup packed brown sugar
  1 cup dark corn syrup
  1 cup chopped pecans
  3 tablespoons bourbon *or* ½ teaspoon vanilla extract
  2 tablespoons butter or margarine, melted
  ¼ teaspoon salt

1. Prepare 9-inch Classic Crisco® Single Crust. *Do not bake.* Heat oven to 350°F.

2. For Filling, beat eggs in large bowl at medium speed of electric mixer. Beat in brown sugar. Stir in corn syrup, nuts, bourbon, butter and salt. Pour into unbaked crust.

3. Bake at 350°F for 40 to 50 minutes or until filling in center is set. Cover edge with foil, if necessary, to prevent overbrowning. Cool to room temperature before serving. Refrigerate leftover pie.
Makes 1 (9-inch) pie

New England Maple Apple Pie

2 pounds all-purpose apples, cored, peeled and thinly sliced (about 6 cups)
½ cup *plus* 2 tablespoons unsifted flour
½ cup CARY'S®, MAPLE ORCHARDS™ or MACDONALD'S™ Pure Maple Syrup
2 tablespoons margarine or butter, melted
1 unbaked (9-inch) pie shell
¼ cup packed light brown sugar
1 teaspoon ground cinnamon
⅓ cup cold margarine or butter
½ cup chopped nuts

Place rack in lowest position in oven; preheat oven to 400°F. In large bowl, combine apples and 2 *tablespoons* flour. Combine pure maple syrup and melted margarine. Pour over apples; mix well. Turn into pie shell. In medium bowl, combine remaining ½ *cup* flour, sugar and cinnamon; cut in cold margarine until crumbly. Add nuts; sprinkle over apples. Bake 10 minutes. *Reduce oven temperature to 375°F;* bake 35 minutes longer or until golden brown. Serve warm. Garnish as desired. *Makes 1 (9-inch) pie*

Sweet Potato Pie with Fruit Topping

Crust
2 (9-inch) Classic Crisco® Single Crusts
    (pages 6 and 7)

Filling
1 can (15¼ ounces) crushed pineapple
    in juice, undrained
2½ cups mashed, cooked sweet potatoes
1 can (14 ounces) sweetened condensed
    milk
2 eggs, slightly beaten
½ cup packed brown sugar
¼ cup BUTTER FLAVOR CRISCO®
1 teaspoon ground nutmeg

Topping
2 cans (8 ounces *each*) sliced pineapple
    in juice, undrained
½ cup granulated sugar
2 tablespoons cornstarch
1 to 2 drops yellow food color
    (optional)
12 to 16 maraschino cherries (red or
    green), drained

1. Prepare both 9-inch Classic Crisco® Single Crusts. Roll and press into 2 (9-inch) pie plates. *Do not bake.* Heat oven to 350°F.

2. For Filling, drain crushed pineapple, reserving juice. Discard 6 tablespoons juice. Combine remaining juice, pineapple, sweet potatoes, sweetened condensed milk, eggs, brown sugar, Butter Flavor Crisco® and nutmeg in large bowl. Beat at medium speed of electric mixer until well blended.

3. Spoon filling into pie crusts.

4. Bake at 350°F for 30 to 45 minutes or until fillings are set.

5. For Topping, drain sliced pineapple, reserving juice. Combine granulated sugar and cornstarch in small saucepan. Add enough water to reserved pineapple juice to make 1 cup. Add to saucepan. Add food color. Cook and stir on medium heat until mixture comes to a boil and thickens. Cool slightly.

6. Cut each pineapple slice in half. Dip in pineapple juice glaze. Arrange half of pieces on each baked pie. Dip cherries in glaze. Arrange half on each pie. Use remaining glaze to cover pie tops. Cool to room temperature before serving. Refrigerate leftover pies.

Makes 2 (9-inch) pies

Apricot Walnut Mince Pie

1 (6-ounce) package dried apricots
1 (27-ounce) jar NONE SUCH®
    Ready-To-Use Mincemeat
    (Regular *or* Brandy & Rum)
1 cup chopped walnuts
1 unbaked (9-inch) pie shell
1 (16-ounce) container BORDEN® or
    MEADOW GOLD® Sour Cream, at
    room temperature
1 tablespoon sugar
1 teaspoon vanilla extract
    Walnut halves

Place rack in lowest position in oven; preheat oven to 400°F. Chop ½ *cup* apricots; reserve remainder. In medium bowl, combine mincemeat, chopped apricots and chopped nuts; turn into pie shell. Bake 25 minutes. Meanwhile, in medium bowl, combine sour cream, sugar and vanilla. Spread evenly over pie. Bake 8 minutes longer or until set. Cool. Garnish with reserved apricots and walnut halves. Refrigerate leftovers.

Makes 1 (9-inch) pie

Sweet Potato Pie with Fruit Topping

Peppermint Parfait Pie

Peppermint Parfait Pie

1 (1-ounce) bar unsweetened baking chocolate
1 (14-ounce) can EAGLE® Brand Sweetened Condensed Milk (NOT evaporated milk)
½ teaspoon vanilla extract
1 baked (9-inch) pie crust
1 (8-ounce) package cream cheese, softened
3 tablespoons white creme de menthe liqueur
  Red food coloring (optional)
1 (8-ounce) container frozen non-dairy whipped topping, thawed

In small saucepan over medium heat, melt chocolate with ½ *cup* sweetened condensed milk; stir in vanilla. Spread on bottom of crust. In large mixer bowl, beat cheese until fluffy. Gradually beat in remaining sweetened condensed milk. Stir in creme de menthe and food coloring. Fold in whipped topping. Pour into pie crust. Chill 4 hours or until set. Garnish as desired. Refrigerate leftovers.

Makes 1 (9-inch) pie

Apple Gingerbread Pie

Crust
½ cup CRISCO® Shortening
¼ cup sugar
1¼ cups all-purpose flour
½ cup ground pecans
½ teaspoon ground ginger

Filling
4½ cups thinly sliced, peeled McIntosh *or* Granny Smith apples (about 1½ pounds *or* 4 to 5 medium)
3 tablespoons honey
2 tablespoons water
⅓ cup golden raisins
⅓ cup currants
½ to 1 teaspoon apple pie spice

Topping
1 cup whipping cream, whipped
2 tablespoons finely chopped pecans

1. For Crust, heat oven to 375°F. Cream Crisco® and sugar until light and fluffy, using spoon. Stir in flour, ground pecans and ginger. Blend until mixture is well combined. Press into 9-inch pie plate. Bake at 375°F for 10 to 12 minutes or until lightly browned. Cool.

2. For Filling, combine apples, honey and water in large saucepan. Simmer, covered, 20 minutes or until apples are tender. Stir in raisins, currants and apple pie spice. Cool. Spoon into cooled baked crust.

3. For Topping, spread whipped cream over filling. Sprinkle with chopped pecans. Refrigerate until ready to serve.

Makes 1 (9-inch) pie

Irish Cream Pecan Pie

¼ cup MAZOLA® Margarine
1 cup sugar
3 eggs
¾ cup KARO® Light Corn Syrup
2 tablespoons Irish cream liqueur
1 unbaked (9-inch) pie shell
1¼ cups whole pecans

Preheat oven to 350°F. In large bowl with mixer at medium speed, beat margarine to soften. Gradually beat in sugar. Beat in eggs, one at a time, until well blended. Beat in corn syrup and liqueur. Pour into pie shell. Sprinkle with pecans. Bake 45 to 50 minutes or until set around edges (filling will be puffy). Cool on wire rack.

Makes 1 (9-inch) pie

Chocolate Macadamia Angel Pie

Angel Pie Crust
  4 egg whites
  ¼ teaspoon salt
  ¼ teaspoon cream of tartar
  1 cup sugar

Filling
  ¼ cup sugar
  3 tablespoons cornstarch
  ½ teaspoon salt
1½ cups milk
  1 cup (6-ounce package) NESTLÉ®
     Toll House® Semi-Sweet Chocolate
     Morsels
  1 tablespoon chocolate-flavored
     liqueur
1½ cups heavy cream, whipped, divided
  1 cup chopped macadamia nuts
    Chocolate shavings and whole
     macadamia nuts (optional)

Angel Pie Crust: Preheat oven to 275°F. In 1½-quart bowl, combine egg whites, salt and cream of tartar; beat until foamy. Gradually beat in sugar until stiff peaks form. Spread meringue on bottom and up side of buttered 9-inch pie plate. Build meringue up around rim, extending 1 inch higher than edge. Bake 1 hour. Turn oven off. Let stand in oven with door ajar 1 hour.

Filling: In medium saucepan, combine sugar, cornstarch and salt. Gradually stir in milk. Cook over medium heat, stirring constantly, until mixture boils. Boil 1 minute; remove from heat. Add Nestlé® Toll House® Semi-Sweet Chocolate Morsels and chocolate-flavored liqueur; stir until morsels are melted and mixture is smooth. (Mixture will be thick.) Transfer to large bowl; cool to room temperature. Fold in 2 cups whipped cream and chopped nuts. Spoon into prepared crust. Chill until ready to serve. Top with remaining whipped cream; garnish with chocolate shavings and whole nuts.

Makes 1 (9-inch) pie

Chocolate Macadamia Angel Pie

Left to right: Raspberry Amaretto Mince Pie, Apricot Walnut Mince Pie (page 179)

Raspberry Amaretto Mince Pie

2 (10-ounce) packages frozen red raspberries in syrup, thawed and well drained, reserving syrup
⅓ cup amaretto liqueur
1 (9-ounce) package NONE SUCH® Condensed Mincemeat, crumbled
1 egg, beaten
1 unbaked (9-inch) pie shell
½ cup sliced almonds

Place rack in lowest position in oven; preheat oven to 425°F. In medium saucepan, combine reserved raspberry syrup, amaretto and mincemeat; bring to a boil. Cook and stir 1 minute. Remove from heat; stir in raspberries and egg. Turn into pie shell. Top with almonds. Bake 30 minutes or until bubbly. Cool. Garnish as desired. Refrigerate leftovers.

Makes 1 (9-inch) pie

No-Bake Pumpkin Pie

1 can (14 ounces) sweetened condensed
   milk
1 teaspoon ground cinnamon
¼ teaspoon ground ginger
½ teaspoon ground nutmeg
½ teaspoon salt
1 envelope KNOX® Unflavored
   Gelatine
2 tablespoons water
2 tablespoons butter
1 can (16 ounces) pumpkin
   (about 2 cups)
1 (9-inch) prepared graham cracker
   crumb crust

In small bowl, blend milk, cinnamon,
ginger, nutmeg and salt; set aside.

In medium saucepan, sprinkle unflavored
gelatine over water; let stand 1 minute. Stir
over low heat until gelatine is completely
dissolved, about 2 minutes. Blend in milk
mixture and butter. Continue stirring over
low heat until butter is melted, about 2
minutes. Blend in pumpkin. Turn into
prepared crust; chill until firm. Garnish
with whipped cream or whipped topping,
if desired.   *Makes 1 (9-inch) pie*

Kahlúa® Eggnog Pie

1½ cups half-and-half
   8 tablespoons KAHLÚA®, divided
½ cup sugar
   Dash salt
5 egg yolks
3 tablespoons cornstarch
1 tablespoon butter
1 teaspoon rum or brandy flavoring
   Meringue Crust (recipe follows)
1 cup whipping cream, whipped
   Ground nutmeg

In medium saucepan, combine half-and-
half, 5 tablespoons Kahlúa®, ½ cup sugar
and salt. Cook over medium heat until
very hot. Beat egg yolks. Dissolve
cornstarch in remaining 3 tablespoons
Kahlúa®. Blend into yolks. Whisk yolk
mixture into hot milk mixture. Cook,
stirring constantly, until thickened, about
1 minute. Stir in butter and rum flavoring.
Cool thoroughly. Pour into cooled
Meringue Crust. Chill at least 1 hour.
Spread whipped cream over filling.
Sprinkle with nutmeg.
                    Makes 1 (9-inch) pie

Meringue Crust

5 egg whites
1 cup sugar
1¼ teaspoons lemon juice

Preheat oven to 200°F. In large bowl,
beat egg whites until soft peaks form.
Gradually add 1 cup sugar, beating until
stiff but not dry. Blend in juice. Reserve
about 1½ cups meringue. Spoon
remaining meringue into well-greased 9-
inch pie plate. With back of spoon, spread
meringue evenly over bottom of pan and
around edges to form pie shell. Spoon
remaining meringue into pastry bag fitted
with #5 star or other decorative tip. Pipe
border around edge of meringue in pie
plate. Bake 2 hours. Broil briefly to brown
decorative edge, watching carefully to
prevent burning. Cool.

Note: This pie is best prepared and served
on the same day.

Fruited Streusel Kuchen with Orange Cream

Kuchen
2¼ cups all-purpose flour
  2 teaspoons baking powder
¼ teaspoon salt
⅓ cup sugar
⅓ cup LAND O LAKES® Butter, softened
  2 eggs
½ cup milk
½ cup orange juice
  1 tablespoon orange-flavored liqueur
    or orange juice
  1 teaspoon vanilla extract
  1 large tart cooking apple, peeled, cored, sliced ⅛ inch thick
½ cup coarsely chopped dried apricots
½ cup dried figs, quartered
½ cup golden raisins
½ cup coarsely chopped walnuts
½ cup fresh *or* frozen whole cranberries

Streusel Topping
½ cup sugar
  2 tablespoons LAND O LAKES® Butter, softened
  1 teaspoon ground cinnamon
  1 teaspoon grated orange peel

Orange Cream
  2 cups chilled whipping cream (1 pint)
¼ cup sugar
  2 teaspoons grated orange peel
  1 tablespoon orange-flavored liqueur
    or orange juice

Heat oven to 350°F. In medium bowl, stir together flour, baking powder and salt; set aside. In large mixer bowl, beat together ⅓ cup sugar and ⅓ cup butter at medium speed, scraping bowl often, until well mixed, 1 to 2 minutes. Continue beating, adding eggs one at a time, until well mixed, 1 to 2 minutes. Reduce speed to low. Continue beating, scraping bowl often and gradually adding flour mixture alternately with milk and ½ cup orange juice until smooth, 2 to 3 minutes.

By hand, stir in 1 tablespoon orange-flavored liqueur and vanilla. Spread into greased 12½-inch tart pan with removable bottom. Arrange apple slices around outside edge of surface. Sprinkle apricots, figs, raisins, walnuts and cranberries around and on top of apple slices. Gently press into batter.

In medium bowl, stir together Streusel Topping ingredients; sprinkle over fruit. Bake 35 to 45 minutes or until lightly browned.

In small chilled mixer bowl, beat chilled whipping cream at high speed, scraping bowl often, until soft peaks form, 1 to 2 minutes. Continue beating, gradually adding ¼ cup sugar and 2 teaspoons orange peel, until stiff peaks form. By hand, gently stir in 1 tablespoon orange-flavored liqueur. Serve with warm Kuchen. *Makes 1 (12½-inch) tart*

Cranberry Pecan Pie

  3 eggs, slightly beaten
  1 cup light or dark corn syrup
⅔ cup sugar
  2 tablespoons margarine, melted
  1 cup coarsely chopped fresh cranberries
  1 cup coarsely chopped pecans
  1 tablespoon grated orange peel
  1 unbaked (9-inch) pie shell

Preheat oven to 350°F. In medium bowl, stir together eggs, corn syrup, sugar and margarine until well blended. Stir in cranberries, pecans and orange peel. Pour into pie shell. Bake 1 hour or until knife inserted halfway between center and edge comes out clean. Cool on rack.
Makes 1 (9-inch) pie

*Favorite recipe from **Pecan Marketing Board***

Fruited Streusel Kuchen with Orange Cream

Macaroon Apple Mince Pie

1 (27-ounce) jar NONE SUCH®
    Ready-To-Use Mincemeat
    (Regular *or* Brandy & Rum)
1 unbaked (9-inch) pie shell
3 medium all-purpose apples, cored,
    peeled and thinly sliced
½ cup BORDEN® or MEADOW
    GOLD® Whipping Cream,
    unwhipped
1 egg *yolk*
1 teaspoon vanilla extract
½ cup coconut macaroon crumbs
    (4 small macaroons) *or*
    ¾ cup flaked coconut

Place rack in lowest position in oven;
preheat oven to 425°F. Turn mincemeat
into pie shell; arrange apples on top. In
small bowl, beat cream, egg *yolk* and
vanilla; pour over apples. Top with
macaroon crumbs. Bake 10 minutes.
*Reduce oven temperature to 375°F; bake 25
minutes longer or until lightly browned.*
Cool. Serve warm or chilled. Refrigerate
leftovers.   *Makes 1 (9-inch) pie*

Tip: Substitute 2 (9-ounce) packages
NONE SUCH® Condensed Mincemeat,
reconstituted as package directs for None
Such® Ready-to-Use Mincemeat, if
desired. Use unbaked (9- or 10-inch) pie
shell. Proceed as directed.

Macaroon Apple Mince Pie

Stained Glass Harvest Pie

Filling
  1 cup quartered pitted prunes
  1 cup dried apricot halves
  ½ cup golden raisins
  1 cup halved cranberries, fresh or
    thawed frozen
  1 cup peeled, chopped tart apples
  ½ cup coarsely chopped walnuts or
    pecans
  ⅓ cup sugar
  ¼ cup BUTTER FLAVOR CRISCO®
  ¼ cup orange flavor liqueur *or* orange
    juice

Crust
  9-inch Classic Crisco® Double Crust
    (pages 6 and 7)

Topping
  ¼ cup orange marmalade
  1 teaspoon orange flavor liqueur *or*
    orange juice

1. For Filling, combine prunes, apricots
and raisins in large saucepan. Add enough
water to cover fruit. Bring to a boil. Reduce
heat and simmer, uncovered, 10 minutes
or until tender. Drain. Return to saucepan.
Add cranberries, apples, nuts, sugar,
Butter Flavor Crisco® and ¼ cup liqueur.
Cook and stir on low heat 5 minutes. Cool.
Cover; refrigerate 2 hours or overnight for
flavors to blend.

2. Prepare 9-inch Classic Crisco® Double
Crust; press bottom crust into 9-inch pie
plate, leaving overhang. Spoon in filling.
Heat oven to 400°F.

3. For Topping, combine marmalade and
1 teaspoon liqueur in small saucepan.
Heat until smooth. Strain and drizzle over
filling. Moisten pastry edge with water.

4. Cover pie with woven lattice top. Bake
at 400°F for 45 to 55 minutes or until
filling in center is bubbly and crust is
golden brown. Cover edge with foil, if
necessary, to prevent overbrowning. Cool
to room temperature before serving.
    Makes 1 (9-inch) pie

Orange Rum-Pecan Tart

2 eggs, slightly beaten
½ cup light or dark corn syrup
½ cup sugar
2 tablespoons frozen orange juice concentrate, thawed
2 tablespoons dark rum
1 tablespoon margarine, melted
1 teaspoon vanilla extract
1½ cups coarsely chopped pecans
1 baked (9-inch) tart crust

Preheat oven to 350°F. In medium bowl, stir together eggs, corn syrup, sugar, orange juice concentrate, rum, margarine and vanilla until well blended. Stir in pecans. Pour into tart crust. Bake 30 to 40 minutes or until knife inserted halfway between center and edge comes out clean. Cool on rack.   *Makes 1 (9-inch) tart*

*Favorite recipe from **Pecan Marketing Board***

Dried Apricot Cranberry Tart

Pastry for 1-crust 9-inch pie
⅓ cup packed light brown sugar
⅓ cup light corn syrup
2 eggs
2 tablespoons melted butter or margarine, cooled
1 teaspoon vanilla extract
¼ teaspoon salt
¾ cup dried California apricots, chopped
1 cup fresh or frozen cranberries
½ cup chopped walnuts
24 dried California apricot halves
Additional corn syrup
Whipping cream, whipped
Mint sprig for garnish

Dried Apricot Cranberry Tart

Preheat oven to 375°F. Press pastry into 9-inch tart pan. Bake 10 to 12 minutes or until golden; cool. *Increase oven temperature to 400°F.* Meanwhile, combine brown sugar, corn syrup, eggs, butter, vanilla and salt; whisk until smooth. Stir in chopped California apricots, cranberries and nuts. Pour into cooled pie crust; bake 30 minutes. Brush California apricot halves with additional corn syrup; overlap apricots around edge of tart. Cool 10 minutes. Serve tart with whipped cream; garnish with mint sprig.

Makes 1 (9-inch) tart

*Favorite recipe from **California Apricot Advisory Board***

Molasses Pumpkin Pie

1 (16-ounce) can solid pack pumpkin
½ cup packed light brown sugar
¼ cup BRER RABBIT® Light Molasses
2 teaspoons pumpkin pie spice
1 teaspoon salt
4 eggs, beaten
1½ cups milk or light cream
1 unbaked (9-inch) pie shell with high
    fluted edge
    Whipped Cheese Topping (recipe
    follows) *or* whipped cream

Preheat oven to 400°F. In bowl, blend pumpkin, brown sugar, molasses, spice and salt. Beat in eggs and milk. Pour into prepared pie shell. Bake 50 to 55 minutes or until pie is puffed and firm in center. Serve warm or cold with Whipped Cheese Topping. *Makes 1 (9-inch) pie*

Whipped Cheese Topping: Blend 3 ounces softened cream cheese, ½ cup powdered sugar, ¼ cup heavy cream, 1 teaspoon vanilla extract and 1 teaspoon grated orange peel until smooth. Chill until serving time.

Holiday Pineapple Tart

1 can (20 ounces) DOLE® Crushed
    Pineapple in Syrup, undrained
1 teaspoon cornstarch
1½ cups milk
½ cup reduced-calorie dairy sour cream
1 package (4-serving size) sugar-free
    instant vanilla pudding & pie
    filling mix
1 container (4 ounces) thawed frozen
    nondairy whipped topping
1 teaspoon *each:* grated orange peel,
    rum extract
¼ teaspoon ground nutmeg
1 (9-inch) prepared chocolate cookie or
    graham cracker crumb crust

- **Microwave Directions:** Drain ½ cup pineapple syrup from can into large glass measuring cup. Stir in cornstarch; microwave on high until glaze boils and thickens.

- Combine milk and sour cream. Beat in pudding mix until well blended. Fold in ½ cup drained pineapple, whipped topping, peel, extract and nutmeg.

- Turn filling into prepared crust. Chill until set.

- Arrange remaining pineapple on top of tart. Spoon cooled glaze over tart. Garnish with orange slices, if desired.
Makes 1 (9-inch) tart

Prep Time: 20 minutes
Chill Time: 4 hours

Mince Cheesecake Pie

1 (27-ounce) jar NONE SUCH®
    Ready-To-Use Mincemeat
    (Regular *or* Brandy & Rum)
1½ teaspoons grated orange peel
1 unbaked (9-inch) pie shell
2 (3-ounce) packages cream cheese,
    softened
½ cup sugar
2 eggs
1 teaspoon vanilla extract

Place rack in lowest position in oven; preheat oven to 425°F. Combine mincemeat and 1 *teaspoon* peel; turn into pie shell. Bake 15 minutes. Meanwhile, in small mixer bowl, beat cheese and sugar until fluffy. Add eggs, vanilla and remaining ½ *teaspoon* peel; mix well. Pour over mincemeat. *Reduce oven temperature to 350°F.* Bake 25 minutes longer or until set; cool. Serve warm or chilled. Garnish as desired. Refrigerate leftovers.
Makes 1 (9-inch) pie

Apple Almond Mince Pie

3 medium all-purpose apples, cored,
    peeled and thinly sliced
3 tablespoons flour
2 tablespoons margarine or butter,
    melted
   Pastry for 2-crust 9-inch pie
1 (27-ounce) jar NONE SUCH® Ready-
    To-Use Mincemeat (Regular *or*
    Brandy & Rum)
½ cup slivered almonds, toasted and
    chopped
½ teaspoon almond extract
1 egg *yolk* mixed with 2 tablespoons
    water (optional)

Place rack in lowest position in oven; preheat oven to 425°F. Toss apples with flour and margarine; arrange in pastry-lined 9-inch pie plate. Combine mincemeat with almonds and extract. Spoon over apple mixture. Cover with top crust; cut slits near center. Seal and flute. Brush egg mixture over crust. Bake 10 minutes. *Reduce oven temperature to 375°F;* bake 30 minutes longer or until golden. Cool. Serve warm. Garnish as desired. Refrigerate leftovers.

Makes 1 (9-inch) pie

Tip: Substitute 1 (9-ounce) package NONE SUCH® Condensed Mincemeat, reconstituted as package directs for None Such® Ready-to-Use Mincemeat, if desired.

Left to right: Apple Almond Mince Pie, Mince Cheesecake Pie

Plum Pudding Pie

Pie Shell (recipe follows)
⅓ cup KAHLÚA®
½ cup golden raisins
½ cup chopped pitted dates
⅓ cup chopped candied cherries
½ cup chopped walnuts
⅓ cup dark corn syrup
½ teaspoon pumpkin pie spice
¼ cup butter, softened
¼ cup packed brown sugar
 2 tablespoons flour
¼ teaspoon salt
 2 large eggs, slightly beaten
    Kahlúa® Cream (recipe follows)

Preheat oven to 350°F. Prepare Pie Shell. Combine Kahlúa®, raisins, dates and cherries. Let stand 1 hour or longer to blend flavors. Add walnuts, corn syrup and spice. Cream butter, brown sugar, flour and salt together. Blend in eggs. Stir into fruit mixture.

Turn into Pie Shell. Bake on rack below oven center 35 minutes, just until crust is golden. Cool on wire rack. Prepare Kahlúa® Cream. When ready to serve, swirl mounds of Kahlúa® Cream around outer edge and in center of pie or press through #8 rosette tube in pastry bag, making large swirls.   *Makes 1 (9-inch) pie*

Pie Shell: Combine 1½ cups sifted flour with ¾ teaspoon salt. Cut in ½ cup shortening until mixture forms coarse crumbs. Sprinkle with 3 to 4 tablespoons cold milk, adding just enough to hold dough together. Shape into a ball. Roll out on lightly floured board to 12-inch circle. Fit into 9-inch pie plate. Trim edge about ⅜ inch beyond rim. Fold under and flute, or decorate edge as desired.

Kahlúa® Cream: Beat 1 cup chilled heavy whipping cream with 2 tablespoons Kahlúa® just until mixture holds a peak.

Clockwise from top: Plum Pudding Pie, Northwest Pumpkin Apple Pie (page 192), Pumpkin & Cream Cheese Tart with Cranberry-Orange Topping

Pumpkin & Cream Cheese Tart with Cranberry-Orange Topping

Pie crust mix for single 9-inch crust
 4 packages (3 ounces *each*) cream
    cheese, softened
¾ cup packed brown sugar
 2 eggs
 1 teaspoon ground cinnamon
¼ teaspoon ground nutmeg
 1 teaspoon grated orange peel
 1 can (16 ounces) solid pack pumpkin
 1 can (16 ounces) OCEAN SPRAY®
    Whole Berry Cranberry Sauce
    Glazed Orange Slices (recipe follows)

Preheat oven to 425°F. Prepare pie crust mix as package directs. Press dough onto bottom and 1½ inches up side of ungreased 9-inch springform pan; set aside.

In large bowl, beat cream cheese and sugar until light and fluffy. Beat in eggs, one at a time. Stir in cinnamon, nutmeg, orange peel and pumpkin until smooth and well blended. Pour into pastry-lined pan; spread evenly. Place in preheated oven; *immediately reduce oven temperature to 350°F.* Bake 35 minutes or until center is almost set. Cool completely in pan on wire rack. Spread whole berry cranberry sauce on top. Prepare Glazed Orange Slices; arrange in overlapping ring on top of cranberry sauce. Refrigerate until serving time. Remove side of springform pan before serving.

Makes 1 (9-inch) tart

Glazed Orange Slices: In medium skillet, combine 1 cup granulated sugar and ¼ cup water. Bring to a boil over medium heat; simmer 1 minute. Add 12 thin orange slices. Cook over low heat, turning frequently, 5 minutes or until slices are almost translucent.

Northwest Pumpkin Apple Pie

3 medium apples, peeled, cut into thin slices
1 teaspoon lemon juice
⅔ cup *plus* 1 tablespoon sugar
2 teaspoons all-purpose flour
1 unbaked (9-inch) pie shell with high fluted edge
2 eggs, slightly beaten
1 cup LIBBY'S® Solid Pack Pumpkin
1 can (5⅓ ounces) evaporated milk
2 tablespoons butter or margarine, melted
½ teaspoon ground nutmeg
⅛ teaspoon ground cinnamon

Preheat oven to 400°F. In medium bowl, toss apples with lemon juice, ⅓ cup sugar, and flour. Arrange apple slices in overlapping circles in pie shell; cover loosely with foil. Bake 20 minutes. Meanwhile, in medium bowl, combine eggs, pumpkin, ⅓ cup sugar, evaporated milk, butter, and nutmeg; mix well. Remove foil from pie shell. Carefully pour custard mixture over apples. Continue baking, uncovered, 10 minutes. In small bowl, combine remaining 1 tablespoon sugar and cinnamon; sprinkle over top of pie. Bake 10 minutes longer or until custard is almost set. Cool on wire rack at least 2 hours before slicing. Serve warm or at room temperature.

Makes 1 (9-inch) pie

Yampricot Praline Pie

Crust
9-inch Classic Crisco® Single Crust (pages 6 and 7)

Filling
¾ cup cooked and mashed sweet potatoes, fresh or canned
⅓ cup packed brown sugar
⅓ cup granulated sugar
¾ teaspoon ground cinnamon
¾ teaspoon ground ginger
⅛ teaspoon salt
1¾ cups sliced peeled fresh apricots or frozen dry pack apricot halves
1 can (5 ounces) evaporated milk
2 eggs, well beaten

Topping
¾ cup finely chopped pecans
⅓ cup packed brown sugar
¼ cup BUTTER FLAVOR CRISCO®
Whipped cream (optional)

1. Prepare 9-inch Classic Crisco® Single Crust. *Do not bake.* Heat oven to 350°F.

2. For Filling, combine sweet potatoes, ⅓ cup brown sugar, granulated sugar, cinnamon, ginger and salt in large bowl. Add apricots, evaporated milk and eggs. Mix well. Spoon into unbaked crust. Bake at 350°F for 25 minutes (if using frozen apricots, bake 35 minutes). Remove from oven.

3. For Topping, combine nuts, ⅓ cup brown sugar and Butter Flavor Crisco®. Mix well. Crumble topping evenly over top of filling. Return to oven 40 to 50 minutes (if using frozen apricots, bake 35 to 45 minutes) or until center is set. Cool. Serve with whipped cream, if desired.

Makes 1 (9-inch) pie

Pennsylvania Shoo-Fly Pie

Pennsylvania Shoo-Fly Pie

Crust
10-inch Classic Crisco® Single Crust
   (pages 6 and 7)

Crumb Mixture
  2 cups all-purpose flour
  ½ cup packed brown sugar
  ⅓ cup butter or margarine, softened

Liquid Mixture
  1 cup boiling water
  1 teaspoon baking soda
  ¾ cup *plus* 2 tablespoons dark molasses
  2 tablespoons light molasses

1. Prepare 10-inch Classic Crisco® Single Crust. *Do not bake.* Heat oven to 375°F.

2. For Crumb Mixture, combine flour, brown sugar and butter in bowl. Mix until fine crumbs form.

3. For Liquid Mixture, combine water and baking soda in large bowl. Stir until foamy. Stir in molasses. Pour into unbaked crust. Reserve ½ cup crumb mixture for topping. Carefully stir remaining crumb mixture into molasses mixture in crust. Sprinkle with reserved crumb mixture. Bake at 375°F for 45 to 55 minutes or until set. Cool before serving.

Makes 1 (10-inch) pie

Linzertorte

Linzertorte

6 ounces unblanched almonds
1 cup butter or margarine, chilled
½ cup granulated sugar
3 egg yolks, slightly beaten
1 teaspoon vanilla extract
    Grated peel of 1 lemon
1 teaspoon ground cinnamon
¼ teaspoon ground cloves
    Pinch salt
1 cup all-purpose flour
1 cup seedless raspberry jam
    Powdered sugar

Preheat oven to 350°F. In food processor or blender, process almonds until finely ground; set aside. In large bowl, beat butter until soft and fluffy. Gradually beat in granulated sugar. Add egg yolks and vanilla; blend well. Stir in lemon peel, spices, salt and almonds; mix well. Stir in flour.

Tightly wrap one fourth of the dough in plastic wrap; refrigerate. Pat remaining dough evenly onto bottom and 1 inch up side of ungreased 9-inch springform pan. (Crust will be fairly thick.) Spread

raspberry jam evenly onto bottom of crust. Roll out chilled dough to ½-inch thickness on lightly floured surface. Cut into 6 strips, each ½- to ¾-inch wide. Arrange strips in diamond-shaped lattice pattern over top of jam.

Bake 45 to 50 minutes or until lightly browned. Cool in pan on wire rack 5 minutes; remove side of springform pan. Cool completely. Sprinkle with powdered sugar.   *Makes 1 (9-inch) tart*

Sour Cream Pumpkin Pie

Filling
1 cup dairy sour cream
3 eggs
⅔ cup sugar
1 can (16 ounces) solid pack pumpkin
    (not pumpkin pie filling)
½ teaspoon ground cinnamon
¼ teaspoon ground cloves
¼ teaspoon ground nutmeg
¼ teaspoon ground ginger
¼ cup chopped pecans
12 pecan halves or chopped pecans

Crust
9-inch Classic Crisco® Single Crust
    (pages 6 and 7)

1. For Filling, combine sour cream, eggs, sugar, pumpkin, cinnamon, cloves, nutmeg and ginger in medium bowl. Stir until blended. Set aside.

2. For Crust, heat oven to 375°F. Prepare 9-inch Classic Crisco® Single Crust; press into 9-inch pie plate. Bake at 375°F for 8 minutes. Sprinkle ¼ cup chopped pecans over bottom.

3. Pour filling over nuts. Bake 40 minutes. Remove from oven. Top with pecan halves. Bake pie 5 to 10 minutes longer. Cool to room temperature before serving.
        Makes 1 (9-inch) pie

Maple Apple Pie

Crust
   9-inch Classic Crisco® Double Crust
      (pages 6 and 7)

Filling
   7 cups sliced, peeled baking apples
      (about 2½ pounds *or* 7 medium)
   ¾ cup pure maple syrup or maple-
      flavored pancake syrup
   2 tablespoons cornstarch

Nut Layer and Glaze
   ½ cup chopped pecans
   3 tablespoons pure maple syrup or
      maple-flavored pancake syrup,
      divided
   1 teaspoon butter or margarine

1. Prepare 9-inch Classic Crisco® Double Crust; press bottom crust into 9-inch pie plate, leaving overhang. *Do not bake.* Heat oven to 375°F.

2. For Filling, place apple slices in large microwave-safe bowl. Cover with waxed paper. Microwave at 100% (HIGH) 2 minutes; stir. Repeat twice or until apples start to soften. Combine ¾ cup maple syrup and cornstarch in microwave-safe measuring cup. Stir. Microwave at 100% (HIGH) 2 minutes. Stir. Repeat until mixture starts to thicken. Pour over cooked apples. Cool.

3. For Nut Layer, combine nuts, 2 tablespoons maple syrup and butter in small microwave-safe bowl. Microwave at 100% (HIGH) 1 minute; stir. Microwave at 50% (MEDIUM) 1 minute; stir to break up. Cool.

4. Spoon filling into unbaked pie crust. Top with nut layer. Moisten pastry edge with water.

5. Cover pie with woven lattice top. Bake at 375°F for 1 hour or until filling in center is bubbly and crust is golden brown. Remove from oven.

6. For Glaze, brush pie with remaining 1 tablespoon maple syrup. Bake 5 minutes longer. Cool until barely warm or to room temperature before serving.

Makes 1 (9-inch) pie

Pumpkin "Pie" Crunch

   1 can (16 ounces) solid pack pumpkin
      (not pumpkin pie filling)
   1 can (12 ounces) evaporated milk
   3 eggs
   1¼ cups sugar
   1 tablespoon *plus* 1 teaspoon pumpkin
      pie spice
   ½ teaspoon salt
   1 package (18.25 ounces) DUNCAN
      HINES® Moist Deluxe Yellow
      Cake Mix
   1 cup chopped pecans
   ¾ cup BUTTER FLAVOR CRISCO®,
      melted
   Whipped cream

1. Heat oven to 350°F. Grease bottom of 13×9×2-inch pan.

2. Combine pumpkin, evaporated milk, eggs, sugar, pumpkin pie spice and salt. Pour into pan. Sprinkle dry cake mix evenly over pumpkin mixture. Top with nuts. Drizzle with melted Butter Flavor Crisco®. Bake at 350°F for 50 to 60 minutes or until golden. Cool completely. Serve with whipped cream. Refrigerate leftovers.   *Makes 16 to 20 servings*

PERFECT PASTRIES

Pastry Chef Tarts

1 package (10 ounces) pie crust mix
1 egg, beaten
1 to 2 tablespoons cold water
1½ cups cold half-and-half or milk
1 package (4-serving size) JELL-O®
    Instant Pudding and Pie Filling,
    French Vanilla or Vanilla Flavor
Assorted berries or fruit*
Mint leaves (optional)

- Preheat oven to 425°F. Combine pie crust mix with egg. Add just enough water to form dough. Form 2 to 3 tablespoons dough into 1- to 2-inch round. Press rounds onto bottoms and up sides of 3- to 4-inch tart pans. (Use tart pans with removable bottoms, if possible.) Pierce pastry several times with fork. Place on baking sheet. Bake 10 minutes or until golden. Cool slightly. Remove tart shells from pans; cool completely on wire racks.

- Pour half-and-half into small bowl. Add pudding mix. Beat with wire whisk until well blended, 1 to 2 minutes. Spoon into tart shells. Chill until ready to serve.

- Arrange fruit on pudding. Garnish with mint leaves.

Makes 10 (3- to 4-inch) tarts

Prep time: 20 minutes
Baking time: 10 minutes

*Use any variety of berries, mandarin orange sections, melon balls, halved seedless grapes, sliced peaches, kiwifruit or plums.

Note: Substitute (3- or 4-inch) graham cracker crumb tart shells for baked tart shells.

Chocolate Chip Tarts a l'Orange

1 (15-ounce) container ricotta cheese
2 eggs
¼ cup sugar
2 tablespoons butter, melted
½ teaspoon vanilla extract
1 cup (6-ounce package) NESTLÉ®
    Toll House® Semi-Sweet Chocolate
    Morsels
2 (4-ounce) packages single serve
    graham cracker crumb crusts
2 (11-ounce) cans mandarin oranges,
    drained
¼ cup apricot preserves

Preheat oven to 350°F. In large bowl, combine ricotta cheese, eggs, sugar, butter and vanilla extract; beat well. Stir in Nestlé® Toll House® Semi-Sweet Chocolate Morsels. Spoon ¼ cup filling into each crust. Place on cookie sheet. Bake 20 to 25 minutes. (Centers will be soft.) Cool completely. Arrange orange segments on top of each tart. In small saucepan over low heat, melt apricot preserves. Brush orange segments with preserves. Chill.

Makes 12 individual tarts

Warm Hearts

1 sheet frozen puff pastry *or*
   4 frozen patty shells
2 tablespoons raisins
1 tablespoon dried or candied fruit
1 cup POLLY-O® Lite Ricotta
   Ground cinnamon to taste
1 teaspoon honey
1 egg, beaten slightly with
   1 teaspoon water

Let pastry stand at room temperature for 20 minutes. Preheat oven to 400°F. Chop fruit coarsely; combine with ricotta, cinnamon and honey in small bowl.

Using 3-inch heart-shaped cookie cutter or cardboard pattern, cut 8 hearts from pastry. Brush 4 pastry hearts lightly with water and top with remaining 4 pastry hearts, pressing together gently. Place 2-inch heart-shaped cookie cutter or cardboard pattern on top of stacked pastry hearts. Using small sharp knife, trace small heart, cutting through *top layer* of pastry only. Brush tops lightly with egg-water glaze. Place pastry hearts on moistened cookie sheet; bake in center rack of oven 15 minutes or until puffed and golden. Remove to rack to cool.

While pastry is still warm, use small knife to cut out small top hearts. Set small

pastry hearts aside; scoop out and discard dough centers of large pastry hearts. Fill large pastry hearts with ricotta mixture; top with smaller pastry hearts. Serve warm. *Makes 4 pastries*

Pumpkin Caramel Tarts

1 (15-ounce) package refrigerated pie
   crusts
12 EAGLE™ Brand Caramels,
   unwrapped
1 (14-ounce) can EAGLE® Brand
   Sweetened Condensed Milk
   (NOT evaporated milk)
1 (16-ounce) can solid pack pumpkin
   (about 2 cups)
2 eggs
3 tablespoons water
1 tablespoon vanilla extract
½ teaspoon ground cinnamon

Preheat oven to 425°F. From each pie crust, cut out 7 (4-inch) circles. Press circles into 3-inch tart pans. In medium saucepan over low heat, melt caramels with sweetened condensed milk, stirring constantly. Remove from heat; stir in remaining ingredients. Pour equal portions into crusts. Place on baking sheets. Bake 15 minutes. *Reduce oven temperature to 350°F;* bake 20 to 25 minutes longer or until set. Cool. Garnish as desired. Refrigerate leftovers.

Makes 14 (3-inch) tarts

Microwave Tip: In 2-quart glass measure with handle, combine caramels and sweetened condensed milk. Cook on 100% power (high) 3 minutes or until caramels melt, stirring after each minute. Proceed as directed.

Warm Hearts

Golden Apple Turnovers

2 cups diced WASHINGTON Golden
    Delicious apples (about 2 apples)
1/4 cup raisins
2 tablespoons chopped walnuts
2 teaspoons grated orange peel
1/3 cup granulated sugar
    Pastry for 2-crust 9-inch pie
    Orange Glaze (recipe follows)

Preheat oven to 400°F. Combine apples,
raisins, nuts, 2 teaspoons orange peel and
sugar. Roll pastry to 1/8-inch thickness; cut
into 10 to 12 (4½-inch) circles. Divide
apple mixture evenly among pastry
circles. Fold circles in half; seal edges with
fork. Cut steam vents into tops of pastry.
Bake 25 to 30 minutes or until golden.
Drizzle with Orange Glaze while still
warm. *Makes 10 to 12 turnovers*

Orange Glaze: Combine 3/4 cup powdered
sugar, 1 tablespoon orange juice, 1/4
teaspoon grated orange peel and dash salt.

Favorite recipe from **Washington Apple Commission**

Chocolate Pecan Tassies

Crust
1/2 cup (1 stick) margarine or butter
1 package (3 ounces) PHILADELPHIA
    BRAND® Cream Cheese, softened
1 cup all-purpose flour

Filling
1 square BAKER'S® Unsweetened
    Chocolate
1 tablespoon margarine or butter
3/4 cup packed brown sugar
1 egg
1 teaspoon vanilla extract
1 cup chopped pecans
    Powered sugar (optional)

Chocolate Pecan Tassies

- Beat 1/2 cup margarine and cream cheese
  until well blended. Beat in flour until just
  blended. Wrap dough in plastic wrap;
  refrigerate 1 hour.

- Heat oven to 350°F. Microwave chocolate
  and 1 tablespoon margarine in large
  microwavable bowl on HIGH 1 minute
  or until margarine is melted. *Stir until
  chocolate is completely melted.*

- Beat in brown sugar, egg and vanilla
  until thickened. Stir in pecans.

- Shape chilled dough into 36 (1-inch)
  balls. Flatten each ball and press onto
  bottoms and up sides of ungreased
  miniature muffin cups. Spoon about 1
  teaspoon filling into each cup.

- Bake 20 minutes. Cool in pans on wire
  racks 15 minutes. Remove from pans.
  Sprinkle with powdered sugar.
  Makes 36 tassies

Prep time: 45 minutes
Chill time: 1 hour
Baking time: 20 minutes

Cherry Fudge Tarts

Cherry Fudge Tarts

3 (1-ounce) bars unsweetened *or* semisweet baking chocolate
1 (14-ounce) can EAGLE® Brand Sweetened Condensed Milk (NOT evaporated milk)
¼ teaspoon salt
¼ cup water
2 egg *yolks*
1 teaspoon almond extract
1 cup (½ pint) whipping cream, *whipped*
14 (3-inch) prepared tart-size graham cracker crumb crusts *or* 14 baked (3-inch) tart-size pie crusts
1 (21-ounce) can cherry pie filling, chilled

In heavy saucepan over medium heat, melt chocolate with sweetened condensed milk and salt. Cook and stir rapidly until *very thick* and bubbly, 5 to 8 minutes.

Add water and egg *yolks;* cook and stir rapidly until mixture thickens and bubbles again. Remove from heat; stir in extract.

Pour into large mixing bowl. Cool 15 minutes. *Chill thoroughly,* about 30 minutes; beat until smooth. Fold in whipped cream. Spoon into prepared crusts. Chill 1 hour or until set. Top with cherry pie filling. Refrigerate leftovers.

Makes 14 (3-inch) tarts

Puff Pastry Apple Pockets

1 package (17¼ ounces) frozen puff pastry sheets, thawed as package directs
1 can SOLO® *or* 1 jar BAKER® Apple Filling
⅓ cup raisins
1 teaspoon ground cinnamon
½ teaspoon grated lemon peel
Milk
Sugar

Preheat oven to 400°F. Sprinkle work surface lightly with flour. Unfold one sheet of pastry and lay flat on floured surface. Roll out to 15×10-inch rectangle. Cut into 6 (5-inch) circles.

Combine apple filling, raisins, cinnamon and lemon peel in small bowl. Spoon 1 heaping tablespoonful apple filling onto each pastry circle, slightly off center. Brush pastry edges with milk; fold pastry over filling to make half-moon shape. Press edges of pastries with fork to seal; place on ungreased baking sheets. Brush tops with milk; sprinkle with sugar. Repeat with remaining sheet of pastry and apple filling.

Bake 18 to 22 minutes or until golden brown. Remove from baking sheets and cool on wire racks.

Makes 12 pastry pockets

Almond Lime Tarts

Tart Shells
½ cup *plus* 2 tablespoons butter,
    softened
⅓ cup granulated sugar
1 egg, beaten
1¾ cups flour

Lime Curd
2 limes
2 egg yolks
¼ cup granulated sugar
3 tablespoons butter

Almond Filling
1 cup BLUE DIAMOND® Blanched
    Whole Almonds, toasted
1 cup granulated sugar
1 egg

Lime Glaze
1 lime, juiced
½ cup powdered sugar

Preheat oven to 400°F. Mix together ½ cup *plus* 2 tablespoons butter, ⅓ cup granulated sugar and 1 egg until just combined. Add flour; work lightly with fingertips to form dough. *Do not overmix.* Shape dough into a ball; chill 1 hour.

Meanwhile, grate peel from both limes; squeeze juice from limes. Combine peel, juice, egg yolks, ¼ cup granulated sugar and 3 tablespoons butter in double boiler. Cook, stirring constantly, until thickened, about 3 to 5 minutes; chill.

Finely grind almonds with 1 cup granulated sugar in food processor or blender. With machine running, add 1 egg and process until well blended; reserve.

To assemble, roll chilled dough out on lightly floured board. Divide dough among 10 (4-inch) tart pans; trim edges. Bake 5 minutes; *do not brown.* Remove from oven; spread bottom of each tart with 2 teaspoons chilled lime mixture. Fill tarts half full with almond filling. Smooth tops; bake 10 to 15 minutes or until lightly browned. Cool completely. Mix lime juice and powdered sugar until smooth; drizzle over tops of tarts.

Makes 10 (4-inch) tarts

Mini Mincemeat Tarts

1 can (20 ounces) DOLE® Crushed
    Pineapple in Syrup
2 cups prepared mincemeat
½ cup toasted slivered almonds
1 teaspoon ground allspice
3 cups all-purpose flour
2 tablespoons sugar
¼ teaspoon salt
¾ cup margarine
½ cup cold water
1 egg yolk
1 tablespoon light cream

- Preheat oven to 375°F. Drain pineapple well, pressing out syrup with back of spoon.

- Combine pineapple, mincemeat, almonds and allspice in medium bowl; set aside. Combine flour, sugar and salt in another medium bowl. Cut in margarine until mixture resembles coarse meal. Add enough water to form a ball.

- Divide dough into 12 pieces. Roll out 6 pieces on lightly floured surface; fit into 6 (3¾-inch) tart pans. Trim edges. Spoon pineapple mixture evenly into each pan.

- Roll out remaining 6 pieces of dough. Cover each tart; trim and flute edges. Make slits on tops. Decorate as desired with dough scraps. Combine egg yolk and cream in small bowl. Brush over tops of tarts. Bake 20 minutes. *Reduce oven temperature to 350°F; bake 20 minutes more.* *Makes 6 (3¾-inch) tarts*

Orange-Filled Cream Puffs

¾ cup granulated sugar
3 tablespoons cornstarch
1½ cups orange juice
3 egg yolks, beaten
1 cup DANNON® Plain or Vanilla
     Lowfat Yogurt
2 tablespoons margarine or butter
6 Cream Puffs (recipe follows)
1 can (11 ounces) mandarin orange
     sections, drained
     Powdered sugar

In medium saucepan, combine granulated sugar, cornstarch and orange juice. Stir over medium heat until bubbly; cook and stir 2 minutes more. Remove from heat. Gradually stir half of the hot mixture into egg yolks. Return to pan. Bring to a boil; reduce heat. Cook and stir 2 minutes. Remove from heat. Stir in yogurt and margarine. Cover; chill 4 hours. Meanwhile, prepare Cream Puffs.

To serve, spoon filling into bottoms of Cream Puffs. Top with orange sections. Add cream puff tops. Lightly sift powdered sugar over tops.

Makes 6 cream puffs

Cream Puffs: Preheat oven to 400°F. Grease baking sheet. In medium saucepan, combine 1 cup water and ½ cup margarine. Bring to a boil, stirring until margarine melts. Add 1 cup flour and ½ teaspoon salt, stirring vigorously. Cook and stir until mixture forms a ball. Remove from heat; cool 10 minutes. Add 4 eggs, one at a time, beating after each addition until mixture is smooth. Drop heaping tablespoons of batter into 10 mounds, 3 inches apart, on prepared baking sheet. Bake 30 to 35 minutes or until golden brown and puffy. Cool slightly. Cut off tops and remove any soft dough inside. Cool completely on wire rack. Freeze unused cream puffs for later use. Makes 10 cream puffs.

Orange-Filled Cream Puffs

Apple Dumplings

Pastry
     9-inch Classic Crisco® Double Crust
          (pages 6 and 7)
Filling
     6 baking apples (about 3 inches in
          diameter), peeled and cored
     ⅓ cup chopped pecans
     ⅓ cup raisins
     ½ teaspoon ground cinnamon
Syrup
     2 cups packed brown sugar
     1 cup water
Topping
     Whipped cream (optional)

1. Heat oven to 425°F. Grease 11½×8×2-inch baking dish.

2. Prepare 9-inch Classic Crisco® Double Crust. Roll two thirds of the pastry into 14-inch square on lightly floured surface. Cut into 4 squares. Roll remaining pastry into 14×7-inch rectangle. Cut into 2 squares.

3. For Filling, place 1 prepared apple in center of each pastry square. Combine nuts, raisins and cinnamon. Divide raisin-nut mixture evenly among apples; spoon into centers of apples.

4. Moisten corners of each pastry square. Bring opposite corners of pastry up over apple and press together. Press pastry seams together along sides of dumpling. Place dumplings in prepared baking dish.

5. For Syrup, combine brown sugar and water in medium saucepan on low heat. Stir until mixture comes to a boil. Pour carefully around dumplings.

6. Bake 40 minutes or until apples are tender and pastry is golden brown, spooning syrup over dumplings several times during baking. Serve warm with whipped cream, if desired.

Makes 6 dumplings

Galbani® Mascarpone Graham Cracker Pies

Galbani® Mascarpone Graham Cracker Pies

1 pound GALBANI® Mascarpone
2½ tablespoons ground chocolate*
2 small firm bananas, sliced
8 (2-inch) prepared graham cracker
    crumb tart shells
24 semisweet chocolate chips *or*
    ¼ cup grated semisweet chocolate

In small mixing bowl, vigorously mix mascarpone with ground chocolate. Place 2 or 3 banana slices in bottom of each tart shell. Evenly divide mascarpone mixture among tart shells. Top with remaining banana slices and chocolate chips. Serve immediately. *Makes 8 (2-inch) tarts*

*Finely grated semisweet *or* milk chocolate chips can be substituted for ground chocolate.

Favorite recipe from **Cucina Classica Italiana, Inc.**

Pineapple Eggnog Eclairs

1 cup water
½ cup margarine
1 cup all purpose flour
¼ teaspoon salt
4 eggs
3 tablespoons cornstarch
2 cups dairy eggnog
1 can (20 ounces) DOLE® Crushed
    Pineapple, drained
¾ teaspoon brandy extract
¾ cup fudge sauce

• Preheat oven to 400°F. Combine water and margarine in medium saucepan; bring to a boil. Add combined flour and salt, stirring vigorously over medium heat about 1 minute or until mixture leaves sides of pan and forms a smooth ball. Remove from heat; cool.

• Add eggs, one at a time, beating with wooden spoon after each addition; beat until batter is smooth. Drop batter by scant ¼ cupfuls 2 inches apart onto ungreased baking sheets. Shape eclairs into 4½ × 1½-inch rectangles.

• Bake 35 to 40 minutes or until puffed and golden. Cool eclairs away from drafts.

• Place cornstarch in small saucepan. Gradually stir in eggnog until blended. Cook over medium heat, stirring, until mixture boils and thickens. Cool. Stir in pineapple and extract. Refrigerate until thoroughly chilled.

• Cut tops off eclairs; remove and discard soft dough inside. Spoon ¼ cup filling into each eclair. Replace tops. Spread 1 tablespoon fudge sauce onto top of each eclair. *Makes 12 eclairs*

Apple Cheddar Turnovers

2 packages active dry yeast
¼ cup warm water (110° to 115°F)
⅓ cup butter
⅓ cup granulated sugar
1 teaspoon salt
½ cup (2 ounces) shredded aged
    Wisconsin Cheddar cheese
1 (8-ounce) carton dairy sour cream
1 egg, slightly beaten
3½ to 4 cups all-purpose flour
1¼ cups apple pie filling
1 cup sifted powdered sugar
½ teaspoon vanilla extract
1 to 2 teaspoons milk

Soften yeast in warm water. In large saucepan, heat butter, granulated sugar and salt until warm (115° to 120°) and butter is almost melted, stirring constantly. Add cheese, stirring until melted. Pour into large mixing bowl. Stir in sour cream and egg; mix well. Stir in *1½ cups* flour; beat well. Add softened yeast; stir until smooth. Stir in enough remaining flour to make pliable dough. Turn out onto lightly floured surface; knead 2 minutes. Cover and let rest 10 minutes. Roll *half* of the dough into 12-inch square. Cut into 9 (4-inch) squares. Place about *1 tablespoon* apple pie filling in center of *each* square. Fold dough over to form triangle; seal edges well. Repeat with remaining dough and pie filling.

Place pastries on greased baking sheets; cover and let rise in a warm place until doubled in volume (about 20 minutes). Bake 10 to 15 minutes or until lightly browned. Remove from baking sheets to wire rack.

Meanwhile, in small mixing bowl, combine powdered sugar and vanilla. Stir in enough milk to make of spreading consistency. Spread onto warm pastries. Serve warm or cooled.

Makes 18 pastries

Preparation time: 1 hour

Favorite recipe from **Wisconsin Milk Marketing Board**
© *1993*

Cocoa Nut Bundles

1 can (8 ounces) refrigerated quick
    crescent dinner rolls
2 tablespoons butter or margarine,
    softened
1 tablespoon granulated sugar
2 teaspoons HERSHEY₀S Cocoa
¼ cup chopped nuts
    Confectioners' sugar

Heat oven to 375°F. On ungreased cookie sheet, unroll dough and separate to form 8 triangles. In small bowl, combine butter, granulated sugar and cocoa. Add nuts; mix thoroughly. Divide chocolate mixture evenly among triangles, placing chocolate mixture on wide end of each triangle. Take dough on either side of mixture and pull up and over mixture, tucking ends under. Continue rolling dough toward opposite point. Bake 9 to 10 minutes or until golden brown. Sprinkle with confectioners' sugar; serve warm.

Makes 8 bundles

Cocoa Nut Bundles

Chocolate-Filled Cream Puffs

1 cup water
½ cup butter or margarine
¼ teaspoon salt
1 cup all-purpose flour
4 eggs
   Chocolate Cream Filling
   (recipe follows)
   Confectioners' sugar

Preheat oven to 400°F. Bring water, butter and salt to a boil in medium saucepan. Add flour; stir vigorously over low heat about 1 minute or until mixture leaves side of pan and forms a ball. Remove from heat; add eggs, one at a time, beating well after each addition until smooth and velvety.

Drop dough by scant ¼ cupfuls onto ungreased cookie sheet. Bake 35 to 40 minutes or until puffed and golden brown. While still warm, horizontally slice off small portion of tops; reserve. Remove any soft dough inside; cool. Prepare Chocolate Cream Filling; fill cream puffs. Replace tops; dust with confectioners' sugar. Chill.

Makes about 12 cream puffs

Chocolate Cream Filling

1¼ cups sugar
⅓ cup HERSHEY'S Cocoa
⅓ cup cornstarch
¼ teaspoon salt
3 cups milk
3 egg yolks, slightly beaten
2 tablespoons butter or margarine
1½ teaspoons vanilla extract

Combine granulated sugar, cocoa, cornstarch and ¼ teaspoon salt in medium saucepan; stir in milk. Cook over medium heat, stirring constantly, until mixture boils; boil and stir 1 minute. Remove from heat. Gradually stir small amount of chocolate mixture into egg yolks; blend well. Return egg mixture to chocolate mixture in pan; stir and heat just until boiling. Remove from heat; blend in 2 tablespoons butter and vanilla. Pour into bowl; press plastic wrap directly onto surface. Cool.

Miniature Cream Puffs: Drop cream puff dough by level teaspoonfuls onto ungreased cookie sheet. Bake at 400°F about 15 minutes. Fill as directed. Makes about 8 dozen miniature cream puffs.

Chocolate-Almond Tarts

   Chocolate Tart Shells (recipe follows)
¾ cup granulated sugar
¼ cup HERSHEY'S Cocoa
¼ cup cornstarch
¼ teaspoon salt
2 cups milk
2 egg yolks, slightly beaten
2 tablespoons butter or margarine
¼ teaspoon almond extract
   Sliced almonds

Prepare Chocolate Tart Shells; set aside. Combine granulated sugar, ¼ cup cocoa, cornstarch and salt in medium saucepan; blend in milk and egg yolks. Cook over medium heat, stirring constantly, until mixture boils; boil and stir 1 minute. Remove from heat; blend in 2 tablespoons butter and almond extract.

Pour into cooled shells; press plastic wrap directly onto surface. Chill. Garnish tops with sliced almonds.

Makes 6 individual tarts

Chocolate Tart Shells: Preheat oven to 350°F. Combine 1½ cups vanilla wafer cookie crumbs (about 45 wafers), ⅓ cup confectioners' sugar, ¼ cup HERSHEY'S Cocoa and 6 tablespoons melted butter or margarine in medium bowl; stir until completely blended. Divide mixture among 6 (4-ounce) tart pans; press mixture firmly onto bottoms and up sides of pans. Bake 5 minutes. Cool.

Napoleons

1 package (17¼ ounces) frozen puff
    pastry sheets
Chocolate Filling (recipe follows)
Vanilla Glaze (recipe follows)
Chocolate Glaze (recipe follows)

Thaw folded pastry sheets as package directs. Heat oven to 350°F. Gently unfold sheets. On lightly floured surface, roll each sheet to 15×12-inch rectangle; trim to even edges. Place on large ungreased baking sheets; prick each sheet thoroughly with fork. Bake 18 to 20 minutes or until puffed and golden brown. Cool completely on baking sheets. Prepare Chocolate Filling.

Cut one rectangle lengthwise into 3 equal pieces. Place one piece on serving plate; spread with one fourth of the Chocolate Filling. Top with second piece of pastry; spread with one fourth of the filling. Place remaining piece on top; set aside. Repeat with remaining pastry and filling.

Prepare Vanilla Glaze; spread on top of each pastry. Prepare Chocolate Glaze; drizzle over frosting in decorative design. Refrigerate at least 1 hour or until filling is set. Carefully cut each pastry into 6 pieces. Cover; refrigerate leftovers.

Makes 12 servings

Chocolate Filling

1 envelope unflavored gelatin
2 tablespoons cold water
¼ cup boiling water
1 cup sugar
½ cup HERSHEY'S Cocoa
2 cups (1 pint) cold whipping cream
2 teaspoons vanilla extract

Top to bottom: Chocolate-Filled Cream Puffs, Chocolate-Almond Tarts, Napoleons

In small bowl, sprinkle gelatin over cold water; let stand 1 minute to soften. Add boiling water; stir until gelatin is completely dissolved and mixture is clear. Cool slightly. In large mixer bowl, stir together sugar and cocoa. Add whipping cream and vanilla; at medium speed, beat, scraping bottom of bowl occasionally, until stiff. Pour in gelatin mixture; beat until well blended. Refrigerate to spreading consistency, if necessary. Makes about 5 cups.

Vanilla Glaze: In small mixer bowl, combine 1½ cups confectioners' sugar, 1 tablespoon light corn syrup, ¼ teaspoon vanilla extract and 1 to 2 tablespoons hot water; beat to spreading consistency. (Add additional water, ½ teaspoon at a time, if necessary.) Makes about ½ cup.

Chocolate Glaze: In small saucepan, melt ¼ cup butter or margarine. Remove from heat; stir in ⅓ cup HERSHEY'S Cocoa until smooth. Cool slightly. Makes about ¼ cup.

Top to bottom: Peanut Butter Tarts, Individual Chocolate Cream Pies

Peanut Butter Tarts

1 package (3½ ounces) instant vanilla
   pudding and pie filling
1½ cups milk, divided
1 cup REESE'S® Peanut Butter Chips
6 single serve graham cracker crumb
   crusts (4-ounce package)
Whipped topping
Fresh fruit

Microwave Directions: In small mixer bowl, blend pudding mix and 1 cup milk; set aside. In top of double boiler over hot, not boiling, water, melt peanut butter chips with remaining ½ cup milk, stirring constantly to blend. (Or, microwave chips and ½ cup milk in small microwave-safe bowl at HIGH (100%) 45 seconds; stir. If necessary, microwave at HIGH additional 15 seconds or until melted and smooth when stirred.) Gradually add to pudding, blending well. Spoon into crusts. Cover; refrigerate until set. Garnish with whipped topping and fruit.

Makes 6 individual tarts

Individual Chocolate Cream Pies

1½ ounces (½ of 3-ounce package) cream
    cheese, softened
6 tablespoons sugar
½ teaspoon vanilla extract
2½ tablespoons HERSHEY'S Cocoa
2½ tablespoons milk
1 cup (½ pint) cold whipping cream
6 single serve graham cracker crumb
    crusts (4-ounce package)
Whipped topping
HERSHEY'S MINI CHIPS
    Semi-Sweet Chocolate

In small mixer bowl, beat cream cheese,
sugar and vanilla until well blended. Add
cocoa alternately with milk, beating until
smooth. In small mixer bowl, beat
whipping cream until stiff; fold into
chocolate mixture. Spoon into crusts.
Cover; refrigerate until set. Garnish with
whipped topping and small chocolate
chips. *Makes 6 individual pies*

Imported Tokay Tarts

1 cup imported Tokay grapes or other
    winter grapes
1½ cups finely ground graham cracker
    crumbs
¼ cup butter or margarine
¼ cup sugar
2 packages (8 ounces *each*) cream cheese
⅓ cup honey
1 tablespoon lemon juice
2 eggs
1 cup dairy sour cream

Preheat oven to 375°F. Halve and seed
grapes; set aside. Combine crumbs, butter
and sugar. Divide crumb mixture among
8 (4-inch) tart pans; press to cover bottoms
and sides. Beat cheese until smooth; beat
in honey, lemon juice and eggs. Pour into
tart shells. Bake 25 minutes. Spoon equal
portions sour cream over each; top with
grapes. Return to oven 5 minutes. Cool.
Makes 8 (4-inch) tarts

*Favorite recipe from **Chilean Winter Fruit Association***

Almond Cinnamon Focaccia

2 packages (¼ ounce *each*) active dry
    yeast
1½ cups warm (110°F) water
2 cups all-purpose flour
1½ cups cake flour
1 cup sugar, divided
½ teaspoon salt
½ cup *plus* 3 tablespoons olive oil,
    divided
1 tablespoon cinnamon
¼ cup butter, melted
1 cup BLUE DIAMOND® Sliced
    Natural Almonds, toasted

Dissolve yeast in water. Combine flours,
½ cup sugar and salt; stir into yeast
mixture. Gradually mix in ½ cup oil,
stirring constantly, just until dough forms.
Cover; let rise in warm place until doubled
in volume, about 1½ hours. Combine
remaining ½ cup sugar and cinnamon;
reserve. Grease 17×11-inch pan with
remaining 3 tablespoons oil; spread dough
into pan. Brush top with melted butter;
sprinkle with toasted almonds, pressing
almonds firmly into dough. Sprinkle with
cinnamon-sugar mixture. Let rise in a
warm place, 15 to 20 minutes. Preheat
oven to 375°F. Bake 20 to 25 minutes. Cut
into squares. *Makes 20 servings*

Raspberry-Filled Chocolate Ravioli

2 squares (1 ounce *each*) bittersweet *or* semisweet chocolate
1 cup butter or margarine, softened
½ cup granulated sugar
1 egg
1 teaspoon vanilla extract
½ teaspoon chocolate extract
¼ teaspoon baking soda
    Dash salt
2½ cups all-purpose flour
1 to 1¼ cups seedless raspberry jam
    Powdered sugar

Melt chocolate in top of double boiler over hot, not boiling, water. Remove from heat; cool. Cream butter and granulated sugar in large bowl until blended. Add egg, vanilla, chocolate extract, baking soda, salt and melted chocolate; beat until light. Blend in flour to make stiff dough. Divide dough in half. Cover; refrigerate until firm.

Preheat oven to 350°F. Lightly grease cookie sheets or line with parchment paper. Roll out dough, half at a time, ⅛-inch thick between two sheets of plastic wrap. Remove top sheet of plastic. (If dough gets too soft and sticks to plastic, refrigerate until firm.) Cut dough into 1½-inch squares. Place half of the squares, 2 inches apart, on prepared cookie sheets. Place about ½ teaspoon jam in center of each square; top with another square. Using fork, press edges of squares together to seal, then pierce center of each square. Bake 10 minutes or just until edges are browned. Remove to wire racks to cool. Dust lightly with powdered sugar.

Makes about 6 dozen ravioli

Walnut Tarts

Cream Cheese Pastry (recipe follows)
2 eggs
½ cup sugar
½ cup KARO® Light or Dark Corn Syrup
2 tablespoons bourbon (optional)
1 tablespoon MAZOLA® Margarine, melted
½ teaspoon vanilla extract
1 cup finely chopped walnuts

Preheat oven to 350°F. Prepare Cream Cheese Pastry. Roll dough into 1-inch balls. Press evenly into bottoms and up sides of 1¾×1-inch muffin cups. Refrigerate. In medium bowl, beat eggs slightly. Stir in sugar, corn syrup, bourbon, margarine, vanilla and walnuts. Spoon 1 tablespoon mixture into each pastry-lined cup. Bake 20 to 25 minutes or until lightly browned. Cool in pans 5 minutes. Remove; cool completely on wire rack. Store in tightly covered container.

Makes about 2 dozen individual tarts

Cream Cheese Pastry

½ cup MAZOLA® Margarine, softened
1 package (3 ounces) cream cheese, softened
1 tablespoon sugar
1⅓ cups flour
    Pinch salt

In large bowl, combine margarine, cream cheese and sugar; stir until well blended. Add flour and salt; stir until thoroughly combined.

Raspberry-Filled Chocolate Ravioli

Apricot-Pecan Tassies

1 cup all-purpose flour
½ cup butter, cut into pieces
6 tablespoons light cream cheese
¾ cup packed light brown sugar
1 egg, slightly beaten
1 tablespoon butter, softened
½ teaspoon vanilla extract
¼ teaspoon salt
⅔ cup dried California apricot halves, diced (about 4 ounces)
⅓ cup chopped pecans

In food processor or blender, combine flour, butter and cream cheese; process until mixture forms a ball. Wrap dough in plastic wrap; chill 15 minutes. Meanwhile, combine brown sugar, egg, butter, vanilla and salt; beat until smooth. Stir in apricots and nuts. Preheat oven to 325°F. Shape dough into 24 (1-inch) balls; place in waxed-paper-lined or greased miniature muffin cups. Press dough onto bottom and up side of each cup; spoon 1 teaspoon filling into each. Bake 25 minutes or until crust is golden and filling is set. Cool; remove from pans. Tassies can be wrapped tightly in plastic and frozen up to six weeks. *Makes 24 tassies*

Favorite recipe from **California Apricot Advisory Board**

Apricot-Pecan Tassies

Old-Fashioned Fried Apple Pies

1 cup cored, chopped WASHINGTON Golden Delicious apples
4 tablespoons orange juice, divided
1 tablespoon granulated sugar
1 teaspoon grated orange peel
    Dash salt
2 teaspoons cornstarch
    Pastry for 1-crust 9-inch pie
    Vegetable oil for deep-frying
    Powdered sugar

Combine apples, 3 tablespoons orange juice, granulated sugar, orange peel and salt; cover and cook gently 10 minutes or until apples are tender. Dissolve cornstarch in remaining 1 tablespoon orange juice; stir into apple mixture. Cook and stir until thickened and smooth. Cool. Thinly roll out pastry; cut into 5-inch rounds. Place 1½ tablespoons filling on each round. Moisten edges with water; fold in half and seal edges well with fork. Prick small holes in tops of pies. Deep-fry in oil heated to 375°F about 3 minutes or until golden brown. Drain on paper towels. Sift powdered sugar over tops just before serving. *Makes 6 individual pies*

Note: Recipe may be doubled.

Baked Variation: Prepare pies as above. Bake in preheated 425°F oven 15 to 20 minutes or until golden. If desired, sprinkle with cinnamon sugar before baking.

Favorite recipe from **Washington Apple Commission**

Blueberry Cream Cheese Strudel

1 package (8 ounces) cream cheese,
    softened
1 egg
¼ cup powdered sugar
2 tablespoons frozen orange juice
    concentrate, thawed
½ teaspoon vanilla extract
12 sheets (8 ounces) phyllo dough
    About ¾ cup unsalted butter, melted
1 can SOLO® *or* 1 jar BAKER®
    Blueberry or other flavor
    Fruit Filling
    Powdered sugar

Preheat oven to 375°F. Grease large baking sheet; set aside. Beat cream cheese, egg and ¼ cup powdered sugar in medium bowl with electric mixer until smooth. Add orange juice concentrate and vanilla; beat until blended. Set aside.

Unfold phyllo dough; place between two slightly damp dish towels to keep from drying out. Place 1 sheet phyllo dough on separate clean dish towel; brush with melted butter. Place second sheet on top; brush with melted butter. Repeat with remaining phyllo and melted butter.

Spread cream cheese mixture down center of dough to within 2 inches of edges on all sides. Spread blueberry filling over cream cheese mixture. Fold both long sides in over filling. Fold 1 short side in 2 inches. Continue to fold strudel over from short side, using towel as aid. Raise towel on short side and use to roll strudel onto prepared baking sheet, seam side down. Brush entire surface with melted butter.

Bake 35 to 45 minutes or until top is golden brown and crisp. Carefully slide strudel onto wire rack to cool slightly. Dust with powdered sugar just before serving. Serve warm.

Makes 1 strudel (8 to 10 servings)

Golden Apple Rum Tartlets

Golden Apple Rum Tartlets

¼ cup butter or margarine
¼ cup sugar
8 cups (6 to 8) WASHINGTON Golden
    Delicious apples, peeled, cored and
    sliced
2 tablespoons grated orange peel,
    divided
¼ teaspoon ground cinnamon
¼ cup light rum*
5 teaspoons cornstarch
16 baked (3-inch) tart crusts
    Mint leaves (optional)

Melt butter in skillet; blend in sugar. Add apples, 1 tablespoon orange peel and cinnamon; simmer 10 to 15 minutes or until apples are tender. Blend rum and cornstarch; stir into apple mixture. Cook and stir until mixture boils and thickens. Cool. Spoon apple mixture into tart shells. Garnish with remaining orange peel and mint leaves. *Makes 16 tartlets*

*Substitute 3 tablespoons water *plus* 2 teaspoons rum extract for the rum, if desired.

Favorite recipe from **Washington Apple Commission**

Individual Spicy Apple Pies

¼ cup butter or margarine
4 to 6 cups sliced peeled baking apples
   (about 4 to 6 apples)
½ cup granulated sugar
¼ cup packed brown sugar
⅓ cup crushed gingersnaps
½ teaspoon ground cinnamon
1 teaspoon cornstarch
6 KEEBLER® Ready-Crust Single
   Serve Graham Cracker Tarts

In skillet, melt butter over medium-high heat. Cook and stir apples in butter until almost tender. Combine sugars, gingersnaps, cinnamon and cornstarch. Sprinkle over apples. Cook and stir until mixture forms a thick, dark sauce, 2 to 3 minutes. (Depending on juiciness of apples, 1 to 2 teaspoons water may need to be added to thin sauce.) Remove from heat. Spoon mixture into crusts. Serve warm with small scoops of frozen vanilla yogurt, custard or ice cream, if desired.

Makes 6 individual pies

Note: Apple amounts vary due to size of apples. After apples have been browned, they will lose moisture and size if overcooked. If you have too many apples, reserve excess and reheat as an accompaniment to dinner or breakfast.

Individual Spicy Apple Pies

Chocolate Tassies

Pastry
   2 cups all-purpose flour
   2 packages (3 ounces *each*) cold cream
      cheese, cut into chunks
   1 cup cold butter or margarine, cut into
      chunks

Filling
   2 tablespoons butter or margarine
   2 squares (1 ounce *each*) unsweetened
      chocolate
1½ cups packed brown sugar
   2 teaspoons vanilla extract
   2 eggs, beaten
      Dash salt
1½ cups chopped pecans

Place flour in large bowl. Cut in cream cheese and butter. Continue to mix until dough can be shaped into a ball. Wrap dough in plastic wrap; refrigerate 1 hour. Shape dough into 1-inch balls. Press each ball into ungreased miniature (1¾-inch) muffin pan cup, covering bottom and side of cup with dough.

Preheat oven to 350°F. Melt butter and chocolate in heavy medium saucepan over low heat. Remove from heat. Blend in brown sugar, vanilla, eggs and salt; beat until thick. Stir in pecans. Spoon about 1 teaspoon filling into each unbaked pastry shell. Bake 20 to 25 minutes or until pastry is lightly browned and filling is set. Cool in pans on wire racks. Remove from pans; store in airtight containers.

Makes about 5 dozen tassies

Cherry Envelopes

2 packages (3 ounces *each*) cream
    cheese, softened
⅓ cup butter or margarine, softened
⅓ cup granulated sugar
⅓ cup milk
2¼ cups all-purpose flour
1 teaspoon baking powder
1 teaspoon grated lemon peel
½ teaspoon salt
1 can SOLO® *or* 1 jar BAKER® Cherry
    or Blueberry Filling
1 egg beaten with 1 tablespoon water
    for brushing
    Powdered sugar

Preheat oven to 350°F. Grease 2 baking sheets; set aside. Beat cream cheese, butter, granulated sugar and milk in large bowl with electric mixer until well blended. Stir in flour, baking powder, lemon peel and salt. Knead dough in bowl 8 to 10 strokes or until smooth. Divide dough into equal halves.

Roll out one half on lightly floured surface to 15×10-inch rectangle. Cut into six (5-inch) squares. Spoon 1 heaping tablespoonful cherry filling onto center of each pastry square. Brush edges of pastry with beaten egg mixture and bring corners in to center to enclose filling. Pinch edges to seal. Place filled pastries on prepared baking sheets and brush with beaten egg mixture. Repeat with remaining pastry and cherry filling.

Bake 20 to 25 minutes or until golden brown. Remove from baking sheets and cool on wire racks. Dust with powdered sugar just before serving.

Makes 12 pastries

Tangerine Tarts

    Pastry for 2-crust 9-inch pie
1½ cups Florida tangerine juice
1 cup sugar
3 teaspoons grated tangerine peel
⅔ cup unsalted butter or margarine
8 eggs, beaten
4 Florida tangerines, peeled and
    sectioned

Preheat oven to 400°F. On lightly floured surface, roll pastry dough to ⅛-inch thickness. Cut out 8 to 10 (5-inch) circles with cookie cutter. Press each circle into 3½-inch fluted tart pan; prick with fork. Place pans on a cookie sheet. Bake 10 to 12 minutes or until lightly browned. Cool on wire rack. Carefully remove shells from pans; cool thoroughly.

In top of double boiler over simmering, not boiling, water combine tangerine juice, sugar, peel and butter. Stir until sugar dissolves and butter melts. Gradually whisk about 2 cups tangerine mixture into beaten eggs, then return mixture to top of double boiler. Stir constantly until mixture thickens. Cover. Chill.

When ready to serve, spoon tangerine mixture into tart shells; top with tangerine sections.

Makes 8 to 10 (3½-inch) tarts

Favorite recipe from **Florida Department of Citrus**

Acknowledgments

The publishers would like to thank the companies and organizations listed below for the use of their recipes in this book.

Best Foods, a Division of CPC International Inc.
Blue Diamond Growers
Borden Kitchens, Borden, Inc.
California Apricot Advisory Board
California Tree Fruit Agreement
Canned Food Information Council
Checkerboard Kitchens, Ralston Purina Company
Chilean Fresh Fruit Association
Contadina Foods, Inc., Nestlé Food Company
Cucina Classica Italiana, Inc.
The Dannon Company, Inc.
Del Monte Foods
Dole Food Company, Inc.
Dreyer's/Edy's Grand Ice Cream, Inc.
Florida Department of Citrus
Heinz U.S.A.
Hershey Chocolate U.S.A.
Hunt-Wesson, Inc.
Kahlúa Liqueur
Keebler Company
Kellogg Company
Kraft General Foods, Inc.
Land O' Lakes, Inc.

Libby's, Nestlé Food Company
Thomas J. Lipton Co.
Nabisco Foods Group
National Live Stock and Meat Board
National Turkey Federation
Nestlé Foods Company
New Zealand Kiwifruit Marketing Board
North Dakota Beef Commission
Ocean Spray Cranberries, Inc.
Oregon Washington California Pear Bureau
Pecan Marketing Board
Perdue Farms
Pet Incorporated
Pollio Dairy Products
The Procter & Gamble Company
The Quaker Oats Company
Reckitt & Colman, Inc.
Red Star Yeast Products
Sauder's Penn Dutch Eggs
Sokol & Company
USA Rice Council
Washington Apple Commission
Wisconsin Milk Marketing Board

Photo Credits

The publishers would like to thank the companies and organizations listed below for the use of their photographs in this book.

Best Foods, a Division of CPC International Inc.
Borden Kitchens, Borden, Inc.
California Apricot Advisory Board
California Tree Fruit Agreement
Canned Food Information Council
Checkerboard Kitchens, Ralston Purina Company
Chilean Fresh Fruit Association
Contadina Foods, Inc., Nestlé Food Company
Cucina Classica Italiana, Inc.
Del Monte Foods
Dole Food Company, Inc.
Hershey Chocolate U.S.A.
Hunt-Wesson, Inc.
Kahlúa Liqueur
Keebler Company

Kraft General Foods, Inc.
Libby's, Nestlé Food Company
Thomas J. Lipton Co.
National Live Stock and Meat Board
Nestlé Foods Company
New Zealand Kiwifruit Marketing Board
Perdue Farms
Pollio Dairy Products
The Procter & Gamble Company
Reckitt & Colman, Inc.
Red Star Yeast Products
Sauder's Penn Dutch Eggs
USA Rice Council
Washington Apple Commission

INDEX

METRIC CONVERSION CHART

VOLUME MEASUREMENTS (dry)

1/8 teaspoon = 0.5 mL
1/4 teaspoon = 1 mL
1/2 teaspoon = 2 mL
3/4 teaspoon = 4 mL
1 teaspoon = 5 mL
1 tablespoon = 15 mL
2 tablespoons = 30 mL
1/4 cup = 60 mL
1/3 cup = 75 mL
1/2 cup = 125 mL
2/3 cup = 150 mL
3/4 cup = 175 mL
1 cup = 250 mL
2 cups = 1 pint = 500 mL
3 cups = 750 mL
4 cups = 1 quart = 1 L

VOLUME MEASUREMENTS (fluid)

1 fluid ounce (2 tablespoons) = 30 mL
4 fluid ounces (1/2 cup) = 125 mL
8 fluid ounces (1 cup) = 250 mL
12 fluid ounces (1 1/2 cups) = 375 mL
16 fluid ounces (2 cups) = 500 mL

WEIGHTS (mass)

1/2 ounce = 15 g
1 ounce = 30 g
3 ounces = 90 g
4 ounces = 120 g
8 ounces = 225 g
10 ounces = 285 g
12 ounces = 360 g
16 ounces = 1 pound = 450 g

DIMENSIONS

1/16 inch = 2 mm
1/8 inch = 3 mm
1/4 inch = 6 mm
1/2 inch = 1.5 cm
3/4 inch = 2 cm
1 inch = 2.5 cm

OVEN TEMPERATURES

250°F = 120°C
275°F = 140°C
300°F = 150°C
325°F = 160°C
350°F = 180°C
375°F = 190°C
400°F = 200°C
425°F = 220°C
450°F = 230°C

BAKING PAN SIZES

Utensil	Size in Inches/Quarts	Metric Volume	Size in Centimeters
Baking or Cake Pan (square or rectangular)	8×8×2	2 L	20×20×5
	9×9×2	2.5 L	22×22×5
	12×8×2	3 L	30×20×5
	13×9×2	3.5 L	33×23×5
Loaf Pan	8×4×3	1.5 L	20×10×7
	9×5×3	2 L	23×13×7
Round Layer Cake Pan	8×1½	1.2 L	20×4
	9×1½	1.5 L	23×4
Pie Plate	8×1¼	750 mL	20×3
	9×1¼	1 L	23×3
Baking Dish or Casserole	1 quart	1 L	—
	1½ quart	1.5 L	—
	2 quart	2 L	—